Juliet Rieden has been a journalist for more than 30 years, working between the UK and Australia for magazines and newspapers as a writer and editor. She is currently Editor-At-Large at *The Australian Women's Weekly*, where she also works as the Royal Correspondent and the Books Editor. Her first book, *The Royals in Australia*, was published in 2015.

The WRITING *on the* WALL

How one boy, my father,
survived the Holocaust

JULIET RIEDEN

MACMILLAN
Pan Macmillan Australia

First published 2019 in Macmillan by Pan Macmillan Australia Pty Ltd
1 Market Street, Sydney, New South Wales, Australia, 2000

Cataloguing-in-Publication entry is available
from the National Library of Australia
http://catalogue.nla.gov.au

Typeset in 12.25/16 pt Bembo by Post Pre-press Group, Brisbane
Printed by McPherson's Printing Group

The author and the publisher have made every effort to contact copyright
holders for material used in this book. Any person or organisation
that may have been overlooked should contact the publisher.

Aboriginal and Torres Strait Islander people should be aware that this
book may contain images or names of people now deceased.

The paper in this book is FSC® certified.
FSC® promotes environmentally responsible,
socially beneficial and economically viable
management of the world's forests.

This book is dedicated to my father's aunts and uncles and their children and especially Ida Hoffer. You are the family I never knew I had, but longed to embrace. To my grandparents Rudolf and Helena whose sacrifice is the reason I am here writing this book and to my father, Hanus, whose quiet dignity in the face of deep trauma and unconditional love for us, *his* family, takes my breath away.

CONTENTS

PART III
NEW BEGINNINGS

FOREWORD

'The struggle of man against power is the
struggle of memory against forgetting.'
– Milan Kundera, *The Book of Laughter and Forgetting*

I first met Juliet Rieden when she interviewed me for *The Australian Women's Weekly* in 2012 after I came out live on television in support of Marriage Equality. I was still very nervous and felt extremely vulnerable. Juliet relayed my story with compassion, fairness and dignity.

Since then we have crossed paths a few times, and when I launched my own memoir Juliet again interviewed me. She mentioned at the time how strongly my family's experiences resonated with her. I suggested that she take the journey to find the truth of her own story.

And this is that story.

Little did I realise just how much her life and history parallels that of my own – and many other refugee families. Like me, she is the English-born descendent of urbane Eastern Europeans who were plunged into hell. Like my father, her father identified as an Englishman. And, like me, she is haunted by questions of what happened to her family.

But there are poignant differences. My family tried to save their Jewish friends and neighbours from the flames of the Holocaust. Many in Juliet's family did not survive. This deeply moving account reminds us that even those who did not perish in the flames were severely burned by their cruel heat.

This brave, intelligent book is also a penetrating investigation into acts of charity. Saving people does not always come from pure altruism and can have complex, mixed motives. Juliet's father John (or actually Hanus) was part of something similar to the famous Kindertransports, only her father travelled to England by plane not train. She uses her journalistic detective skills and storytelling ability to bring to life the terrible loneliness and exile that was the cost of his survival.

Families usually keep secrets for one, or perhaps both, of two reasons – pain and shame. Unbearable pain. Unbearable shame. It takes great courage and compassion to prise open that locked door of the heart. To set about answering those awful questions: what happened to my family and, maybe even harder, what did they do to survive? What did they do in impossible circumstances?

Understandably, much of the telling of the Holocaust has been about Auschwitz. But it was not the only hell on earth. Juliet also takes us into the bizarre world of Theresienstadt, the model 'show' camp that provided a mask for the horror of the Final Solution.

Walking in the footsteps of her extended family, many of whom did not survive, Juliet paints vivid, heartbreaking pictures. She provides names, dates and places.

As the last generation of Jewish survivors of the Holocaust pass from this earth, their stories will not disappear with them. They will not fade into oblivion, unremembered. Through Juliet's diligence and love, 'they exist once more, proof that not even Hitler can erase my family without a trace'.

Memoirs such as this will ensure we do not lose the struggle against 'forgetting' – that sly accomplice of tyranny.

Magda Szubanski

LIFTING THE CURTAIN

As I stare at the wall of Prague's Pinkas Synagogue, I feel a blaze of heat flush through my body and my heart begins to pound and stutter. The etched letters are dancing in front of my eyes, the red now taking on the ghoulish taint of dried blood. My knees buckle and I grasp the railing in front of me, gripping it white-knuckle tight, eager not to make a scene. An uncomfortable tingling is running up and down my spine, tapping through each vertebra. Is someone there looking over my shoulder? I check behind me but no one is interested in me; all are transfixed by the wall, lost in their own torment. Retreating, I turn away and bend secretively over my phone for a frantic internet search.

And then everything changes.

It makes me sad and a little angry that I discovered the family I never knew from Google. I think I held my breath as I jabbed in the names I had just discovered on the wall – Emil Rieden, Berta Rieden, Felix Rieden, Ota Rieden – and then added 'Holocaust' to my internet search. Could these really be my people on the wall of this memorial to Czechs murdered by the Nazis?

1

The answers came at one click. It was that easy.

Emil was my great-grandfather, Berta and Felix my great-aunt and great-uncle, and Ota ... well, Ota (an innocent spelling error from the calligrapher who painted the names) should have read Otto, who was their brother, another great-uncle. All three were siblings of my grandpa Dr Rudolf Rieden; Emil was *his* father. And all, I later discovered, lived with my dad, Hanus Rieden, before he fled to England from Czechoslovakia in March 1939, only a week before Hitler's troops arrived in Prague, part of an elaborate and desperate escape when he was aged just eight. He never saw them again.

It was the first day of September in 2016 and I was 52 years old. How could I have been ignorant to their fate all this time? Why didn't my father tell me?

I turn back to the writing on the wall, now feeling ownership, but still incredulous. Next to each name, dates of birth and death are carefully painted. And as I push my brain to work out their ages, tears start to roll down my face.

——

I always knew our family was different.

For a start, while we lived in the heart of commuter-belt Surrey, on London's outskirts, both our parents were only children and our grandparents lived in other countries – Mum's parents 17,000 kilometres away, on the other side of the world in Australia; Dad's trapped behind the Iron Curtain in Eastern Bloc Czechoslovakia. Our Australian grandparents, Flo and Roy, came over every few years in a big flourish with exotic gifts for my two brothers and me, and tales of stopping off at places like Singapore and Ceylon.

But Rudolf and Helena were inaccessible, shadowy phantoms whom I imagined huddled under blankets, speaking in foreign whispers, always looking over their shoulders. We had one of their blankets – smart, camel-coloured with *Rieden* embroidered in bright-red chain stitch in the corner. I used it occasionally as an extra layer in winter. It was only decades later that I discovered this was one of the few remnants from home they were allowed to keep with them when they were imprisoned for three years in Theresienstadt concentration camp, north of Prague. This was the very blanket that had provided a meagre barrier to one of them in the bitterly cold winters.

Rudolf died when I was barely a toddler, but Helena was constantly in my thoughts, rattling around my head. I was told she had come over to see us when I was almost three. I think I remember it, but I don't really. She was given my bedroom and, so the story went, I screamed and screamed until I made myself sick when I saw her in pink winceyette pyjamas smoking in my bed. After which, apparently, we got on famously – even though she spoke very little English – until she had to go back to Prague, beyond reach, again.

It made me think of the big metal and PVC concertina curtain at school that could be pulled across to create two classrooms from one. This was the sort of structure I imagined separated my grandmother from me – one long meandering barrier stretching right across Europe. If I went to the edge of West Germany and just lifted the corner of the curtain a little, I might be able to sneak in and find her. I knew Grandma wanted to see me because she sent us presents: traditional wooden toys, thick brush-cotton romper suits, slightly gruesome hand-crafted string puppets (which I now know are typical Czech souvenirs; string puppets abound in the tourist shops of Prague's old town), and indestructible water glasses that never broke no matter how many times we dropped them on the floor.

I also knew that she and Grandpa had been through a really tough time in the war, and that they'd managed to smuggle Dad out to England before the Nazis deported them, which is why he was here with us and they were there, but he never went into details. I always thought it was strange that they didn't come with him, and the answers I was given didn't feel right somehow.

Evidently, like many Czech Jews, they thought the Nazi threat would be over in a matter of months and they would all soon be reunited. They were wrong. They ended up being stripped of the comfortable life they knew: Grandpa's job with the government, their flat in Prague, holidays in the mountains. And, along with approximately 155,000 other Jews, they were sent on trains to Theresienstadt. Unlike most, they survived. How they managed this and what went on in that place was never discussed.

Nor was why they didn't come back for Dad after liberation, something I never understood. He was their only son, serious-minded Hanus, who was born in 1930 and was separated from them when he was eight years old. And although my mother liked to hypothesise and criticise, it wasn't something Dad liked to talk about.

I thought if I could squeeze behind that curtain, reach Grandma and bring her over then we could sort it all out. My brothers and I were told that Dad couldn't go to his mother now because the Communists probably wouldn't let him out again and he would never risk that – we were too precious to him. Whenever I brought it up he seemed genuinely fearful that his life might be snatched away.

As I grew older I would regularly berate my parents for not providing me with relatives. It became a family joke, one I trotted out like a bratty child every birthday, Easter and Christmas without fail. My best friend Mandy had loads of them – grandparents, aunts, uncles, cousins of all ages – always free for endless entertainment: games, parties, dinners, outings. So I adopted hers and regularly went to stay with Mandy's nanna or her aunt and uncle. I had no idea that there *had* been relatives – so many – but they had all been murdered. It must have cut deep for Dad when I moaned about a lack of extended family. But still nothing was said.

When I pressed further, Mum did tell me that Dad's wider family had been killed in the gas chambers, but no names were mentioned. No one was identified, no numbers given, no stories told. My sense was that these were people Dad didn't know, a few random distant cousins he had nothing to do with. One might have been a rabbi, I recall Mum saying, which made me think they can't have been terribly close to Dad, because his family, though Jewish, weren't really religious. Dad had never attended synagogue – his father preferred him to play football in the fresh air on The Sabbath – and he knew nothing of things like Passover and Hanukkah. At least that's what he said.

His memories of Prague were all about going to coffee houses with his mother; listening to classical music and playing the piano; eating gluggy bread dumplings, which he adored, and frankfurters, rollmop herrings and sauerkraut . . . and travelling on the tram. He showed me a photo of him skiing in the mountains – a tiny boy in a woolly hat on wooden skis – and I was sure he said they had a family house somewhere out there in the countryside.

When I say I had no relatives it's not entirely true; there were people, some we even called aunts and uncles. They called my father Hans or Hoss rather than John, the name we knew him by. It was an undiscussed fact that various strange Eastern Europeans were surrogate relatives to our nuclear family. Some seemed to feel as if they needed to nurture us – my 'aunt' Fine, whom I knew very little, left me a gold garnet ring in her will. I remember going to the funeral somewhere in north London and being given the ring. Fine and her husband, 'Uncle' Lud, were friends of my grandparents from Prague, the only ones from Helena and Rudolf's group who had chosen to flee (at least this was the story I was told). They left with the clothes on their backs and a couple of suitcases but had to abandon everything else – their home, their money, their possessions. Fine told Mum everyone thought they were crazy. As it turned out, they were the smart ones.

There was also 'Uncle' Willi, who would visit in his smart Mercedes car and take us out. From the scant details we heard, I gathered he might have had something to do with Sigmund Freud, the celebrated psychoanalyst, and I later found out he became quite famous in his own right. And then Dad had a couple of much closer friends whom we saw a good deal. They were fellow Prague refugees – Annalisa, Theo and Klaus – all with strong accents. None of them discussed their past in any real detail; all were measured in what they revealed.

We knew they had been together in 'The Mission' with Dad. This was a curious children's home called The Barbican Mission to the Jews (BMJ), where Dad was raised. The children had arrived there by a sort of religious kindertransport run by an evangelical preacher who had personally saved 68 Czech Jewish children from Hitler on the proviso he could convert them into Christians. Dad didn't talk about this place much either.

But unlike Annalisa, Theo and Klaus, my father's accent was almost imperceptible, and so I always assumed his story was very different from theirs and somehow less tortured.

I was wrong.

======

On the night before Dad died, in 2006, when we were all sitting around his bed with his favourite Mozart sonata playing, he looked straight at Nick, my eldest brother, his firstborn, and said in a clear voice: 'The plane is in the hangar.' He was hallucinating, morphine and cancer playing tricks on his brain. But what was he talking about?

Was this the plane that had taken him away from his parents and his homeland in 1939? I have a photograph of Dad, aged eight, climbing the stairs of the KLM (Royal Dutch Airlines) charter, a little cloth knapsack on his back. Was he going back to that pivotal moment when his life changed forever?

When I started the research for this book I had no idea what, if anything, I would uncover. My main aim was to find out what had happened to my relatives and if there were others. I especially wanted to solve the mystery that had always baffled me about how my grandparents managed to survive so miraculously when so many others around them were sent away for execution. Did they collaborate to save their skin or was my grandfather one of the Elders in the controversial Ältestenrat, the Jewish council of Elders that ran Theresienstadt and chose those who were transported and those who were saved? And then, having gone through all that, why oh why didn't they come back to get their only son?

My investigations uncovered far more than I imagined. What I found was shocking, revelatory and deeply personal. I learned about family I never knew I had and the dark and twisted tales of their fates. The more I found the more I needed to know, and it started to become a pilgrimage to remember my kin, to pay homage to their stories. I headed to Czechoslovakia and Poland to seek them out, to follow in their footsteps.

But it then also became something else. It became about getting to know my dad all over again, about really understanding what he went through – for the first time, with my eyes wide, wide open and my journalist's brain on high alert. There was so much Dad experienced and didn't talk about. I know now he was protecting us from it – he didn't want to pass on the weight of the misery – but I always hankered to know more.

In my research I came across letters from my grandparents sent to Dad's guardians in the Mission just after liberation, which explained a great deal. I also stumbled upon a locked box in the British National Archives with Dad's name on it: John Rieden. This was astonishing; a whole box file all about my father that was locked in 2012 and was intended not to be opened until 2040. I had to file a Freedom of Information request to gain access to it, and in the 172 documents inside that box my father's struggle was laid out.

This is his story.

PART I
DISCOVERIES

CHAPTER ONE

THE DAY EVERYTHING CHANGED

I was born in 1963 in Surrey, one of England's green and pleasant home counties, an hour's drive from London. I was the youngest of Elizabeth – always known as Betty – and John Rieden's three children and the only girl. Initially Mum and Dad had wanted four children, but when I was born they decided to stop. Mum told me that following two sons, she and Dad had really wanted a girl but she was certain it wouldn't happen. So they were so shocked and delighted when I came along that they reconsidered their plans for a fourth child. As a precocious teen I would joke that I was so fabulous there was no need for a new arrival, while my brothers would quip it was more likely that I was such a handful it put our parents off procreating further. This was typical of our sibling scraps.

It's true that I was a fairly lively child, prone to temper tantrums when I couldn't get my own way, which, with two elder brothers ganging up against me, was often. But I always knew I was treasured. My mother told me when I was young she feared she would lose me because somehow she felt she didn't deserve me, which was a surprisingly irrational emotion for Mum, who was always grounded and unsentimental. Around age four or five I contracted mumps and Mum told me she was sure I was going to die. She sat up for three nights watching me breathe, afraid to leave my side.

Mum was born in Australia. Her father was a ship's engineer who served in the navy during the bombing of Darwin in World War II; her mother, a teacher and gifted musician. After studying at the University of Western Australia, Mum trained as a dietician and worked at the 1956 Melbourne Olympics in the athletes' kitchen before sailing for Britain: the ubiquitous Australian trip to the mother country. She'd bought a one-way ticket to London and was looking for adventure. In England she landed a great job working for the Flour Advisory Bureau, travelling around the country giving cooking demonstrations to women's institutes. She met my father – who by then was an insurance underwriter working in the City of London – on a skiing holiday, ironically in Austria (Hitler's birthplace), and from the photos I'm pretty sure the attraction was instant. They married in 1959 and settled in the south of England. After having children, Mum retrained as a teacher and taught biology and chemistry at one of the local state schools.

As an adult my father didn't identify as Jewish, and even if he had wanted to raise my brothers, Nick and Peter, and me in the faith, we wouldn't have been considered true Jews since Judaism follows matrilineal descent and Mum wasn't Jewish. We certainly never grew up with any Jewish traditions. In fact, we didn't grow up with religion at all. My mother had been raised with a nominal nod to the Anglican church. She went to Sunday school, knew all her hymns – and recently I was surprised to find a leather-backed prayer book as her ninth birthday gift from her mother in her library. But she was the most confirmed atheist I have ever known and, if anything, this was the family credo.

In our comfortable home in suburban Surrey, we five were a tight-knit unit with no nearby extended family. Mum's parents were a very long way away in Perth, Western Australia; Dad's were in Czechoslovakia and both were only children. Though money was always tight, our parents worked hard and ensured we always went on an annual holiday. These trips, usually to Europe, were the highlight of our year and planned in intricate detail by my father at least six months in advance. But it was on these sojourns, when we would often encounter Germans, that I also sensed some dark shadows in Dad's past. They were definitely connected to his Czech childhood but were not something he readily discussed.

I loved school and was a hard worker, often stressing too much around exams. Both our parents were mighty serious about education, and the pressure was at times intense. Dad would check my homework and frequently test me on my French vocabulary and Latin declensions. Theatre was our family's guilty indulgence, and even though my parents could only afford tickets up in the 'gods', we went up to the West End and the National Theatre in London, and visited the local repertory companies regularly. This was the Rieden mind food. My first outing, aged three and a half, was to a three-hour production of *Toad of Toad Hall*. Mum was worried I might get fidgety, but afterwards I famously announced that the play 'wasn't yerry yong!' (very long).

Theatre developed into a passion for me and I studied English literature and drama at university with the firm intent of becoming a newspaper theatre critic. With an honours degree secured, I then took a postgraduate diploma in journalism. Despite freelancing as a theatre reviewer for the newspapers, I quickly realised the established critics kept their coveted jobs for life and none were looking like they would be falling off their perch any time soon. So I would have to expand my journalistic horizons. I worked mostly in entertainment journalism, where I met my partner, Katie. Later, when she was offered a magazine editorship in Australia, I also found a job on a magazine there and we headed for the sun.

Dad was diagnosed with cancer in 2001. He and Mum assured me the prognosis was good as he started treatment. And at first he responded well. But by 2004 he was becoming very sick. I was heartbroken, and Katie and I moved back to the UK so I could help care for him. For the next two years I worked as a senior journalist at a UK national newspaper in London, and most Fridays and weekends headed to Surrey as Dad battled his illness with dignity. Losing him hit me hard, and after his funeral we scurried back to Sydney. We bought a flat in the Eastern Suburbs and I began working for the venerable *Australian Women's Weekly*, travelling Australia and the world to interview fascinating people and adding Royal Correspondent to my list of reporting duties.

Every year since 1997, we have returned to England to see our family and friends, and we were in Prague that day in 2016 for a three-day stopover on the way back to Sydney. Prague was bulging with tourists, the sun was out and the city was achingly beautiful.

And then I went to the Pinkas Synagogue in the heart of the Old Jewish Quarter and everything changed.

———

Out back at Pinkas Synagogue is the famous Old Jewish Cemetery, where graves, some ten deep, are piled on top of each other, stabbing through the earth, reaching, reaching for a shaft of sunlight. The headstones are packed in, jostling and tumbling in what at first glance seems to be utter chaos. The deep layering and overcrowding in this burial ground is the result of limited space in what was once part of an ancient ghetto, a testament to shameful centuries of legalised anti-Semitism.

Here, apart from a brief flourishing of tolerance around the turn of the twentieth century, Jews were forced to live in segregation, banned from other Prague neighbourhoods, and though this cemetery was expanded a couple of times, it still proved far too small for the community's dead. There are some 12,000 tombstones crowded in, dating back to the fifteenth century, some just poking up their heads above ground level as others grandstand above. It's an unsettling sight that, in the context of the names on the synagogue wall, can't help but conjure up ghostly echoes of the pyramids of twisted bodies in Hitler's gas chambers, each gasping for a last breath.

Between the tombstones, wildflowers and grasses have claimed the topsoil, delivering a softness to this arena of death. So despite the pall, there is serenity here. This historic place, this tiny patch of religious calm and respect in a city of Baroque gilt excess, Gothic flying buttresses, swirling romantic Art Nouveau and intellectual sharp-edged Cubism, belongs to the Jews – and today it felt as if it belonged to me.

Pinkas, the second-oldest synagogue in Prague, was turned into a memorial back in the late 1950s for the 80,000 Jewish victims of the Holocaust who came from Bohemia and Moravia. Two painters took on the Herculean task of inscribing the victims' names on the walls, an epitaph for those who had no real graves, many no longer families even, to remember them.

And it was here, in this synagogue, for the first time in my then 52 years, that I grasped the point of tombs and memorials, or at least how they related to me. For this simple, eloquent evocation gave voice to the intellectual hearts, the deep thoughts, the conversation, the vibrant lives, the sartorial style and the soaring musicality of so many, brutally snuffed out and carelessly tossed in pits or rivers, shot in the head or back, choked by gas and engulfed in flames.

Here the inhumane became human and my family took shape. Pieces of who my father was and who I am were all thrown up in the air, and I felt a searing need to grasp them and pull them back together. After reading the names of my relatives on the wall, I crouched down in the courtyard outside the synagogue and started to search the internet feverishly and email my two brothers, Nick and Peter, in England. I felt dizzy and a little lost. Something elemental had shifted.

While I knew that my grandparents, Rudolf and Helena Rieden, had been sent away to Theresienstadt (Terezín in Czech), my understanding had always been that they had survived the Holocaust relatively unscathed by the horrors so many others had endured. Dad preferred to call Theresienstadt a ghetto rather than a concentration camp. He said it was a sort of walled town where his mother and father lived, not in comfort and not willingly, but it wasn't a death camp and they got through it. Indeed, at the end of the war they came out and simply resumed their lives back in Prague. Or so I thought.

The existence of a wider family – of Rudolf and Helena's brothers and sisters, Dad's aunts and uncles, of their parents, of cousins – this was never mentioned. But here they were, and as my crude internet dredge started to reveal, they were not only murdered, but their various journeys to that full stop took nearly all of them through Theresienstadt, that name

I knew so well. Grandma and Grandpa would have been there in the camp when their kin were sent East to their deaths. What's more, Emil Rieden, Rudolf's father, Dad's grandpa, actually perished in the ghetto just four months after Rudolf and Helena were transported there. Were they with him when he died, I wonder, and did Emil have any sense of what lay ahead for his children?

I couldn't take it all in. Who were these people and why didn't I know more about them?

I raised myself back on my feet and headed back inside Pinkas, drawn to that spot in the heart of the synagogue where six lines up from the bottom I had spied *Rieden*, a personal hieroglyph pregnant with meaning. I needed to check what I had seen was still there. That I hadn't imagined it. But there was no mistake.

After staring at the letters compulsively I eventually turned away and followed the crowds to the rooms upstairs, unaware of what lay ahead. It was an exhibition of children's drawings, evocative paintings and sketches by the children who were sent to Theresienstadt. They have become incredibly important to those who want to understand the Holocaust and what went on, because from the innocence of youth comes a poignant and powerful dialogue depicting exactly what the inmates knew about what was happening to them, how they felt and the brutal conditions of their incarceration.

If Dad had not escaped to England, his drawings would have been in this exhibition and I would not be here. Nine thousand children under the age of 15 passed through Theresienstadt, 1633 lived there when the camp was liberated. Most of these young artists were all murdered.

Their pictures are of Nazi soldiers with guns, buildings with black smoke pumping from chimneys, emaciated prisoners crammed into dark, dirty dwellings with ragged clothes, bunk beds piled high. And then there's another world painted here: of life before Theresienstadt, an exaggerated imaginative paradise with butterflies, green meadows and naive houses where families live happily together.

They stay with you these drawings, they reach into your soul . . . and I had seen them before.

＝＝＝

It was 1990 some months after the Velvet Revolution, when the Communists were finally overthrown in a bloodless coup and, like a page from a children's fable, playwright Václav Havel was elected as president of a new Czechoslovakia. Only this wasn't fiction, this was reality and everyone was rejoicing. Now for the first time, Dad could go back to his birthplace without fear of reprisal.

It was my idea that he, Mum and I book a holiday as soon as possible, and when I mentioned it to Dad he was surprisingly eager. By this time his parents, Rudolf and Helena, had both died and there was no mention of any other kin we should be checking on, but Dad really wanted to see Prague again. He was aching to show it to us, and Mum and I wanted to be with him when he was at last reunited with his homeland. It didn't feel like a sombre or tortured pilgrimage, but a chance to celebrate Czechoslovakia's emancipation and enjoy the beauty of this place that was so much part of our family – and, as I was soon to discover, so much part of Dad.

It was early October and the air was crisp. The city was in the throes of waking up after grey Communism had cramped its style. Hotel rooms were in high demand, mostly from young West German tourists, whose Deutschmark made them very rich in this secret land that had been shut away from Europe for so long. These large groups of beer-swilling holiday-makers seemed oblivious to the part their Fatherland had played in Czechoslovakia's painful history, and I sensed that their presence irritated both my parents.

We could only secure five days in the Intercontinental Hotel, and our travel agent then promised he could arrange a further three nights in a private house. We'd receive the final details when we arrived, Dad was told, and we had to pay the owners in person in Deutschmarks, presented in a sealed envelope. It all felt very shadowy and underhand, and the reality, sleeping in a cramped one-bed flat while the occupants and their baby moved in with their parents a few doors down, was pretty awkward.

This was my first step behind the Iron Curtain I had thought so much about as a child. And it was another world, one to which I was definitely connected but had no knowledge. Communism hadn't dulled Prague's charisma, the squares twinkling with golden baubles atop spires, the cobbled streets and painted houses straight out of a Bohemian fairy tale, the medieval astronomical clock striking on the hour, a ghoulish delight with its skeleton turning the hourglass on life. The only upside of occupation was that Prague wasn't bombed during the war, and though updated a little and with new grey concrete buildings added from the Communist era, Dad's homeland was right there, in all its resplendent glory, as it always had been, waiting for him to come back.

The hotel was dated and beige, stuck in the 1970s with a brutalist concrete exterior. Service was clipped, verging on rude. Like most of Eastern Europe at the time, consumerism in Prague was virtually non-existent. Shops were empty, with one sad dusty item on display in the window, and restaurants were basic and always supposedly fully booked – even when they seemed half-full. These establishments were all still government run and they catered for one booking per table per night. There was no incentive to serve more, so they turned hungry tourists away. It was all very strange to a child of capitalism.

What was most surprising though was the effect Prague had on Dad. He was proud, comfortable and confident. He seemed immediately at home, with a deep-seated contentment, as we meandered around the streets, across the bridges and up through the parks heady with trees.

Dad loved trees. When a neighbour once wanted one of the trees in our garden cut down because it created too much shade, Dad was pained and agitated. It was as if some part of him was being attacked – the severed branches were his limbs. When I saw the richness of the urban forests of oaks, limes, plane trees and giant sequoias along the banks of the Vltava below the castle, I wondered if this was what Dad was trying to recreate when he settled in verdant Surrey in England.

Very quickly my father's Czech started to come back; he understood the announcements on the trams and read the street signs with ease. He taught my mother and me some words, and our nightly dinner game was to see if we remembered them. Otherwise he spoke German.

As children we'd had many holidays in Austria when Dad easily spoke German to all we met. His accent and command of the language were exemplary, although he faltered at times trying to remember.

Early on in my research I discovered why; this was actually his mother tongue – a punishing irony considering his family's fate. The Rieden family hailed from the Sudetenland, part of the Austrian empire before the formation of Czechoslovakia, and at home, to his parents, Dad spoke German. Even after the war, after all that had happened to them, Rudolf and Helena spoke German to each other. Interestingly, on a form I discovered hidden in the British National Archives, Dad was asked to list the languages he spoke. He wrote 'English and a little French', even though his German never left him.

Although Dad spoke little of his parents on this trip, he did want to find out if his childhood home, the apartment he was raised in and had been bundled out of in such frightened haste, was still there. To my astonishment he didn't consult a map or ask for directions. He simply guided my mother and me onto a tram heading into the suburbs.

After 20 minutes or so we hopped off onto a tree-lined street, walked a few blocks, turned left and Dad went straight to the door. He said he'd made this journey all the time with his mother and it was just as he had remembered it, right down to the tram route number.

The door to the apartment block was ajar and I persuaded Dad – who was a little nervous – that we should head on up to his apartment and knock. Eventually he agreed, but no one answered. I think Dad was relieved. I don't think he wanted a confrontation, and when I went back on my research for this book I think I understood what Dad's reticence was all about.

On our third day in Prague we went to the Old Jewish Cemetery. The Pinkas 'writing on the wall' was not there then. In 1967 the Communist government had shut down the memorial and removed the names from the wall. They were painstakingly redrawn between 1992 and 1996, but that was too late for Dad, who I don't believe ever saw this memorial, although he did return to Czechoslovakia on a later, more extensive, visit with Mum.

But the exhibition of children's drawings was in situ, and the hour we spent walking round was the first time I glimpsed Dad's anguish. We were all floored; even my mother was uncharacteristically silent. At times she took her husband's hand as he paused to assimilate each drawing. We couldn't speak, only look and learn.

So this was Theresienstadt, that mythical place where my grandparents had spent the war. This was the 'ghetto'. It wasn't the 'easy option' I had always thought my grandparents had been lucky enough to end up with. It was brutal, terrifying. It was a vision of hell.

When we regrouped outside, darkness was falling and we were all crying. Dad said simply, 'It could have been me.' If we discussed it more I don't remember, but our conversation over dinner that night I will never forget. It was about the new Germans who were all around us in Prague, gleefully throwing their money around, and equally cheerfully visiting the sites commemorating especially brutal incidents during Nazi occupation. Dad questioned their presence here and their sense of ownership and joy. I said they couldn't be blamed for what their ancestors had done and suggested it was good that they at least wanted to visit and understand. History was the most powerful educator.

'Perhaps,' said Dad quietly, but I could sense he didn't agree, and very quickly Mum retorted: 'No, it was something in the German race, something that has not gone away, that created that evil. If you'd lived through it you'd understand.'

I had never heard either of my parents talk like this. They were innate socialists, natural sharers and certainly never racist. But today, here, they were filled with rage.

Mum had been in Australia during the war; her father had served with the Australian Navy, protecting the coastline from

Japanese attacks. What did she know of Germans? And what about all those holidays when we regularly met Germanic families? Dad was always very careful around these people. Courteous but controlled. He certainly never revealed his Jewish background and he avoided any talk of the war, which at times took some tap-dancing. He never tried to stop me forging friendships with the children of these families, and one girl from Frankfurt remained a penpal of mine for years. So why did these young Germans with their brash ways and innocent vitality still have the power to strike fear into my parents' gentle hearts?

The next day Dad wanted to go to Karlovy Vary (known as Karlsbad in German), where he had deep-seated and happy memories of childhood holidays. It's a picturesque and historic riverside spa city, where thermal springs spout high jets and people take the waters hoping to cure all sorts of maladies. It was too hard to go on our own. The Communist authorities' control of tourism was still in evidence and so we had to book a day tour. Unfortunately, the other tourists on our trip included a clutch of Germans. We climbed on the coach and after an hour or so were a little perplexed to find we were stopping en route at a place called Lidice. We hadn't planned on this and definitely weren't prepared for the story of this place.

On 10 June 1942, the village of Lidice was demolished, the houses were razed to the ground. All the men over 15 years old were systematically shot, their bodies left piled up on the ground, and many of the women and children too. Those who remained were sent to concentration camps and some of the very young children, who were considered racially suitable, were 'Germanised' – sent to be raised in Aryan families.

Lidice was not a Jewish village. The attack was retribution for the assassination of Reinhard Heydrich, the brutal

SS officer who had been appointed Acting Protector of Bohemia and Moravia and was one of the most powerful and vicious men in Nazi Germany. Heydrich was behind the 'Final Solution', which planned to deal with the 'Jewish question'. He was also one of the architects of Kristallnacht (crystal night, or the Night of Broken Glass – named after the shattered shop, synagogue and house windows), the attacks which, I later discovered, forced my relatives out of their homes and businesses and started their desperate flight from the Nazis.

When Heydrich was ambushed by members of the Czech Resistance and a week later died from his injuries, the reprisals were horrific. Hitler ordered his SS to 'wade in blood' through Czechoslovakia in pursuit of the culprits. A letter falsely linked the assassins to Lidice, and an example was made of the village. It was prisoners from Theresienstadt – could it have been members of my family? – who were made to bury the bodies of those murdered and clear the ground as if nothing had ever been there, while drunk Nazi soldiers watched on.

Dad had known nothing of this story and as we were taken through every step of the massacre he turned whiter and whiter. There is now a rose garden memorial on the site of the original village of Lidice with 24,000 roses donated by 32 countries around the world.

We were taken into a cinema in the visitor centre at the memorial and there on the screen we saw photos of each man, woman and child who had been killed and each face disappeared from the screen to the soundtrack of gunshots.

Dad couldn't take it and left on his own to make his way back to the coach.

Many of the Germans were already there. I'm not sure if they hadn't wanted to see the memorial or if they were starting to feel uncomfortable, but as we drove on to Karlovy Vary the bus was at last silent.

———

In Karlovy Vary we could breathe again. The pretty painted houses, the hot springs, the forested valleys, the grand architecture take your breath away.

In his pre-war childhood, Dad spent his holidays here. We have a family photo of him promenading along the esplanade with his mum and a lady I later realise is his Aunt Ida, Helena's eldest sister who I now believe was very close to her nephew, little Hanus. Dad is almost six in the photo, with long socks and a smart wool coat, and the two sisters look so elegant in their outfits as they walk towards the camera. This was 1936 and as far as I can tell from the photo the family is happy, close-knit and prosperous.

Less than three years later Dad was in a Christian mission in England, and Helena and Ida were trying to hang on to their lives, property and belongings in Prague as the Nazi net tightened around them.

Ida was unmarried, I later discover, one of eleven brothers and sisters born to Rabbi Moritz Hoffer and his wife, Ruzena. They were all raised in the town of Žlutice in the Karlovy Vary district, so this was very much Helena and Ida's stamping ground. I think the family had a home in this part of Bohemia that my father tried – and failed – to find on a subsequent visit.

Although Dad never talked about his numerous aunts and uncles on his mother's side of the family, and certainly never mentioned Ida, she appears in three of the very few photos of his family we have. An especially poignant one is of Ida by herself, taken in 1937 in Karlovy Vary. Ida looks incredibly stylish, with a fashionable cinched-in jacket and a jaunty beret. This one was made into a postcard and under the photo of Ida is the slogan 'Karlsbad restores your health', written in German. On the back is a note written to Dad at his preparatory school in England.

Curiously there is no stamp or postmark on the card. I assume this means it may have been sent via a central system set up by the Czech Refugee Trust or the Czech government, or even from a concentration camp. Dad definitely received it and cherished it, as we have it along with his meagre belongings from that period. Ida writes in German and says 'A photo taken in Karlsbad in late summer 1937. Dedicated to my beloved Hansi to remember. From his aunt Ida.'

And yet on our day trip to Karlovy Vary, Dad didn't mention Ida at all. We walked along what could well have been the very same colonnade where she is photographed for that postcard. I now suspect Ida was one of the reasons we were there. It must have been so emotional for Dad taking in this beautiful place again, a city that was such a crucial part of his childhood – and yet he kept it inside.

Thinking of that trip now, I wonder if Mum knew what was going on. My parents were incredibly close. Every evening when Dad came home from work, they would pour themselves an aperitif and walk around the garden together sharing the day they had spent apart. I can't imagine he didn't tell her about this, but if he did, Mum knew it wasn't something she could divulge even to us, their children.

═══

When I returned home to Sydney after my discovery at Pinkas Synagogue, I had no clue that Ida and the Hoffer family would also become part of my search. I certainly couldn't forget those names on the wall, and became consumed with

THE WRITING ON THE WALL

a need to unlock their stories. I talked to my brothers, who knew little more than I did, and started to contact a few of my father's friends who were still around to see what they knew. The answer was unanimous: Dad just didn't talk about it. The journalist in me went into full research mode and, as a Rieden, the daughter of a Holocaust survivor, I couldn't let this go. I have never believed in fate, but here it felt as if something was suggesting it was my time to step up.

I wondered if Dad had known what happened to his family, but it was no longer possible to ask him. What did this family go through? How did I end up with no relatives in England when Dad had so many in Czechoslovakia? Could I still have living relatives? There was a photo in our family album of a family on a beach in Israel, which Dad identified as simply 'distant relatives who managed to escape'. Was this family still around, I wondered?

I felt compelled to start my own investigation and resolved to devote all my spare time for the next 18 months to unlocking the truth. The heart of my mission was to answer four burning questions:

1   How did Grandpa and Grandma manage to survive, and what had happened to everyone else?
2   Why didn't they come to England to collect their only child – my Dad, their Hanus – in 1945?
3   Do I have any relatives at all from my Dad's side anywhere in the world?
4   How did my father manage to make his way in Britain as a Jew, forcibly converted to Christianity, with no family to help him?

Everything had changed for me.

CHAPTER TWO

FILLING IN THE BLANKS

Back in Sydney in 2017, I began my research in earnest, tentatively at first and then in fevered flurries. I felt like a detective as I sifted the internet and fired off enquiries and records applications to archives in the Czech Republic, Poland, Austria, Israel, Germany, the United States and Britain. I was astonished and heartened to see the rigour of the Holocaust resources around the world, and I am ashamed to say that initially answers came thick and fast, with relative ease. Ashamed because the facts had been right there waiting to be read, all this time. What had I been waiting for?

And yet these records told me only so much – I yearned to learn more. There was no question I was in this now; there was no turning back. I was determined to find out the truth, not just for me, my brothers and my nieces, but for my murdered relatives.

I very quickly realised that absolutes were going to be hard to find. Lists were the foundation of the Third Reich. The Nazis loved the finality of them, the idea that once something was written down, once someone's fate had been determined on the record it became fact; this was how their dispassionate system worked. I therefore assumed my family stories would be minutely documented, which no doubt they would have been had the perpetrators not also been cowards. For it was these files, reams of paperwork painstakingly filled out, cataloguing the genocide Hitler fervently believed he had a mandate to exercise, that the Nazi officers clamoured to destroy when they saw victory slipping from their grasp.

The records of those horrendous acts, of which they were so proud and certain, now needed to be erased along with the six million Jews they had massacred. Documents were destroyed along with the gas chambers themselves and a great deal of evidence.

Of course, what the Nazis couldn't erase were people's memories, and so history sees the backbone of the Nazi machine through the passionate, angry and bereaved eyes of witness testimonies. Holocaust archives around the world have gathered these accounts for decades to fill in the gaps created by Hitler's henchmen on the run, and their statements come with all the emotion and trauma those bureaucratic records deemed so irrelevant.

For me this meant that while initial local and state government records could tell me some things, I would have to dig a lot deeper to unpick what Hitler did to each member of my family and the excruciating details of their struggle. The more layers I peeled back, the more I realised how painful the stories were going to be, and I began to glimpse the yoke my father had been carrying. But he still never once let on or allowed himself to off-load on his family or friends.

As I worked, a niggling doubt quivered like a butterfly's wings fluttering on the edge of my consciousness. Was I doing the right thing? Was this classic Pandora's box exuberance that

I would live to regret? Why *had* Dad hidden so much from us, his three children to whom he gave everything?

I started to wonder if there may in fact have been a dark secret, an ignominious truth or incident that prevented him from mourning his family's deaths in the open. Or was it simply all too much for Dad to face? I confess I couldn't and wouldn't have stirred this up when my father was alive, so was it really appropriate to do it now when Dad was no longer with us to raise protest? But I couldn't stop.

When Dad was diagnosed with cancer, he slowly disappeared in front of my eyes. On the way there were so many sudden hospital stays for serious medical procedures followed by reprieves. And each time, the joy at little recoveries, stable blood tests, positive reactions to radiotherapy, filled us with hope. But deep down we all knew the end was just over the hill. Mum buckled in for the ride, always pragmatic but optimistic, devoting every hour of every day to the rehabilitation of her husband.

It was harrowing to go through, and when my father died at just 75, there was definitely a 'why him, why us?' moment for me. Why John Rieden, Hanus, the refugee who had been through so much? Where was the justice in that?

My mother and brothers were much more considered and rational. They said we were lucky that we'd had 'the real Dad', with his intellect and sense of humour intact, right to the end, even though he was confined to a hospital bed in the living room and had to face the indignity of being hoisted up and down from bed to chair by carers twice a day, tubes from his bladder filling a bag with urine that was strapped to his lower leg.

My father was accepting, kind and gentle to the end, and while he complained like hell about the uncomfortable pillows and pains in his back, he never once considered the hand he had been dealt was unjust. He took his illness on the chin, just as he had managed his shattered childhood, separated from his parents, from his homeland, from his culture.

I certainly couldn't accept his death, and looking back I think I have never fully understood how he could be so seemingly calm about his past. So perhaps this mission of mine, this meticulous no-stone-unturned investigation of where he came from and what happened to his kin, became my way of keeping Dad with me . . . I hope he understands.

———

The first thing I learned was yes, Dad did have aunts and uncles on his father's side whom he certainly knew, some very well, because for a while they actually lived with him in Prague. And, yes, the 'writing on the wall' was unquestionably correct: the majority of his family were murdered by the Nazis.

At first the facts were bald: dates of transports, dates of birth and addresses. Almost immediately after the Nazi occupation of Czechoslovakia, this living breathing close-knit family became reduced to a series of numbers on lists as they were moved like cattle, always on the brink of slaughter. But as I delved deeper, into archive records, into testimonies, I started to uncover little details about who they were and what really happened. And while the birth dates on the wall were correct and could be verified by certificates, the deaths were for the most part approximations based on the dates of their various transports to death camps.

Each relative's path was different; there was no single mass Rieden extermination but death by a thousand tiny cuts, which in some cases became a game of cat and mouse as first the Protectorate, and then the Schutzstaffel (literally

31

'protective echelon' and abbreviated to the notorious 'SS'), hunted them down. Their destruction was systematic, as it was for millions of Jews, but also seemingly random, with little rhyme or reason as to why each was called when they were and why some suffered so intensely.

It was a lot to take in, but even amid the misery I felt a certain salute of triumph as I stepped back in time to immerse myself in the lives of these people, my people, who until that moment in the Pinkas Synagogue I hadn't even known existed.

Aside from the Riedens on the wall, there were other Riedens, I learned. Paul, Anna, Hedwig and Elsa were also Grandpa's siblings, and didn't seem to be on the registers of Holocaust killings. In total Dad seemingly had seven paternal aunts and uncles. Could any of them have survived? Or did they perhaps have children who had escaped like Dad? This news gave me fresh hope – here was a very real possibility that I may yet have living relatives.

I recall my mother telling me that when my grandmother Helena had visited us in 1965 – the first and last time we ever saw her, and the only time Dad was reunited with her after they had been so cruelly separated in 1939 – she had tried to ask her mother-in-law about what happened in Theresienstadt.

It wasn't easy. Grandma's English was very poor, Mum's German was terrible and Dad didn't want any part in quizzing his mother about those years. I'm not sure if he was protecting Helena or himself or us. But as Mum recalled, Helena never discussed the Holocaust with her son, at least not within her earshot.

But after my father died, Mum told me that late one afternoon on that visit, when she and Helena were together and

Dad was yet to return home from work, Helena did reveal that many times she and Grandpa – Rudolf – had been listed for transport East and even found themselves in queues, but each time they were pulled out of the line just in time. Mum told me that at some point in their conversation 'Auschwitz' was mentioned in a German sentence from Grandma that Mum didn't understand. She never managed to find out if Dad's parents had been there and somehow managed to escape or if Helena was talking about others, and Mum didn't feel she could pry further.

From what I found out later, I suspect this was one of the few times Grandma talked about what happened to our family, and here she may well have been discussing not just the Riedens but her own brothers and sisters, the Hoffers.

When I was growing up Dad had always refused to watch films and television programs about Auschwitz and wouldn't engage in any talk about what happened there, so as a child I believed Grandma and Grandpa might have been sent there after Theresienstadt. As my research started to reveal, thankfully this was not the case. But it was highly likely that Helena and Rudolf would have found their names on the transport lists to the death camps many times and also that their names were removed. Others in the family weren't so lucky. Auschwitz, I later discovered, was very much part of the family story, and I am certain now that Dad knew this.

Theresienstadt camp, which was intended to 'concentrate' Jews from all over Europe, before their inevitable journey to the death camps in the East, was established in November 1941. There were typically 1000 Jews on each transport to the camp, but numbers varied. The journey was arduous, the victims crowded into passenger cars after three or four days spent trapped in the makeshift departure zone in the trade-fair hall in central Prague, guarded by police. My early research into the Riedens showed that most of them had passed through Theresienstadt at some point.

Helena and Rudolf's is a wonderful story of triumph in a very dark catalogue of horror, but how on earth did they avoid the fate of the rest of our family?

═══

My internet searches had come to a full stop and I decided the only way to move forward was to go back to Prague, visit Theresienstadt and Auschwitz myself, and then follow my father's path to England. I started planning my journey.

In the meantime, I became obsessed with everything to do with the Holocaust, devouring books, films and documentaries. Early on I headed to Sydney's Jewish Museum. I had never been inside before, even though I drove past it most days. I never thought it relevant to me but perhaps also the time wasn't propitious.

When I ventured inside I quickly realised the museum is more than a historical archive, it's a meeting place and haven of solace. I felt an almost spiritual aura, which was all the more powerful in light of my recent discoveries about my family. I was surprised to see the museum had an entire exhibition about Theresienstadt. Even though I had grown up knowing that my grandparents spent the war in Theresienstadt, I had no idea what their life was actually like there. I also didn't know how and why Grandma and Grandpa came to be in Theresienstadt and what that journey entailed. Here, laid out before me, however, was the essence of my grandparents' life in that place. Although it was not a death camp, the myth that life in this camp was somehow less brutal was quickly extinguished for me by the avalanche of testimonies depicting the indignities, the fight for survival and the appalling conditions. And hanging over every minute of every day was the terror of being selected for transport East.

Did Dad know all this? Certainly, he never talked about it, nor were there any books in our home about Theresienstadt. And we were a family with books on everything. When we wanted to learn about something we'd buy a book – so this was surprising. Even considering the shocking subject matter, I can't see how my father could have *not* sought out this vital part of his parents' life story. But I also suspect that in discovering the truth, Dad pushed it as far as he possibly could into that corner of his mind where I now understand he must have locked away so much of the pain of what happened.

One of the staff members at the museum told me that her family was also in Theresienstadt, while another shared that her kin were sent to Auschwitz. As I imparted the little I knew of my grandparents' story, I mentioned the blanket that was currently sitting in my brother Nick's garage in England, the one Rudolf and Helena had had with them in Theresienstadt. This sparked a flurry of excitement. Did I have any other memorabilia? Could they see the blanket? Might I consider donating it to the museum?

I was initially taken aback and rather perplexed. How could my family blanket be of value here in Sydney? But as we talked more, I came to understand that every skerrick of life in the camps has become the lifeblood of the Jewish ownership of what they call in Hebrew 'Shoah'. And with Holocaust deniers and anti-Semitism on the rise again, it is these artefacts that give veracity to what I now see as our story. It is here in Sydney that for the first time I started to feel part of the struggle. I was not only welcome, I was cherished.

At the Sydney Jewish Museum, Theresienstadt became real. From many memoirs, histories and especially H.G. Adler's unparalleled and utterly comprehensive *Theresienstadt 1941–1945: The Face of a Coerced Community* (which was first published in 1955 in German and only translated into English in 2017) I filled in the terrible details. I also had the privilege of talking to three survivors from Theresienstadt, all of whom had been there as children, and through various means escaped and were now living in Sydney. For a couple of hours one afternoon a few weeks later, Paul, Litzi and Tomas shared their stories and their pain. Survival, they told me, was a matter of sheer luck in a world where nothing made sense and brutality hovered around every corner. From all this I pieced together my first glimpses of my grandparents' three years in the camp.

═══

Rudolf and Helena would have received their call-up papers late at night, hand-delivered by someone from the Prague JKG (Jüdische Kultusgemeinde, the Jewish Cultural Organisation). During occupation, the JKG was forced to ensure that Protectorate rules with regard to the Jews of Bohemia and Moravia were carried out to the letter. It would have been a grim task for sure.

The papers they delivered included a transport number for both Rudolf and Helena and instructions. Their personal number, they were told, was to be written on hard cardboard and hung on string around their necks for easy identification. This was the beginning of what I now see was a systematic dehumanising process that allowed the Nazi persecution to run more smoothly, stripping each Jew of their sense of self in a series of carefully choreographed indignities. From this moment on, Dr Rudolf Rieden, decorated war veteran, doctor of law, civil servant with the Czech government and father, and his wife, Helena Riedenova, who had worked in a bank and was the daughter of a rabbi and a mother herself, were reduced to mere numerals.

There was no question of not adhering to these demands; the punishments were known to be severe and potentially fatal. Fear was their ruler now, and even though my grandparents would have been expecting that knock on the door, they must have been utterly terrified. I suspect all they had to hang on to at that moment was the knowledge that their son, Hanus, though no doubt scared and confused, was safe in England.

The papers summoned Rudolf and Helena at an allotted hour on an allotted day, in probably a week's time but maybe sooner, to Prague's trade-fair grounds, where a leaky wooden barn-like structure would have become their prison for three or four days while they were processed and before they were put on a train for Theresienstadt.

They were allowed 50 kilograms of luggage each in total – their life's possessions reduced to the equivalent of a bag of cement. Their main bag, they were told, would not be accessible on the journey, so blankets and food for five days should be packed in hand luggage of a knapsack or small suitcase. In their larger bags they were advised to pack clothes, bed linen, bowls and pots, preserved food, washing and sewing equipment, writing paper and candles. They were even told to include small appliances such as an oven and iron, and tools such as a pickaxe, a saw and more. Much of this was then confiscated or stolen at the camp, but they wouldn't have known this then.

Many sewed money and jewels into the lining of coats, jackets and frocks. And in desperation they gave jewellery, valuables, expensive items of furniture, private letters and the like to non-Jewish friends to return to them in better times. I don't know if Helena and Rudolf did this, but I suspect they may have, as when my grandmother died her estate included valuable gold jewellery with real diamonds, gemstones and pearls, which she would never have been able to afford after the war.

All luggage had to be indelibly marked with their names, destination Theresienstadt and their transport number, and a duplicate piece of paper with these details put inside the case, as a back-up should the markings somehow be rubbed off. This reassured some Jews that they would be reunited with their possessions, a largely erroneous assumption, but it also established the idea that any transgressions, attempts to break the rules and slip in impermissible keepsakes or valuables, could and would be traced. The prospect of punishment was a powerful and effective Nazi tool.

My grandparents were also told to bring all of their cash, bank books, insurance policies, ration cards, property deeds and the keys to their home. A detailed eight-page 'property declaration' form had to be filled out, declaring all assets and handing them over to the state. I think my grandparents would have imagined all this to be temporary, but they certainly would have been rattled. Would they have listed everything on these forms? It seems unthinkable that you would blithely hand over your livelihood, but in the end it didn't really matter, for everything was seized anyway. What they were left with was their ID cards stamped with 'ghettoised'. In effect Rudolf and Helena were now no longer citizens of Prague but evacuees.

Jews were told to leave their apartments with the furni-ture intact; selling, giving away or lending items was strictly forbidden. They were caught in a net, and while many chose optimism over despair, I am sure everyone deep down understood what was happening.

What lay ahead, however, was unthinkable.

After a depressing and uncomfortable first few nights of incarceration at the transport point in Prague, Helena and Rudolf, possibly together with Rudolf's sister Berta who was on that same transport, would have been marched to the railway station, heavily laden with their belongings. Here they stayed for several hours while the train was loaded up and their main bags were taken away and piled into freight wagons.

What was running through their minds when they were bundled into passenger carriages with their hand luggage, some 50 or 60 people per carriage? Rudolf wore a prosthetic, having lost his right leg in the First World War, so it would have been doubly difficult for him. For many I have talked to, it is the sheer terror of these train journeys that has stayed with them, and I'm sure this was the case for my grandparents. A picture of their lifetime nightmares was starting to build for me, as I'm sure it must have done for my father when he discovered what his parents had endured. The notorious journeys in cattle carts were the transports East, which many experienced all too soon after this.

Fortunately, Prague to Bohušovice, then the nearest station to Theresienstadt, was just three hours. While the journey was no doubt gruelling it was at least relatively swift. Jews transported to Theresienstadt from further afield in Czechoslovakia, Austria and Germany, endured days of horror on the trains.

On arrival, Rudolf and Helena, dirty and exhausted, would then have had to embark on the three-kilometre tramp, carrying their luggage, from the station to Theresienstadt itself, little knowing that this would be their last taste of life outside the camp for three years. Would Rudolf with his artificial leg have been offered a ride? Or did they join the route march with his sister Berta, I wonder? Those who remember this process talk of cruel SS officers who would lash out at the newcomers on a whim, shouting and beating anyone who wasn't keeping up.

At Theresienstadt the selections started, a process that was going to dominate their lives in the days, months and years ahead. Luggage was off-loaded and the first port for all new inmates to the 'ghetto' was the arrivals centre – the aptly named Schleuse (sluice). Here registration cards were filled out, there were medical examinations and inmates had to strip and be washed in delousing solution. The Nazis, and in some cases the Jewish ghetto officials, raided suitcases, leaving only the bare essentials for those who remained in Theresienstadt. Some of these stolen items ended up being sold back to the inmates in quasi-shops or on the black market. The newcomers then received their vouchers for food, baths and laundry.

The Schleuse was crowded and unpleasant, and mostly inmates slept in the dirt on the floor for days until their fate was revealed. Those first few days in the Schleuse, which could stretch to a week or more, must have been horrendous, with everyone crammed together not knowing what lay ahead.

Rudolf and Helena, I later discovered when I visited Theresienstadt myself, were separated and sent to different barracks. And from this moment on their lives changed forever. I'm sure that my father had no clue until many years after about what was happening to his parents at this time.

———

Today we know exactly what Theresienstadt was like thanks to the testimonies of some of the approximately 23,000 who witnessed and survived the ordeal, and to what was found there by the Russian Army, who liberated the camp at 9 pm on 8 May 1945.

In four years approximately 155,000 prisoners were brought here. Although it wasn't a death camp and had no gas chambers, 35,088 died in Theresienstadt and a further 88,196 were sent to Auschwitz and other extermination camps. And according to historian H.G. Adler, who was an inmate himself, of the 9000 children under the age of 15 who were in Theresienstadt, just 1633 made it to liberation. More than 80 per cent of prisoners who went to Theresienstadt were killed.

The statistics are too huge to comprehend, and now they related directly to me. Most of my family came to this place, this holding pen of anguish and abuse. That Rudolf and Helena came out the other side seemed miraculous.

It was in 1941 that the barbaric Nazi head of the Protectorate, Reinhard Heydrich, picked Theresienstadt to be the linchpin of the Nazi's 'Final Solution of the Jewish Question'. The garrison town and military fortress, originally built between 1780 and 1790 by the Austrian Emperor Joseph II and named in honour of his mother Empress Maria Theresa, was perfect. It was just 60 kilometres from Prague, close to a railway station, surrounded by a moat and impregnable with high walls. There were barracks that could be used to house inmates, and local houses that were appropriated to provide further accommodation. Over the river was also the Small Fortress, a chilling prison where the Nazis incarcerated political prisoners and anyone who crossed them in the ghetto.

This was a city built for the Jews to keep them away from the 'stresses' of the war – or so Hitler told the world. The idea was to present a façade of humanity, but the reality was very different. The first few transports of Jews, selected for their fitness and skills in areas like engineering and building, were tasked with converting this place intended for 7000 to house 50,000 at any one time.

The historic eighteenth-century barracks from the original Terezín fortress would house tens of thousands in a parody of community life. From here the transports East began in 1942, and Theresienstadt's true purpose as a purgatorial waiting room, a cog in the Nazi killing machine, became evident.

Key to this machine running smoothly was maintaining a climate of uncertainty and terror. Prisoners had no idea what was coming next, and the constant removal of possessions, of sustenance, of family ties, of the nuts and bolts of human existence, of basic humanity, ensured Jews clung on to what vestiges of life they were given rather than risk fighting back. Psychological trauma was at the heart of the 'Final Solution', a mind game used with sickening brilliance by the Nazis.

Theresienstadt was ostensibly run by the SS, who issued orders that had to be obeyed to the letter, but its internal administration was controlled by an appointed Jewish Council of Elders or Ältestenrat. The council was in charge of housing, water, food and all the workings inside the camp. This was a clever move by the Nazis, intended to pitch the inmates against each other and shift the blame for what was to come.

The Jews on this council were protected. They lived in more comfortable lodgings, they could choose the top jobs. But being on the council would have been both a privilege and a curse – these Jewish Elders had a lot of power and not all of it was welcome. These men had to make up the transport lists. The leader was appointed by one of Hitler's main Holocaust architects, Adolf Eichmann himself, and he would be told the numbers required for deportation East, their breakdown by age and nationality, and sometimes the skillsets or physical condition necessary. But the actual names of who went and who stayed, which, although it is believed wasn't fully appreciated at the time, decided who lived and who died, was the council's call, and ultimately the leader of the council's call.

There is some debate over how much the council understood about the transports and what they meant. Mostly prisoners were told they were being moved to labour camps, where they would work for the war effort or, in some cases, for the sick and elderly, to places of rest where they might recuperate. But no one really believed this. Whether the elders actually knew about the existence of gas chambers in Auschwitz is unclear. It's possible that they didn't, but what they did know was that those who left Theresienstadt rarely returned, and as time went on and stories filtered back, the idea grew that transports meant death, filling hearts with terror. Thus, as the architects of the lists, the elders could and did try to save their family and friends, removing and replacing names.

As I learned more about the council I started to wonder if Rudolf was indeed one of its members. After all, he was a war veteran, a doctor of law and held a good job with the government before invasion. Is this perhaps how he saved himself and Helena from being transported?

But while the names of the top few elders are known, those of the others in the Jewish self-administrative body, which was a hive of bureaucracy, divided into departments and sub-departments including housing, finance, sewerage and so on, are not readily available to researchers. As I quickly discovered, many survivors and relatives of those who were murdered see these people as collaborators who betrayed their own kind and only sought to help themselves. Consequently, even today, their names are protected. In the circumstances I certainly could not condemn anyone who tried to save themselves and their loved ones, and if this was what Rudolf did I wouldn't blame him. But finding a list of the council names was already proving to be incredibly difficult.

Inside the ghetto life was grim. Housing was damp, freezing and very cramped, with tiered bunk beds for some and stone floors for others. Most inmates lived in dormitories with 60–80 people. Men and women were separated, and children had their own, slightly better, separate accommodation. Heating, via a stove at the end of the room, was scarce, as were cooking pots and bowls. Food mostly took the form of watery soup with one piece of potato swilling around the bottom of the pan and a morsel of bread. Everyone over the age of 15 had to work, and the best work was certainly in the kitchen, where you might be able to purloin extra scraps.

Disease and infection were rife, and the makeshift hospital and sick rooms incredibly basic and ill-equipped. Inmates died every day, and each morning the bodies of those who hadn't made it through the night would be laid out on the streets, their heads covered. They would be collected and left outside the gate in hastily built coffins. These boxes piled up beside the path used by new arrivals en route from the train station – a horrific welcome to their new home. Ultimately, there was no space to bury the bodies and the ground was too boggy anyway, so in time they were burned in cremato-rium ovens.

There was one positive in Theresienstadt and that was the cultural life. Somehow, amid all this squalor and despair, music, art, books and theatre thrived. There were secret performances in dormitories that lifted spirits immeasurably. In 1942 a central library was established with more than 100,000 books. And the community of high-profile and famous artists painted themselves and ensured the children of Theresienstadt were taught well.

In 1944 a bizarre thing happened in Theresienstadt when 466 Danish Jews arrived in the camp and the Danish Red Cross insisted on a visit to check on them. The Danish King, Christian X, had heard that Jews were being gassed and wanted proof that this was not the case. Hitler saw a propaganda opportunity. Theresienstadt was to be 'beautified' and the result would be filmed to show the world how well Nazi Germany was treating the Jews.

First, more transports were ordered to Auschwitz so the ghetto didn't look overcrowded, and then a whole new city was created, with fake shops, a bank with its own ghetto currency, a school and even a coffee house. Flowers were planted and picket fences painted. Everything was meticulously planned for the visit, and for the film a whole fake scenario – with a football match, a concert, happy workers and laughing women and children seemingly loving life – was played out.

At the Sydney Jewish Museum, I stared at excerpts from the film incredulous at the travesty, but also desperately searching for Helena and Rudolf. Were they in there somewhere, hiding in the background of a shot?

After it was all over, the main actors in the film were sent to Auschwitz where they were killed in the gas chambers.

How had my grandparents managed to get through this?

CHAPTER THREE

BREAKING THROUGH THE WALL OF SILENCE

Arriving in England on 8 March 1939 alone, with no family to turn to, must have been bewildering and traumatic for my eight-year-old father. An only child, he was used to spending his days in the coffee houses of Prague with his mother, eating plates of ham and strudel. His parents had managed to secure his passage out of Prague with just days to spare. It would have been a nerve-racking scramble and then, just seven days later, the Nazi tanks rolled in.

The city went into shock, the streets were silent; no one was cheering as jackboots thundered through Prague's elegant city centre. I can't imagine what Rudolf and Helena were thinking when, on that first evening of occupation, the Führer, Adolf Hitler, appeared at the window of Prague Castle, staring down with pride over the beautiful city below, the latest acquisition of his Third Reich. The photograph of that day was immortalised on a Nazi stamp released to celebrate Hitler's birthday a few years later, and is now a rare collector's item. Clearly Hitler believed this was his destiny.

I later discover that as a young man Rudolf had lived in

rooms in the cobbled street that climbed up to Pražský hrad (Prague Castle), but in this moment no doubt his worst fears would have been realised as his family was torn apart by the man who had seized the city's historic palace of power. It's a bitter irony that Rudolf had lost his leg fighting for the Austrian Army in the First World War and now it was an Austrian – Hitler – who was intent on destroying his world.

When we were growing up, Dad never mentioned that tumultuous week and certainly never discussed the plane journey that brought him to England. It was only when I started putting the dates in context that I realised what a narrow escape he'd made.

As children, my brothers and I knew that Dad had fled Prague with the help of an organisation to assist refugees called The Barbican Mission to the Jews, that he had been raised in a Christian children's home somewhere near London and that he had then won a scholarship to an English private school, which took him away from the Mission in term-time. What we didn't know were the details.

The Barbican Mission to the Jews, a rather dubious Europe-wide organisation, turned out to be the brain-child of an evangelical missionary called Reverend Isaac Emmanuel Davidson, who organised Dad's complex escape from Hitler. In an impassioned bid to save Czechoslovakia's Jewish children – and also seizing the opportunity to pros-elytise – the Reverend had already flown one group of children over in January 1939. Dad was in the second and, as it turned out, final batch. In total the Mission saved 68 Czech children from Nazi clutches, educating them and raising them as Christians in children's homes in the leafy suburb of Chislehurst in Kent, on the outskirts of London, and later, when bombing forced evacuation from London and its environs, in Tiverton, Devon, in England's south-west.

The Czech airlift happened before British businessman and philanthropist Nicholas Winton rescued a further 669 children from Czechoslovakia with his now famous Kindertransport. Winton and his team had brought the children over on trains, while Davidson had somehow found the means to charter KLM planes.

There's no question that had these men not acted as they did, the children would have been murdered, victims of the gas chambers. The tragedy for both missions was that they hadn't been able to save more lives, and a distraught Winton later said he felt he had failed. My father was always clear that he owed his life to the Mission, but he rarely expanded on what sort of life the Mission gave him. Looking back, I don't think this was deliberate, but rather an unconscious impulse to not revisit those difficult years.

═══

The door to my father's childhood was pushed ajar for me when my mother and I persuaded him to attend the 50-year reunion of The Barbican Mission to the Jews in 1989, in Kent, England. I think the main reason Dad agreed to go was that fellow refugee and our good family friend Annalisa, who became our adopted aunt when we were growing up, had helped organise the event, and that she and Dad's friend Klaus, another refugee who was on that plane out of Prague with Dad, were going to be there.

It was a Saturday afternoon when we drove up the rather well-heeled suburban Lubbock Road in Chislehurst to the towering spire of Christ Church at the end of a cul-de-sac. The modest celebration with refreshments took place in the very church hall where Dad and the other refugee children had spent their first night in England. Dad recalled they had all slept lined up on the floor in sleeping bags, since the home they were later to move into wasn't yet ready.

Christ Church had played an important part in Dad's childhood, for it was here that these Jewish children were brought to pray. The regime of devotion at the Mission was zealous and strict, which must have been quite a shock for the refugees. Apart from raising the children in the Christian faith, Reverend Davidson made a deal with their parents that in return for saving the children's lives the youngsters would be baptised – should both the child and parents agree – when they reached 16.

Some of the refugees returned to their Jewish faith in adult life and some were happily converted to Christianity, but most didn't express views one way or the other at the gathering, and I got the feeling that, like Dad's family, organised religion had never really played a huge part in their Czech lives and that had continued into adulthood.

The mood of the reunion was joyous, with a lot of animated chatter around a few tables, but, like my father, most people spoke little of what had happened to their families back in Czechoslovakia. Some, I gathered, had returned in 1945 to try to find their families, and I wondered why Dad hadn't done this. He had always said his parents had wanted him to stay and finish his education, but there was something about the way he said it that made me both doubt that this was the whole story and appreciate that he wasn't going to discuss it further.

The Mission didn't only save the bodies and souls of Jews from Czechoslovakia; there were also Jewish children from London's East End, some of whom came from one-parent or poor, underprivileged homes. For these children the Barbican

Mission offered warm, clean accommodation, a structured upbringing and regular meals. I'm unsure what they thought of the Czech children and their foreign ways, but in the Mission Home they were all thrown together and some were here at the reunion.

There was a bespoke cake proudly piped with '50 Years Re-Union'. Curiously it had the Jewish Star of David at its centre, which was surrounded by the piped names of the Mission's four homes in which all the children lived at different times – Seven Trees, Mount Zion, Naomi and Craddock.

I had no idea at the time that Seven Trees, the huge house that became the girls' home and where Dad also spent some time, was actually right next door to the church we were in – we would have driven right past it – and Mount Zion, where he slept in a dormitory with the other boys and had his meals, was just over the road. Dad didn't point out either house.

Our journey to the event took just a couple of hours from our family home in Surrey, but many of the other refugees had come from much further afield – some even from Europe, where they had relocated after the war. Everyone was encouraged to pin photos of themselves and their families on a noticeboard, which also displayed two incredible photos I had never seen before. They were posed group shots of the children taken not long after they had arrived. They all look incredibly smart and well turned out in thick winter clothes.

The first photograph was of those refugees who had arrived in January, and showed Reverend Davidson in the centre with one of them on his lap. The second, in which my father featured, was of the final plane load of children and had the Reverend's wife – Mrs Lucy Vyvyan Davidson – at its heart. Dad was second in from the left in the first row, his legs tucked awkwardly to one side. He wore a wool jacket, long socks, laced leather boots, a tie and white collared shirt and, through his wire-rimmed spectacles, he was staring straight ahead.

I couldn't take my eyes off these photographs, trying to understand from the perplexed faces what they were all feeling. Dad looked neither happy nor sad, but seemed somewhat stunned, an emotion that I suspect stayed with him for years.

Funds were raised among the refugees – and I'm sure my father had donated – for a memorial bench dedicated to the Reverend and his wife. It was erected at the entrance to Lubbock Road and is still there today with an inset plaque:

Rev. & Mrs. I.E. DAVIDSON & FRIENDS

GRATEFULLY REMEMBERED

BY ALL THE BMJ CHILDREN

(68 OF THEM RESCUED FROM CENTRAL EUROPE 1939)

The formality of the message I think reflects the discipline of the Mission, but the warmth for the Reverend and his wife is clear.

Dad told me he spoke no English when he first arrived and that he couldn't remember at what point he had made the transition from his native tongues of German and Czech to this new language, only that it seemed to come naturally and very soon he was thinking in English. The children weren't allowed to talk to each other in Czech, which sounded a little harsh to me, but everyone I spoke to at the reunion thought this was a good thing that helped them assimilate. Otherwise, I suspect fitting in was a little more troubled. The Mozart and Chopin of Dad's childhood was now replaced with church hymns, which along with prayers twice a day became an integral part of Mission life.

One man came up to Dad in a flurry of excitement and said he thought he had my father's knapsack at home. 'Hansi, Hansi,' he uttered. It was the first time I had heard Dad addressed in this way. We knew him as John – he told us he had changed his name when he came to England because Hans or Hanus, as he was known in Czechoslovakia, was too German-sounding. Otherwise I had heard him called 'Hoss' by his refugee friends Klaus and Theo, but never Hansi.

But I knew the bag this man was talking about because Dad was carrying it on his back in one of the very few photos we had of him as a child. In it, little Hanus is walking up the steps of the plane that flew him to England. Rudolf and Helena are no doubt behind the barriers in the crowds waving the children off at Prague airport. Evidently Dad had lent the knapsack to this man when they were together in the Mission and then Dad went off to school and was never reunited with the bag.

Dad was surprised; he seemed to barely remember handing over the bag or much about the Mission in those early years. Later, when I questioned him more, Dad said he wasn't being coy, it was simply that he had blocked it out. I probed further and he said that all he knew was that from age eight to 12, he didn't have a happy time. He couldn't elaborate because the memories were locked away. Dad did recall playing football with the other boys outside the church hall, which he said was good fun, and he remembered the staff being kind and that his jumper, handknitted by his mum, was very scratchy, but that was about it.

I asked if he was angry at his parents for sending him away and he said it wasn't like that. There was no room for judgement; this was just how it was, and like everyone else he accepted it. He said if anything he felt guilty for leaving them.

In the beginning Dad received letters from them, and the Mission made all the children write to their parents regularly, which he was ashamed to admit he found a chore. Dad was never a natural letter writer and as a young boy, he told me, he just didn't know what to say. But then those letters stopped. Did he worry about what was happening to his parents? He said he tried not to think about it and focused on one day at a time and his studies. He didn't mention anyone else, any other family members who were on his mind, trapped back in Czechoslovakia. Were they also locked away in his head?

Annalisa, at 12 years old, was one of the oldest children in the Mission. She and her young brother Theo, then eight, had actually escaped from Prague in July, after Hitler had arrived. Anna, who at the time of writing is 92, and living in North London, remembers that day clearly. Though happy to talk about her mother and their beautiful life in Prague, memories of what happened after Nazi occupation still hold a power to traumatise my aunt. But she wanted to help me understand *her* Prague and what was taken away from them all that day. So when I was in London, Anna, who is still as sparkling, elegant and compelling as I remember her when I was a child, treated me to a fish lunch in her favourite local restaurant and slowly, calmly, took me back to 15 March 1939.

Anna was at home with her mother, brother and their mother's help, and remembers her mother turning up the radio, which had an announcement telling everyone to 'carry on as normal – to go to work, everything is normal. They just kept saying it again and again.' Annalisa's mother Eleonore ran out into the street without her hat – 'and that was when I knew something was wrong,' she says. It was Anna's uncle who took her to school, and she then saw the tanks. 'I'd never seen a tank before and certainly never seen a gun,' she tells me.

The Nazi soldiers looked arrogant and cocky sitting astride their tanks with their guns, driving up the streets of Prague triumphant. Eleonore tried everywhere to get an exit visa for the family, but the authorities wouldn't give it to her, and that was when she managed to get Annalisa and Theo onto one of Nicholas Winton's Kindertransport trains. She'd hoped to follow her children to England herself, where she had secured work as a housekeeper/cook, but ultimately the Germans wouldn't let her out. Annalisa remembers they were all very practical and just got on with it, their goodbyes at the railway station unemotional, but her mum did tell Annalisa: 'Look after your little brother.'

Most of the children on the Kindertransport trains were sponsored by individual English families, but Anna and Theo joined the Mission children, where both became friends with my dad and later with us, his family.

Theo, who now lives in Somerset in England's West Country and whom I spoke to later on the phone, says he remembers my father as a 'quiet, shy and rather reserved little boy' in the Mission. While Theo went to the local school, Dad was sent away on his own to a private school in another part of England, which Theo thinks possibly put him at a disadvantage in the Mission, since he only came back in the holidays. For Theo, the atmosphere in the home was generally 'very convivial', especially once they were evacuated to Craddock House in the countryside, which he really enjoyed, but the religious side of their new world was a bit of a shock.

'Quite a lot of children from the Mission were resentful of the brainwashing we had to put up with,' Theo told me when I chatted to him about his memories of that time. 'It really was intense Christianity. We had morning and evening prayers every day of the week for half an hour before we went off to school and before dinner in the evening. And then a lot of church at the weekend. It was very intense proselytising. In hindsight you have to realise that it was only people's charity that kept me alive, and Reverend Davidson's relentless preaching. That's what he did. He used to go around the country and preach in churches and the collection would go to the Mission. That's how we were kept alive. You have to be grateful for that aspect of it.'

My father didn't talk about the religious teaching, and as I said, he and my mother didn't raise my brothers and me in any faith, but he did tell me that since he was bright and his school grades were good – especially in divinity and the classics – the Mission had decided he would become a minister and they were happy to put him through university to study theology. He waited until the last moment to tell them this wasn't what he intended, and that was when he left their care.

CHAPTER FOUR

ON A WING AND A PRAYER

Still in Sydney, but rapidly building on my plans for a major European trip, I now became fascinated by The Barbican Mission to the Jews (BMJ), by Reverend and Mrs Davidson, and by what went on in the homes they established for these Czech refugee children in the heart of suburban England. I wondered if Helena and Rudolf had any idea about their son's new life. The Mission itself is hardly mentioned in the media stories of refugee escapes to England; these 68 Jewish children literally flew in under the radar. Was anyone monitoring what went on behind closed doors?

I wanted to see if I could uncover the records of the BMJ, if it still existed, in the hope that these would explain the details of my father's escape. There must have been thousands of Jewish children trying to get out of Prague at that time; how did Rudolf and Helena manage to secure this precious passage for their little boy?

I had always understood that my grandparents paid the Mission, but I started to think that this was possibly an erroneous assumption. I couldn't imagine a Christian missionary charity would have run this evacuation as a business. They wouldn't take money from desperate families, surely, and they certainly couldn't have sustained receiving payment from the parents, who were all no doubt eventually sent to concentration camps.

That said, chartering two planes from Prague to England – they were actually KLM planes organised directly with the Dutch airline – and then housing, educating and taking care of 68 children for what turned into seven years or more would have been unfeasibly costly. Could this really have been funded by Reverend Davidson's travelling preaching and by BMJ donors alone?

I was also hoping that the records would throw some light on exactly what happened to my father in the Mission's homes in Chislehurst and Devon, and go some way to explaining why he blocked out so many of his memories from this time. Talking to my 'aunt' Annalisa and her brother Theo, I appreciated that the Mission was a well-meaning and on the whole beneficent place with dedicated staff, so I wondered if my father's problems came from school – or was it simply the agony of an only child separated from his parents and worrying about their fate?

I quickly discovered that today the BMJ has morphed into the Christian Witness to Israel (CWI), a global organisation dedicated to converting Jews to Christianity. Their evangelism has grown in popularity and it now has bases in countries far and wide, including Australia, the United States, France and Hong Kong. It seems incredible to me that such a body would exist at all, let alone still be plying its trade, but from its website it is clear the CWI feels justified in its work. In a nutshell, the CWI wants to share the Messiah with the Jewish people: 'We believe that to preach the Good News of Jesus to everyone but the Jews is an act of spiritual anti-Semitism.' It's a clever argument but still sounds very odd to me, especially since attempting to convert Jews who are historically so deeply fixed in their faith would seem to be a very tough call, notwithstanding an act of notable arrogance.

After extensive trawling I came across the publication *For a Future and a Hope: The Story of the Houses of Refuge in Chislehurst* by Lucy V. Davidson and John S. Ross. Reverend Dr Ross was chief executive officer of CWI in the UK until 2002. It's a slim volume, produced by John Ross in the lead-up to the 50-year anniversary of the Barbican Mission's airlift of the Czech children. He edited Mrs Davidson's original impressive and detailed account of how the idea to save these children came about in the first place, and annotated it with additional information about what happened to the children. It also includes some revealing and poignant correspondence with the children's parents. This is gold, and as I read on I couldn't believe it – my father, referred to as 'Hansi Rieden' – is in there!

The publication has received very limited exposure outside the BMJ turned CWI community, but it reveals a story that deserves more attention for the sheer heroism involved. Reverend Davidson's risky evacuation of the children takes your breath away, both in its execution and in the Reverend's unflinching determination to see it through.

It turns out the BMJ actually already had offices in both Poland and Prague before Hitler started to carve away at Czechoslovakia. The annexation of the Sudetenland in the Munich Agreement signed on 30 September 1938 had created a subculture of stateless Jews trying to find refuge outside German territory. Things worsened with the shocking Kristallnacht on 9 and 10 November, when Nazi Stormtroopers were let loose in Germany. And it was at this point, writes Mrs Davidson, that the BMJ's work became 'new and vital'.

The now infamous Kristallnacht was nominally in response to the assassination of a German embassy official in Paris by a Polish-Jewish youth who was angry at his family's expulsion from Germany. The Kristallnacht outburst of murderous thuggery involved the destruction of thousands of Jewish homes and 7500 businesses; more than 1000 synagogues, along with their sacred Torah scrolls were burned; Jews were beaten and at least 96 killed, while some 30,000 Jewish men were transported to concentration camps.

With terror raining down on the Jewish community, the BMJ was deluged with terrified families seeking help. The Reverend's wife doesn't shy away from the tricky issue of conversion, the elemental basis of the Mission's work, and her argument exposes the extent of righteous piety driving the organisation. At the time the BMJ only had Naomi Home in Mitcham, south London. 'Hundreds of times I have been asked the question, "How do you get children for the Naomi Home?"' writes Mrs Davidson:

> On the surface this question cannot be answered, because it is unlikely for Jewish parents to commit their children into Christian hands, with the full understanding that they will be brought up in that faith. Jewish charities are ample, and there is no lack of orphanages or other refuges for children in need. We can only reply with the simple truth that in answer to prayer God sent children, who by this means might find salvation in the Lord Jesus.

It was a pretty inadequate response to my mind, but one thing was clear, the Mission knew exactly what they were hoping to achieve – to save Jewish souls by showing them the light. In Czechoslovakia, where fear was feeding hysteria within the Jewish community, the BMJ's light suddenly became a beacon of hope.

I think initially the Mission had felt compelled to save those Jews trapped in the mechanism of Hitler's 'Final Solution' who had already become Christians, either as born-again converts or through marriage. Hitler defined Jews based on the religion of their grandparents, so even those who were baptised into Christianity were being persecuted along with practising Jews. Then there were 'ethnic Jews' who were not practising and barely attended synagogue, and certainly many of the parents of the Jewish children Reverend Davidson managed to save fell into both of these categories.

But ultimately labels didn't matter. When Reverend Davidson visited Europe and travelled overland to Czechoslovakia by train in the autumn of 1938, he was disgusted by what he saw. I suspect he was also made painfully aware of his own nation's part in what was going on. Czechs were appalled when British Prime Minister Neville Chamberlain declared 'peace in our time'. The British leader had signed away Czechoslovakia's future with the Munich Agreement – known to Czechs as the Munich Betrayal – which handed over Sudetenland on the western border of the nation to Germany, leaving the Jews there exposed to brutal persecution. This was part of a policy of appeasement by Western European leaders and specifically Chamberlain towards Germany, who believed that if they allowed Hitler to annex the Sudetenland he wouldn't invade Czechoslovakia. It proved to be a deeply flawed assumption with devastating consequences. 'Everyone realised that the state of affairs and so-called peace would not, and could not, be long protracted,' writes Mrs Davidson.

This single act set the country on a course to occupation by the forces of the most depraved dictator the world had ever seen. Essentially, Britain had handed the Czech Jews over to Hitler on a plate. Reverend Davidson was one of many who realised the gravity of the situation. 'Escape, before the iron heel of Germany stamped out the last atom of freedom and security from this little country, was the one thought in every mind,' writes Mrs Davidson.

I think it would be unfair to suggest that her husband's immediate impulse to save lives was anything other than humanitarian and altruistic, but of course saving their souls would be an added bonus, and was after all at the heart of his personal ethos. I don't think this mattered one jot to those, including my grandparents, who handed their children over to Reverend Davidson. All they wanted was a safe haven, which they believed, or at least naively hoped, would be short-lived.

In the BMJ's magazine, *Immanuel's Witness*, the Reverend vividly described his own chilling encounter with Nazi officers, which sparked his concern:

At eleven o'clock at night we passed the Dutch-German frontier. Already, in our sleeping compartment, we were interviewed first by the Dutch authorities, then the German. The ordinary German official is quite decent, but Hitler's Gestapo is another matter. One in mufti, and three uniformed savage creatures entered my compartment, after the ordinary official was gone, with the threat, 'We are going to take our time here!'

'Where are you going?' snarled one at me.

'To Prague.'

'Oh! We shall see about that! What literature have you?'

'None.'

'What are you going for; business?'

'No, I am a clergyman.'

'Are you an Aryan?'

'No.'

'Are you a Jew?'

'Yes.'

'Are you stopping in Germany?'

'Oh no! I am only passing through.'

'Are you not getting out in any town in Germany?'

'No, not at all.'

In giving my answers I was scrutinised by four pairs of devilish eyes. Down came my bag; its contents turned out, and my clothes most minutely searched. Having found no reason for asking me to accompany them they left me with a ferocious curse.

It's interesting that Davidson declared himself to be Jewish at this juncture. It's true. The Reverend was indeed a Jew born in Poland who found his way to Christianity, and the idea of being a 'Jewish Christian', as St Paul (and of course Jesus) had been, definitely inspired and informed his evangelism and his work with the BMJ. But why would he say to a scary and very hostile Nazi interrogator that he was Jewish?

When I later spoke to John Ross who had edited this book and is now retired and living in Scotland, he told me that he saw this 'as a spirited riposte to the unpleasant attitudes Reverend Davidson was outraged to encounter as an English clergyman. Holding a British passport made him confident of his safety as a subject of "his Britannic Majesty" (as his passport stated). I suspect he travelled wearing a clerical collar, and that may well have added to his defiant confidence. Even the Nazis wouldn't dare interfere with the safety of an Englishman!' If Ross is right, it certainly indicates the fearless personality of the Reverend. It would have been an incredible asset on both this journey, which frankly sounds utterly terrifying, and his evacuation mission to come.

When Davidson finally reached the BMJ office in Prague, he was besieged by thousands of petrified Jews, all wanting conversion and a way out. He told them he had no authority to bring any adults to England and could 'only promise to help their children if the necessary permission could be obtained for their emigration to England.' It was a promise he had no idea if he could keep. Even if he did manage to arrange the paperwork and permissions, where would the funds come from?

'But to say no was absolutely unthinkable,' writes his wife. 'At once these waiting people were told that a transport for fifty children to be taken to England would be arranged. Tear-stained faces were covered with smiles, parents and children were sent home to pack.'

Mrs Davidson goes on to explain that a mysterious Englishman who heard of the project offered to pay that very afternoon for the passage of the 50 children. It was quickly decided that an overland journey was far too risky, and so the Reverend returned to the UK to try to organise both the logistics and the paperwork. I have been unable to identify the marvellous benefactor, but suspect he also paid for my father's flight out.

Back in Britain, the Reverend had his work cut out for him. Although initiatives to rescue German and Austrian Jewish children were already underway and supported by the British government through the establishment of official bodies, Czechoslovakia had not been considered, and the rules would not bend. Reverend Davidson found himself battling rigid bureaucracy at every turn. What's more, the existing committee was 'governed almost entirely by Jews from whom, naturally, we could expect no favour', notes a dejected Mrs Davidson.

The parents in Prague continued to write. Time was of the essence, they appealed, soon it would be too late. Meanwhile the BMJ offices, both in Prague and London, were also under siege from yet more Czech parents pleading for help.

Eventually – and Mrs Davidson notes 'miraculously' – 50 permits went through, arriving in the post two days after Christmas. As for funds, Mrs Davidson says 'the question of money was not one that troubled us. The certainty that God would provide for every child *He* sent us was a conviction which completely delivered us from all anxiety. How gloriously we have since proved His faithfulness in this as well as every other respect.' It's worth adding that she was of course correct, and even with my sceptical hackles on high alert, I can't deny faith won out here. Mountains were moved in a quite extraordinary way.

The BMJ started looking for properties near their base in Chislehurst and found Seven Trees, a huge mansion in leafy Lubbock Road, right next to the parish church. With the Lord as their neighbour, this would be perfect. Mrs Davidson says that while their search was successful, the barking opposition they faced from many of the householders in Lubbock Road, who didn't want 'undesirable aliens' in their vicinity, threw up another roadblock.

As I read this, I resolved to investigate further on my planned visit to the British Library and the UK National Archives. Evidently the whole issue went through endless ugly council meetings, which reflected the shameful existence of significant anti-Semitism in the UK at the time.

Mrs Davidson's description of the arrival of that first plane load of refugees to Croydon aerodrome is incredibly poignant. The girls would go to Naomi Home, where extra beds had been squeezed in and space for more seats found in the dining room. The boys were going to be put up in the church hall and parish rooms, since approval for their children's home in Lubbock Road was still being fought over. 'Darkness had already fallen when at last the great plane swooped down and I shall never forget my first look at the children about whom I had been thinking and praying almost ceaselessly for so long,' wrote Mrs Davidson.

There were customs officials, passport officials and a medical inspection to be got through. The children were stiff with cold, tired, excited, and sick with their journey. The babble of German and Czech was confusing. Two little boys, aged three and four, clung hopelessly to the Dutch stewardess who had been extremely kind to them on the way; with her departure it seemed as though the last link with home was leaving them and they cried bitterly.

The youngest of these two little boys, aged three, was a particularly manly and self-contained little fellow. He looked almost square as he walked from the aeroplane, in his thick grey overcoat, scarf and woolly hat muffling him to the eyes; his little face was very white and his great dark eyes brim full with uncertainty.

He had been very sick on the journey and was utterly weary. He had never heard English before and the strange tongue confused and frightened him. There was something about him which gripped my heart from the first moment, but he sternly and resolutely repelled every advance.

For an hour we stood and he still maintained his self-control, then it was time for him to see the official doctor who had to pass all new arrivals as non-infectious and fit to enter the country. This meant considerable undressing; he clung desperately to his coat and his chin began to quiver ominously.

The doctor was weary and harassed at the end of what had been for him a very long and trying day. He told us to hurry, and it meant that sheer force had to be used before this child, who resisted every inch of the way, could pass the examination.

But at last we were in the waiting motor coach. At least there was no black-out then and the older children found both interest and amusement in their first sight of London. We drove first to Naomi Home at Mitcham, where the girls' luggage had to be sorted out and the girls themselves deposited, and then on to Chislehurst to settle the boys in their quarters.

The language question during those first few days was naturally one of considerable difficulty ... Looking back, one realises with what extraordinary fortitude and adaptability they bore themselves during those early weeks.

Our way of life was so utterly strange to them, so completely different from anything to which they had been accustomed; and outstanding in this strangeness was our attitude toward religion. Their early training had done absolutely nothing to prepare them for this; with the great majority it held no place in their lives whatsoever. A few of those who were purely Jewish, had grandparents who still observed Jewish customs, but this the children considered to be entirely out of date and only of interest to old people. Quite a number of the others were children of mixed marriages. Their parents, by mutual consent, seemed to have left the question of religion entirely out of their calculations;

the children had received no teaching whatsoever, and neither Church nor Synagogue held any place in their lives. That it should now become the vital centre of everything was to them an extraordinary change.

It was far from easy for many of them to become accustomed to Grace before meals, prayers morning and evening, Church on Sunday and Bible classes, an environment in which the Bible was always on hand. It was regarded by most of them with sheer amazement, just another of the extraordinary English customs; to some it was a source of amusement and to others irksome.

But even from the very first there were a few who seemed to realise that it was here that their great need would be met and their hearts seemed to open naturally and with wonderful response to the very first teaching that was given.

While the accent on religion is heavy, it doesn't feel domineering, and I am mindful that whatever I may feel about Reverend and Mrs Davidson's motivations, without them my brothers and I would not be here today. What's more, Dad did not turn into a bible-carrying Christian; he actually developed a deep-seated mistrust of all organised religion and married a confirmed atheist – my mother.

For the second batch of children, Reverend Davidson went over to accompany the children himself, driven by the urgency of the situation. 'That was a terrible day,' writes Mrs Davidson of Hitler's appearance in Prague one week later.

Reports and rumours reached the children's ears at school. I went into the boys' dining room at 'Seven Trees' while they were having dinner and was struck by the terrible gloom which hung over the room. The dinner was almost untouched and, as soon as they realised my presence, they sprang from the table and surrounded me repeating again and again the one question, 'Is it true?'

Their distress was very painful and the utter despair on one boy's face as he pushed his plate aside and buried his face in his arms was so unnatural in a child that I shall never be able to forget it.

This was heartbreaking to read. My father would have been acutely aware of the fear mounting back at home. I expect his escape was hurried and chaotic, with no time to assimilate what was happening, or its implications for this close family unit being ripped apart. I cannot imagine what he was thinking and now, as I pore over the photographs I have of him from that time, I am overwhelmed by the courage displayed both in my grandparents' painted-on smiles and my father's dogged acceptance.

There is one in particular in which his parents are standing with Dad by the door of the bus that took all the children and their families to the airport. They look so happy together, a united threesome. Dad is animated and beaming. Little did he know that this was the last time he would ever see his father, feel his touch, hear his voice. His Prague childhood is over forever. Did his relatives, who I later discover were numerous and Dad knew well, hold a fond farewell party, I wonder, or was it all kept low-key so as not to worry little Hanus or alert the authorities?

Taken just hours later, the final photograph of Dad as a child in his homeland sees him, head down, climbing aboard the KLM plane, knapsack on his back, bound for England.

The next photo we have of Dad, which we were given at the BMJ reunion and now have in our family album, was taken a few weeks later in the Chislehurst church hall with the other children in the Mission, Dad sitting in the front row, staring out, but somehow separate from the others. The change in his demeanour is stark. From this moment on my father had to rely on his own wits, and part of that coping mechanism I now realise was to withdraw into himself and shut out the noise.

My father lived in the home only during school holidays; in term time he was at private boarding schools. He must have felt very isolated as he headed off alone, especially at his secondary school, where he was a scholarship boy mixing with regular fee-paying English children in the British 'public'-school system. As a result, he lost his accent very quickly and sounded much more English than the rest of the Czech refugees. His command of English was always word perfect, and it was a family joke that Dad would regularly correct our grammar; it took a foreigner to really appreciate how the English language should be spoken!

———

As the children settled in, the BMJ began to face criticism from both the Jewish and Christian communities. Evidently the BMJ homes were regularly inspected and the children found to be well cared for, but from Mrs Davidson's account it's clear there was scrutiny of what they were up to. Bishops were approached, and some of the boys 'waylaid on their way to or from school, and also outside the Church on Sunday'. It isn't clear exactly who was responsible, and the Reverend and BMJ staff didn't find out until later so couldn't intervene. And while I'm sure motives were pure, it must have been pretty confusing for the refugees.

What this opposition achieved was to prevent Reverend Davidson from bringing over a new wave of children from Prague. 'All Jewish families desirous of sending their children to England were circularised and asked to sign a declaration that they would not allow their children to be brought up in the Christian faith and that those who had already undertaken to do so would not place them under the care of the Barbican Mission,' writes Mrs Davidson.

> The parents were most unwilling to do this and only in one case did parents withdraw their consent to their children remaining with us. Nevertheless, the granting of permits lay very largely in the hands of these people and they succeeded in holding back some eighty little ones who were all ready to proceed to England and to us.
>
> We had full particulars of all these children and still hold a number of papers concerning them. It is impossible to look at their photographed faces unmoved as one thinks of conditions on the Continent at the present time. In one case, two children's permits, stamped by our Home Office, were torn up before the eyes of their aunt when she acknowledged that they were to be placed under the guardianship of the Mission.

As I continued to read of the Davidsons' battles with the authorities and the fate of specific children, my heart skipped a beat when Dad's name suddenly came up. We have jumped forward to the end of the war and some miraculous news: 'In June 1945, the joyful news was received that Hansi Reiden's [sic] parents had both been liberated from the concentration camp at Terezín after three years internment.' And here is John Ross writing with details he had gathered from the BMJ archives:

Hansi's mother, due to her weakened condition, was unable to cope with an early reunion with her son. His father, Dr Rudolh [sic] Ridden [sic] wrote from Prague that October, lamenting the present state of things in Czechoslovakia and explaining that while it had always been their hope to have be [sic] reunited as soon as possible the world outside the camps had collapsed and offered little prospects for an intelligent young boy. 'Hansi has forgotten the Czech language,' argued Dr Rieden, 'it would be better for him to stay in England to continue his studies. Please, would you tell me if it would be possible for Hansi to get British Nationality?' He speculated if Hansi could have a new life, perhaps as a teacher, a technical engineer or a physician, as favoured most of all by Dr. Rieden.

This was not only fantastic news about my grandparents' liberty but it immediately went to the heart of the pressing issue of why my grandparents did not return to collect their 'Hansi'. I was intrigued – this meant that John Ross must have found letters from my grandparents. I was now burning to see those missives.

I set about trying to track him down – this Reverend was going to be key to my investigation. I found him living in Scotland and, after years away from the work of the CWI, fortuitously reconnecting with the organisation to work on a talk for the body's 150th anniversary.

We communicated via email, and Reverend Ross was incredibly helpful and knowledgeable. He told me that there was indeed a file on my father, and on a number of the other children in the CWI archives, and he was certain these would be of interest to me. He managed to persuade the CWI to allow me to visit the archives, which had recently relocated to a relatively new building near Oxford in England, so that I might undertake my own research.

And in the meantime, aware of my eagerness, John Ross thoughtfully arranged for my father's file to be photocopied and emailed to me.

CHAPTER FIVE

HANUS BECOMES JOHN

I was four months into my investigation and the information was mounting up. The itinerary for my proposed trip to Eastern Europe and England three months later was filling up, and my pilgrimage was taking shape. I would need to be away for at least a month, and my partner Katie, who speaks German, agreed to come along with me to help in the archives and take photos.

As I counted down the days and continued my research, Dad's BMJ file arrived from the CWI. I'm not sure what I was expecting – perhaps a few official papers, certainly not the deeply personal, poignant letters, detailed school reports, a Christmas card made by my father and much more. The CWI had copied every item in the file, even the buff folder in which they were catalogued. As I opened the file I almost couldn't breathe. For a second I had a crisis of conscience. Was I doing the right thing meddling in my father's personal life?

I sat down at the dining-room table, my laptop open in front of me with the file icon flashing. On the shelf behind me sat one of the framed photos I have of Mum and Dad, their faces staring back, kind and warm. I couldn't read Dad, but Mum seemed to be telling me to get on with it. Patience was never one of her virtues.

On the outside 'Hans Rieden' was inscribed in beautiful lettering, and then, scribbled above it in pencil, 'Parents arrived Teresen [sic] concentration Camp'. What a find! I am sure that the children never saw these files, then or as adults. And when I talked to Annalisa and Theo, whose files I later uncovered on my visit to the archives, both confirmed that they had no idea these dossiers even existed.

The very first item in my father's file was a photo, slightly larger than head and shoulders. He had a smart striped tie and pinstripe shirt, and if he wasn't age eight, you might think he was off to work in an office. His hair looked as if his mum had slicked it down in that stereotypical lick-your-fingers-and-iron-out-the-kinks way. Dad's hair was naturally crinkled and wiry, and it must have taken some attention to smooth it out with such perfection. There was a neat parting on one side and Dad was looking straight at me, his eyes seemingly searching for something (or am I being fanciful?).

I was pleased to see he already had the dimple in his chin that became a feature and we always used to joke was the result of eating too many vegetables, and his ears were sticking out slightly, possibly the result of the sleek hairdo. This was a set-up photo, taken in a studio in Prague, which I soon realised was for his passport.

The passport, which his parents must have organised in haste in order to facilitate their son's escape, was also in the file. The document was written in Czech (and French – still used in passports as the international diplomatic language): 'Hanuš Rieden, born in Praha. Date of birth 18.7.1930. Profession: student. Face: oval. Eyes: blue. Hair: chestnut brown.'

Interesting, because my father's hair was black, but perhaps at that age it was lighter. It was signed by an official on behalf of the police president, and on the cover is the Republika Československá coat of arms with a majestic crowned, double-tailed lion that seems to be mid-roar.

The next item was a child's handmade Christmas card with the artist *Hans Rieden* signed in the top corner. On the front Dad had created coloured-in letters that read 'A Merry Christmas' and drawn an aeroplane with 'Christmas Plane' written in English along its fuselage and the red, white and blue of a national ensign on its tail. Was this the Czech flag colours or the Union Jack colours, I wondered, and was this the plane that brought him from Prague or the plane little Hanus hoped would be taking him back home, the perfect Christmas present for his parents? Inside Dad had written, 'I wish you all a very happy Christmas', along with drawings of a couple of Christmas trees, and a pink Christmas ribbon glued onto the front and inside.

Was this Dad's first homemade Christmas card? As a Jew I imagine he was unlikely to have celebrated Christmas before, but when I asked Aunt Annalisa about this she said that they observed Christmas as well as Hanukkah as children in Czechoslovakia. She said the Czechoslovakia that was created in October 1918 was a very progressive democracy, embracing all cultures and creeds. It really was ahead of its time, she mused, and while, yes, she and my father were nominally Jewish, their race didn't separate them. How quickly that changed!

If the card was intended for his parents, it was never sent, which struck me as rather sad. But perhaps it was for the Reverend and Mrs Davidson, who I later discovered Dad saw as surrogate parents.

A typed document in German on sepia paper appeared to be my grandparents' application lodged with the BMJ in Prague on 24 January 1939. It gave a brief CV for Rudolf and Helena and then outlined why they were hoping the Mission would agree to save their son. This document alone answered a lot of my questions.

My grandfather was born in 1894 in Reichenberg, which is the German name for the beautiful city of Liberec in North Bohemia surrounded by the Jizera Mountains, where I later discovered the Rieden family had been quite prominent. Rudolf went to a German grammar school and in 1913 enrolled at the German University (part of Charles University) in Prague to study law.

But most illuminating was my grandfather's war record. Grandpa wrote that he was called up on the outbreak of war in 1914 and served as an officer until 1919 in the Austrian Army. He was a war hero and injured veteran aged just 25, and I feel sure this must have counted for something with his Nazi persecutors. Grandpa had fought on the German side in the Great War, and valiantly so. He was decorated several times for bravery and during a battle on the Russian front was so badly injured that his right leg had to be completely amputated. After several operations in 1920, Grandpa continued his studies at the German University, and in 1922 obtained a doctorate in law. After this he joined the Czech civil service, where at the time of writing he was still employed.

My grandmother Helena was born 1893 in Luditz (Žlutice) near Karlsbad (Karlovy Vary). She was the daughter of Rabbi M. Hoffer and one of 11 children. Like Rudolf, Helena went to a German grammar school, and until her marriage in 1927 had worked in a law office, so I imagine my grandparents probably met through work. At the time of writing, Helena was recovering from a serious stomach operation, which had left her in a physically weak state.

What was notable here, and not surprising given Liberec and Žlutice were both in Sudetenland, was that to all intents and purposes it seemed both sides of the family were in fact of German descent – the irony is palpable – and while my father told me he wasn't raised in a strict Jewish home, his maternal grandfather was actually a rabbi, so religion must have been at least a part of family life. It was the first I'd heard of Grandma's ten siblings. Could some of the Hoffers have survived? If they did, I may well have living relatives after all.

But it was in Rudolf and Helena's grounds for application that I learned of the desperate plight facing my family. Here Rudolf explained that since they were born in Sudetenland and had German nationality, they should have been able to stay as citizens there, but as Jews, following the Munich Agreement in 1938, they had been expelled. The whole family had been forced to flee the Sudetenland, leaving all their property and possessions behind.

With his war injury, Rudolf said that emigrating to a new life was unthinkable, although Helena was trying to find a position as a nanny or teacher abroad. But there were also sick octogenarian parents and seven siblings to consider. I wonder which seven siblings he was talking about. From later research I discovered Rudolf had five siblings still alive in 1938 and Helena had ten. Were these seven some combination from their total of 15 siblings who were somehow dependent on Rudolf and Helena?

In conclusion, wrote Rudolf, 'The future education and development of our eight-year-old son, who is well brought up, talented and a boy of the best character, would be utterly compromised by the conditions that have been introduced and we see his acceptance into your protection as the only way to save the child from this chaos.'

Rudolf was concise, unemotional and direct in his request, which filled a little over a page. There was no mention of Davidson's faith, of possible conversion or of what would happen to Hanus should he be accepted. Maybe they knew this information or maybe they didn't want to rock the boat and jeopardise the application.

But from this single page a picture of what had happened to my family was starting to build. Anti-Semitism had continually stripped them of their livelihoods and forced them to flee. They were caught in an ambush which soon would entrap them completely.

Next, I turned to pages and pages of school reports for Dad, by which I was initially very perplexed because they were from two different schools. I always knew Dad had been awarded a scholarship to Blundell's School in Devon in England's south-west for his secondary education, but before that, I now discovered, he had been sent to a private preparatory school called Winterdyne, in Birkdale, Lancashire, in the north of England.

He must have started at this school within weeks of his arrival in England since his first school report is for the term ending Friday 28 July, 1939. This is also where his Aunt Ida's Karlsbad postcard was sent, addressed to 'Herr Hans Rieden'. The school was some 370 kilometres from the Mission, a nearly five-hour drive, and Dad was the only Czech refugee to be sent there. He must have felt so lonely heading off into the unknown by himself, and I wondered who had paid for the school. Did my grandparents give the Mission funds for private education? If so, I can't imagine this school, so far from the BMJ home, would have been the best option.

Or was this a charitable gift, and if so why and how was Dad chosen from the other refugees? There was nothing in the file to enlighten me.

The reports showed that my father stayed at this school until 28 July 1943. In the holidays he returned to the Mission, where I imagine he would have been at a disadvantage as he tried to find his place amid the other children who had been together throughout the term. Theo, Dad's lifelong friend from the home, said that my father was always quiet and never spoke of his parents, even later as an adult, and that he had assumed they weren't close.

Academic study was clearly paramount at Winterdyne, and the pupils sat examinations in every subject most terms, and were graded on their ongoing work. They were then allocated a position in the form. It seems pretty brutal compared to today's softer approach, but was very typical of the education ethos of the era.

In the first report, completed just four and a half months after his arrival in England, Dad was listed as eighth in a form of eight boys. His work scores ranged from 45 per cent in scripture (I am guessing this is Christian scripture, not Judaism) to 80 per cent in French and arithmetic. Astonishingly, he scored 80 per cent in his English language and composition exam, and it is noted that he 'has shown marked progress in his English'. Not bad for a boy who spoke no English only months before.

While back at the Mission for summer holidays, my father would have been with the other Czech refugee children when their regular Sunday-morning service at Christ Church was interrupted on 3 September 1939. Annalisa remembered that someone, possibly the verger, came up to the vicar with a message, which the vicar read out. He announced that Prime Minister Neville Chamberlain had just declared war on Germany, following Hitler's refusal to withdraw his troops from Poland. Annalisa has no memory of the children discussing the situation or of her immediate feelings, only that she hated the Germans and this was before 'the horrors that were to come'. I wondered if my father fully understood what was happening. His world was at sixes and sevens, and this was another blow.

Looking at his reports, it's clear my father buried himself in his schoolwork. In his next report, six months later, Dad had soared to second in a form of 16 boys, with 95 per cent in his scripture exam and 100 per cent in Latin! And then, just a year after his evacuation from Prague, Dad, aged nine, was top in a class of 14 boys, a position he maintained for three terms, consistently excelling in History, Geography, Literature, Recitation, Algebra and more.

In the last quarter of 1942, Dad's report notes that he had been absent, and then I realised that there is actually a report missing for the May–July 1942 term. Dad missed a whole term. This prompted me to sift through the dates, and what I discovered made me mull over whether his parents might actually have funded this private prep school and at this moment their money had ran out.

Helena and Rudolf were transported to Theresienstadt on 12 September 1942 and would have received their summons a few weeks before. In July, Rudolf's 82-year-old father, Emil, and Helena's eldest sister, Aunty Ida, had been rounded up and sent to the camp. I imagine Dad knew little of the details of what was happening to his family, but he would have been aware that his parents were no longer in Prague. Until then he had received letters from them, and the last one must have told him – or perhaps they only told Reverend and

Mrs Davidson – that they had been called for transportation. It was probably the last letter Dad received from them until liberation. Dad must have been paralysed with anxiety – and then he didn't go back for the summer term. Did the money stop or was my father gripped by fear and depression?

But Dad returned to Winterdyne the following term and it was noted that he took his College of Preceptors Preliminary Exam, which I suspect might have been crucial for his application for a scholarship to a private secondary school. If my grandparents' funds had ceased, I wonder who paid for this final year at Winterdyne. Perhaps Reverend Davidson and the BMJ helped out, mindful that this was crucial to my father's further education.

Dad's grades were still incredibly strong – 93 per cent in Divinity. And yet in that first report after his term away, Dad's class position plummeted to fifth of five.

Dad also took piano lessons, something he had done back in Prague as well. There was a certificate in his file showing that he passed Grade III, and in his final report, in 1943, Miss Hibbert gave Dad a 90 per cent grade and wrote that he was 'a musical boy and should continue with his studies'.

Also in that final report, ten days after my father's 13th birthday, the headmaster wrote, 'We shall miss Hans. Every success to him.' It's the sort of report every parent would be so proud to receive, only Rudolf and Helena were fighting for survival in Theresienstadt and I can't imagine ever saw it.

Next in the file was a baptism certificate. It shocked me a little, even though I suspected it might be in there. It recorded that on Saturday 23 January, 1944, when Dad was just 13, he was baptised by Reverend Davidson in All Saints Parish Church in Culmstock, Devon. Dad never mentioned this breach of the Reverend Davidson's agreement to baptise him at 16 with parental approval. His parents couldn't possibly have been consulted, given their current situation.

By this time Dad had started at his senior school, Blundell's, the public school where he was a scholarship student. It was located in Tiverton just 15 minutes' drive away, so I imagine Reverend Davidson collected my father from school for the baptism and then drove him back afterwards. I guess my father agreed to this to keep the peace, but as his school reports from Blundell's show, religion was ceasing to be his top subject. Possibly Reverend Davidson saw this and picked his moment. Or perhaps I am being paranoid.

Dad's reports for Blundell's continued to chart his progress. They ran from 1943 to 1948 and made for fascinating reading. At Blundell's I think standards were tougher. At the start Dad excelled at Latin and French and later in Geography and Ancient Greek, while his interest in Divinity definitely waned. Winterdyne, like the Mission, had a heavy emphasis on Christian teaching; at Blundell's the boys' spiritual devotion was left more as a personal matter, and I suspect my father's attention to the academic subject fell away naturally, along with his faded interest in going to church. His piano prowess, however, remained impressive. A recurrent issue seemed to be not 'talking up' in class, but it was clear my father was a very academically talented pupil and also pretty handy at cricket.

In July 1945 the headmaster mentioned that he expected Dad to work for a university scholarship, and in the same month he passed his School Certificate with three distinctions in Geography, Latin and French and four credits. This meant my father was exempt from the entry requirements for Oxford, Cambridge or London universities, and free to apply for a scholarship after the Sixth Form.

Dad would have been sitting his School Certificate exam just as Victory in Europe was announced and his parents were liberated from Theresienstadt. That eight-year-old Czech Jewish refugee was now an impressive English schoolboy with a promising future.

When I contacted Blundell's archivist, Mike Sampson, to see if he had any details of my father's time there, along with his academic achievements, he sent me a witty farewell notice from the school magazine: 'We say our good-byes to ... Rieden (with an average of 80!) has been the cavalier of House Cricket. He also claims to have stuck a tip on a billiard cue sufficiently firmly for it to last the whole term – a notable achievement.'

Also in the newsletter for his House – the Francis House Recorder – Dad is listed as House Captain of billiards and cricket, and as representing the House in shooting and table tennis. It also stated, 'HR played Chopin's Prelude in D flat and Waltz in A flat on the piano in an FH concert.' The tone was typical of English public schools and gave nothing away about my father's state of mind, though some photos of the cricket team show Dad looking very grown-up but rather awkward.

There was one notable blip in Dad's school reports from Blundell's. It was for the summer term of 1946, from May to the end of July, when Dad's work literally fell off a cliff. His Geography teacher wrote 'his work has lost that real class which it had last term and has become quite ordinary'. While in Latin, usually a stand-out subject for Dad, the teacher penned 'not very good at present'. His form master berated my father for lack of 'vitality'. His housemaster wrote, 'A disappointing report as I had expected so much of him, I hope it will prove only a temporary affair.' And, incredibly, the headmaster offered, 'I know of no particular reason to explain this disappointing term. I should be glad to hear if it is thought that there is any particular cause.'

I am astonished at the insensitivity shown here. Dad was one of only two Jewish Czech refugee boys in the school. Surely the headmaster and teachers had stepped outside their ivory towers, read about the fate of the Jews in Dad's homeland and wondered what had happened to Hans Rieden's family? I welled up with tears of rage as I read the report.

When I looked at the letters that followed, it became obvious that Dad must have been going through at best shock and disappointment, and at worst a nervous breakdown at this time. So yes, his 'vitality' would have been seriously compromised.

When it was time to send my brothers and me to school, my father was always vehemently against private boarding schools and fervently for state-funded comprehensives. I suspect his hatred of the British 'public'-school system stemmed from these brutal experiences at Blundell's.

═══

The first letter in Dad's dossier was one of those quoted by John Ross in Lucy Davidson's book *For a Future and a Hope*. It was from someone called Mary, who was not with the BMJ but worked possibly for a refugee or Jewish or Czech charity based in North London. The news it delivered must have filled my father with joy.

Dear Mr Davidson

I have just received word from Prague that Hansi Rieden's father and mother have returned there safe and sound from the Concentration Camp of Teresen [sic].

I am giving you this very cheerful news and would ask you to be good enough to impress on Hansi to whom I have written separately to write at once in English and to post his letter to me so that I can forward it through the Czech Embassy to Prague in the event of his not having written yet.

I think it would do a lot of good if your goodself [sic] would address a few lines to those poor sufferers in Prague. I am glad to be at your disposal if you require any assistance.

Wishing you all the best, I remain,

Yours faithfully

Mary

This letter was dated 18 June 1945, just weeks after Theresienstadt was liberated. My father must have written immediately to his parents and sat for his School Certificate in a state of unbridled happiness. But it would have been short lived.

The next letter in the file was addressed to the Reverend and Mrs Davidson and jointly signed by my grandparents, dated 13 October 1945, and received on 19 October, some four long months after that initial news. It seems Rudolf and Helena had received a letter from my father and probably wrote back to him privately, but what they are conveying here, in broken English no doubt painstakingly translated with a dictionary to hand, is that they can't take my father back ... It makes me gasp as I read it, and all I can think about is how heartbroken my father would have been.

Dear Reverend & Mrs Davidson

Don't worry please that our answer will be late. Mrs Rieden left yesterday the hospital, where she has been so many weeks in follows of 3 years concentration camp

Terezin. Now she is not recovered and has still pains, it will have a long time till she get back her strength.

We can't say, how thankful we are for all you do our child, he found a second home, what we will never forget. You saved him his life, you give him such a good education, either you haven't one but a hundred of children.

Just now we have learned how dreadfully you have been bombed in 1940–1 and V and V-1 and V-2 and how splendid did the English Nation under such horrid conditions.

We got a long letter from Hans, where he describes his life and now his school during the last 6 years. He enclosed 2 fotos where we see that he gets well and is a good pupil. Please change his name 'Hans' – in Czech we call him 'Hanus' – in 'John'.

When we have been deported we said to take back our child at once we came home. Only 10% of Jews came back. Later we learned, not to do it, the conditions they are here in the moment are not so well to take back our child. Hansi has forgotten the Czech language and it would be better for him to stay in England to continue his studies. Please, should you tell me it would be possible for Hansi to get the British Nationality?

Hansi writes that you will be so kind to try to get for him a Stipendium [scholarship]. He prepares himself for a Schoolmaster. What do you mean [i.e. think] about it? Would not be better to become another stadium [stage (up)], a technical, an Enginieur or Physician?

Sorry we ask you so many questions, but we hardly [i.e. badly] need your advice.

We remain dear Reverend & Mrs Davidson,

Yours thankfully

Dr Rieden & Helena Rieden

I always thought that it was either the Mission or my father who had chosen to change his name. Dad had said it was to take the English form since Hans, Hansi or Hanus all sounded too German. But here I saw it was his parents' wish, and by this time Dad was almost a man, 15 years old, and the war was over. I can only assume that Rudolf and Helena were petrified of standing out in any way.

My traumatised grandparents were handing their only son over to England. There was a tiny bit of humour in this desperately sad letter when, even after all they have been through, these high-achieving parents still criticise their son's choice of career. For the first time they seemed very Jewish to me, and amid all this pain it made me laugh out loud.

My father probably never saw this letter, but he would have received a version of it written to him. I can't begin to imagine its effect on him.

Three days later, Reverend Davidson responded. His letter was practical, outlining some home truths, and I think also shows significant sensitivity. The Reverend now knew Hansi Rieden better than his parents.

Dear Dr Rieden

Thank you for your letter which we received safely. We are so glad to know that you feel satisfied about Hans. It will be difficult to get into the habit of calling him John, and I must write and ask him what he thinks about the name being changed, or rather translated.

There is no possible chance of him obtaining British nationality at present. He could not even apply for it until he is twenty-one. Certainly it would be of very great advantage to him, and I am hoping with him and others that the fact that they have lived since children in this country, and that their interest and future seems to lie here, may be taken into consideration by the Government when it comes to the time. I certainly think you are studying the boy's best interest in allowing him to remain here for as long as possible, though I do most deeply sympathise with you in the continued separation from him. You must deeply long to have him back after all you have been through.

In regard to the profession he has chosen, we do not try to push our boys into one direction more than another. We certainly never suggested to Hans that he should take up teaching, and for some time I had no idea that he was thinking of this. The medical profession is very much over-crowded, and I am glad that he has not chosen this. Not only is the training terribly expensive, quite beyond our power to give him, but, as I said, there are too many taking it up. This last applies even more to engineering, as thousands of trained engineers are coming out of the Forces, but there is a shortage of teachers.

With kindest regards and all good wishes,

Yours very sincerely

Reverend Davidson was right that my father could not apply for British citizenship until he was 21. With his parents alive, Dad was unable to claim the 'orphan of the state' status that some of his fellow refugee children could. And this non-British status did prove a problem for him. It prevented him from applying for a university grant and government aid. Instead, his only option was to seek out specific scholarships, and this greatly reduced his opportunities, as I later discovered.

I don't know what Dad felt about giving up his name. After we went to Prague together and I realised his name was actually Hanus, not John, I used it from time to time and it always made

Dad smile, but he never said anything. And while I am certain he would have been crestfallen at not being reunited with his parents, he seemed to have been so immersed in his studies that part of me does appreciate the wisdom in his continuing.

My mother told me that Dad's parents had also told him, directly after the war, that it was still difficult being Czech and Jewish, and that he was an 'Englishman now', the inference being that he should forget them and his homeland. This must have been in one of their letters to him and it must have cut deep.

The next letter, written on 30 January 1946 and notable for the improvement in Rudolf's English, certainly suggested that Dad had heeded his parents' call and knuckled down to study, but it also broached the thorny issue of money, something that I later discovered became a huge problem for my father. Rudolf and Helena are already calling their son John, so I am guessing my father agreed to the name-change. I am unsure who the mentioned Mr Korff is, but I imagine another intermediary from either the Czech Embassy or a refugee charity. The letter was not sent from my grandparents' pre-war home address, but from somewhere in the neighbouring district in Prague. Rudolf and Helena would have been utterly destitute, having had their property and bank accounts seized when they were transported to Theresienstadt, and there was now no hope in sight of regaining that wealth. Again they were trapped.

Dear Mrs Davidson

I hope you have received my last letter and waiting for an answer we omitted to send you in time the most sincere and hearty wishes for Christmas and the New Year. Please accept now our very true wishes. Mr Korff sent us a letter, written to him by John, in which he describes his Christmas-holidays and we thank very much for the beautiful holidays you have prepared for him, and for the presents.

It seems he is very happy and satisfied with his study, that he likes apparently and it would be a pity if he could not complete his study. I beg to ask if he is diligent enough and if his progress is so good that his teachers are satisfied with his work.

We are longing so much for seeing again the child after so many years and to be able to live together with him. But unfortunately my wife is, at the time being, not yet able to travel, on account of her illness, so that a visit is not yet possible for the moment.

In consequence of my Sudeto-German descent I have also difficulties concerning the compensation of the confiscated property, the flat and my former position.

I cannot repeat it often enough, that we are so much grateful to you, that you have saved our child's life by accepting him in your home and we are as much indebted for the good education, he enjoys.

I hope you are quite well and please accept once more my deeply felt thanks, and compliments to Mr Davidson.

Yours very devotedly

Dr Rieden

My father at this time was now in the sixth form at Blundell's and his reports showed that he was back on form academically, though his housemaster noted 'he has not developed powers of leadership' but is 'a pleasant boy'. Dad was clearly hoping to go to university, where he wanted to do a degree in Geography.

In our family albums there is a photo of Helena dated November 1946. She must have continued to write to her son and sent this with her letter; on it she has written 'with love your mother' in English. I think it is an official photo, maybe taken for an identity document. As I stare into Helena's eyes, I try to imagine what she must be thinking and how unnatural it would have been for her to write to her boy in a foreign tongue. My father had another couple of photos of his mother that he kept all his life, which were taken in August 1924. I wonder if Helena sent these to him or if she put them in his suitcase to keep with him throughout the war. They are studio photos with an air of theatricality. Helena looks beautiful and very fashionable, her hair piled into a bun, and she's wearing what looks like a silk dress. The only postwar photo Dad had of his father is from June 1951, which I suspect was also sent to him in a letter. Rudolf is smiling and standing in a suit that is now too big for his meagre frame, with a flamboyant tie. I think he may be in front of the columns outside Prague's State Opera House, where people are spilling out onto the streets after a performance. Rudolf looks thin and gaunt but happy to be home enjoying the riches of Prague's cultural life. I imagine such a photo would have made Dad a little homesick, a precious reminder of all that he had lost.

The next letter, sent on 16 October 1947 from his parents to the Davidsons, showed again their desperation over money.

Dear Mrs and Mr Davidson

We haven't written you for a long time because we didn't want waste your time with our letters. We thank you very much for your kind information and would like to bother you again with our sorrows.

John writes regularly about his interest and his doing at school. He writes in his last letter 'I have been advised by

my form-master to go in for a scholarship to Cambridge-
University which takes place next March; he says that this
is the best scholarship to try for in Geography and so I will
probably enter for it.' We would like to know the kind of
the scholarship he was going in for. Would he get a sum of
money enough to live on it or would he get accommodation
and board in a College? We should be glad, anyhow, if he
should be successful and so we should be very thankful if you
could help him.

We haven't seen our child for about 8 jears [sic] and are
longing to see him. But we don't see any possibility to come
to England as we aren't in good health and as it is almost
impossible to get here a passport and a moneytransfer for
such purposes.

We thank you from the depth of our heart for jour [sic]
great kindness and for all you have done for our child for
such a long time.

With the best regards from us both

Yours very sincerely

Dr Rieden

Reverend Davidson must have replied swiftly – though
his letter was not in the file. My father always said that the
Mission had hoped he would study Theology at university
and become a minister with them. I suspect the news that Dad
was looking to Geography for his degree would have caused
a bit of a commotion and curtailed any offers of financial
support the Davidsons may previously have proffered. This
follow-up letter from my grandparents on 29 October 1947,
just 13 days after the previous letter, was again heartbreaking.
Should Dad not get a scholarship to study at university, they
don't think he should return to Czechoslovakia.

Just four months later, on 25 February 1948, a Soviet-backed Communist coup d'état in Czechoslovakia triggered more than 40 years of totalitarian rule. My father's window of opportunity to be reunited with his homeland and his parents slammed shut.

Dear Mrs and Mr Davidson

We thank you so much for your kind letter. It is very good of you to write the whole truth. It is necessary for us to know it, even if it is not agreeable. For the time being we have to wait until the question of the scholarship has been decided and we beg you to let us know the decision as soon as you know it. We should be glad if you could let us know your opinion what would happen with the boy in the case if he shouldn't get any scholarship. We would like to think the thing over just now. The difficulty is that the boy has forgotten all his Czech. We are very thankful for all you are doing for our son. We are sure you have saved his life and you have given him the best education he could get. We shall be glad to hear your opinion about his future, we beg for your help to him.

With the best regards and wishes

Yours sincerely

My father's penultimate report from Blundell's showed that he tried really, really hard to win a scholarship to Oxford or Cambridge but didn't quite make it. 'The term has largely been taken up with work for his scholarship examination at Balliol College, Oxford. I am glad that he went up for an interview as this means that his standard was high,' wrote the housemaster. Dad clearly passed the exam but not the interview. His Geography tutor wrote, 'He has worked with his usual quiet industry on his scholarship work ... he did reasonably well at Cambridge, but not well enough for an interview.'

Of course, had he not been a foreign refugee, he would have been able to apply for a grant in the usual way along with his fellow English schoolmates, rather than battle for the very competitive scholarship places. But without a scholarship, Dad had no means of putting himself through university.

The final two letters in my father's file were in his own hand, which I recognised so well and they went some way to explaining what happened next. It was now 1 October 1948, the Iron Curtain had fallen in Czechoslovakia, and my father, age 18, was writing to Mrs Davidson from a school in Maidenhead in the south of England. He seemed to be pretty pleased with himself, having landed a job as a teacher with bed and board.

Winbury School
Hightown Road
Maidenhead

Dear Mrs Davidson,

I write this letter sitting in a classroom, confronted by six boys. Four of them are working, one is gazing out of the window, and the sixth occasionally peeps up at me from his book in the hope that he will get a chance to whisper something to the boy on his left. It is Friday evening, and I am taking Prep. From this, and from the address at the top of the page, you will have gathered that I have got a post as teacher in a Prep. School. It is a small school containing about 50 boys, of whom 6 are boarders. I am the form-master of Class IV (the lowest form), in which there are 11 boys aged 7 to 8. I spend over half my time teaching this form, but I also teach some subjects to higher forms. I find that the boys are quite easy to manage, but the difficulty is to know exactly what and how to teach them. I am finding this a little difficult to start with, but now, after a week here I am already getting into my stride and I think I am going to like it. The chief advantage of this school over most others is that, owing to the small number of boarders, I have very little supervision duty to do. Saturdays and Sundays are all completely free, and so are all the evenings of the week except Friday from 4 o'clock onwards, on Friday I take Prep and get off at 6. Thus, I have got quite a lot of time for studying. I have got a small but quite nice room, and there is also a smallish Common Room for the two other masters (excluding the Head) and myself. My salary, including residence, food, laundry etc, is £200 p.a., so I think I have done quite well. My one grudge at the moment is against Maidenhead, which for shopping, libraries etc. is a dump of the first order. Its one asset is the river, which is lovely in the nice weather we are having now.

It is time for the end of Prep. now, and I must close. I think I have managed to settle down quite well, and I now have a busy week-end ahead of me as I must work out a programme of work for the term. Hoping that you and Mr Davidson are very well,

Love from, Hans

P.S. Please address letters to J. Rieden.

Reading between the lines I think after he finished at Blundell's my father had been left on his own. His parents had not come to get him, nor did they want him to move back to Prague. The Davidsons and the BMJ could no longer house him at the Mission home, and since Dad was not going to study divinity or pursue a career in the Church, they wouldn't be funding his university ambitions. So Dad found a job and in this new outside world he became John Rieden.

But my father hadn't given up on university, and set about applying to study as an external student at London University. This would have been a correspondence course, which he would have had to work at in addition to the day job he needed in order to earn the money to pay the fees and to live. But he seemed to be up for the challenge.

In his last letter to Mrs Davidson – I think it's interesting that he is writing to Mrs Davidson, who Annalisa told me preferred the boys over the girls in the Mission – my father, then an 18-year-old, said: 'I am waiting for a copy of the syllabus for the exam from London University. I have got a Prospectus and entry form . . . and it seems to me to be a good course. I hope I get the syllabus soon, as I want to spread the course out over as long a period of time as possible.'

He also seemed rather bothered by his lack of status now in Britain. 'Please could you also tell me what the position is about my Guardianship,' he wrote.

I have just had a letter from the 'Christian Council for Refugees', in which they inform me, among other things, that Sir Herbert Emerson [League of Nations High Commissioner of Refugees and Director of the Inter-Governmental Committee on Refugees] has now become the Guardian of Orphan Minors, but I am not an Orphan Minor, I wonder how they got hold of my address.

Dad's tone was a little accusatory and no wonder. If he were an orphan he would have been able to apply for citizenship and therefore a university grant. As it was, he was in no-man's-land. But, I would later discover, he had a plan . . .

CHAPTER SIX

YOU CAN RUN
BUT YOU CAN'T HIDE

Ahead of my trip to Prague, now five months away, I start trawling for as much information as I can gather. Very quickly I realise how little I know about my father's family – not just what happened in the Holocaust, but before that: where they were from, what jobs they had, how they lived, what they looked like. Having discovered my grandfather was of German descent, I now wonder how they all ended up in Prague.

On Grandma's side I am still astonished by the revelation that her father was a rabbi who had 11 children. Judaism was nowhere in my upbringing. My mother would sigh heavily when I said I wanted to go to our local Church of England service in our home town on Sunday with my fellow Brownies, and would then giggle disparagingly at the back of the pews as I proudly carried the troop's flag up the aisle. Mum was very much of Marx's 'opium of the people' school of thought where religion – whatever creed – was concerned.

As for my father, I always believed he had a more spiritual soul, but he abhorred the idea of organised religion telling you how to live your life. I think his credo would have been that the impetus for good comes from the power of the human spirit and an innate sense of what's right and wrong, and certainly in his own life that was true.

Dad was naturally kind, with an acute social conscience, and selflessly generous. One time when we were together in Nairobi, he couldn't stop giving money to every child beggar who tugged on his arm. I had been travelling for a while in Africa and felt myself to be a little wiser in matters of street philanthropy. I told Dad the money would probably end up in someone else's pocket, a Fagin controlling the children. But Dad said, 'You don't know that for sure,' and continued to give. Soon he had a trail of children following him.

When I look back now I realise how much of Dad's personality was informed by his past; what happened to him came out in all sorts of ways, and this spurs me on to uncover the truth about who his/our family were and what happened to them.

While the Nazis did destroy a lot of Jewish records and evidence from the camps, I discover that the Czech National Archives – Národní Archiv – in Prague is a treasure trove of documents, albeit mostly in Czech. In a nation torn apart by despotic occupation, ancestry searches for missing relatives are common, and the records that have survived are well catalogued. At this juncture I still only had the names of the Rieden side of the family, along with the 'transport' information I had gleaned from the Czech Holocaust database and other Shoah online records. In the National Archives I hoped to understand more about what had happened before they became part of Hitler's 'Final Solution'.

Since I don't speak Czech, I paid for one of the Czech National Archives archivists to carry out the search and copy any material found. Two months later I received more than 50 documents from the very efficient Ilona Dvořáková along with a bureaucratic summary in English. The documents, in a combination of German and Czech, present a telling dialogue about a family constantly on the run.

The first thing I learn is that Rieden is not actually our family name at all. This is quite a bombshell. I can't explain why – it shouldn't matter – but somehow the charade of a name that has no roots throws me off kilter and adds to the shifting sands of who we are as a family. It's as if the carpet has been pulled from under my feet, part of my identity ripped away with it. And then I realise that this is how my relatives must have felt when they were reduced to numbers on a list. This is how you wipe out a race. Or is it? The name-change actually tells its own very potent story.

Before Rieden, the family surname was Rindskopf, and we were not originally from Prague but from Liberec. In the winter this place turns into a popular ski resort, a short hop from Prague; in the summer it's an elegant city of culture, with endless outdoor music festivals filling the long, warm nights. Historically, Liberec is known for its textiles and manufacturing.

The city's population was always largely German and initially the Jewish community struggled; it wasn't fully established until 1872. By 1930, Jews made up three per cent of the city's population and lived side by side with their gentile neighbours, not exactly in harmony, but rubbing along. Then, after Hitler's annexation of the Sudetenland and the Munich Agreement in 1938, Liberec was handed over to Nazi Germany and became the capital of the region. And it was at this point that the Riedens were forced to flee.

It was my father's grandfather, Emil, who changed his surname from Rindskopf to Rieden in 1913. Emil, who had seven siblings, was the only one in his family to do this. But why? I cannot find any reference to the reason for the change in my archival papers, but on further investigation I discover that many Jews in Bohemia at this time changed their names to conceal their Jewishness and avoid persecution. Was this his intention?

Tracing back through the centuries, Jews traditionally didn't have surnames or family names, but instead would use their father's name. So Emil, for example, would be known as Emil ben Joachim (Emil, son of Joachim). But in Austria in 1787 – when Bohemia was part of the Austro-Hungarian Empire – Jews were forced to adopt German surnames. It was a form of control. I suspect that Rindskopf, which is German for 'ox-head', was given to the family as a term of derision and ridicule – anti-Semitism was rife well before Hitler.

Indeed, in 1787 and 1799 the local nobleman, Count Clam-Gallas, issued a decree to expel the Jews from Liberec. This was to try to quell the success of Jewish tradesmen in the linen industry. Even though Jews made up a tiny percentage of the workforce, they were disproportionately successful, and this angered non-Jewish businessmen. The municipality officials did not cooperate fully with their feudal lord and allowed a few tradesmen to stay – after all, how else could they access their premium goods? – but by 1823 there were just six Jewish families in Liberec. Later the bans were lifted and the Jewish population slowly grew, but anti-Semitism was never far away.

The Rindskopf name would have immediately identified Emil as a Jew (and who wouldn't want to get rid of 'ox-head' as a name?). Changing it to Rieden – which is also the name of a town in the Tyrol in Austria, a village in Bavaria and a Swiss municipality (to all of which I jokingly laid claim as a child, ignorant of the truth about our name) – would make Emil and his children less conspicuous and help them flourish in their work, unhampered by prejudice . . . or so he hoped.

So while Rudolf and his siblings were all born Rindskopfs, by the time they were teenagers and young adults they had become Riedens. It's sad to think that even going back more than a hundred years my ancestors were finding ways to hide who they really were. And even more poignant is that in the end, of course, it didn't work.

I am transfixed by the paperwork, much of it in ornate writing. There's something about this handwritten work, and even the typed documents with the idiosyncrasies of old typewriters, that feels warm and personal, even though many of the documents are heralding tough times. At last these lives I have uncovered, my family, are being recognised, and for me they are becoming living, breathing individuals with homes, jobs, a community and shared experience. What is clear from these documents is that settled family life in Liberec ended abruptly in 1938.

As soon as I realised Liberec was the family home I wrote to the local archives, and what I found there made me realise that this Bohemian city was as close to a Rieden base as I was going to find; this was home. The Rindskopfs/Riedens had a whole life and community there, with a family business and property.

Emil, son of Joachim and Regina, owned a jewellery shop selling colourful glass-beaded Bohemian 'bijouterie'. Rindskopf, I soon discover, is actually pretty important in the history of Bohemian glass. Iridescent, crackle and etched glass in the Art Nouveau style was made in factories owned by a Josef Rindskopf and some of his brothers, and has become highly collectible. While I can't find any direct link to Emil, the coincidence of surname, location and profession seems too strong to ignore, and I imagine it's highly possible that Emil's bijouterie business used glass beads made in the Rindskopf factories.

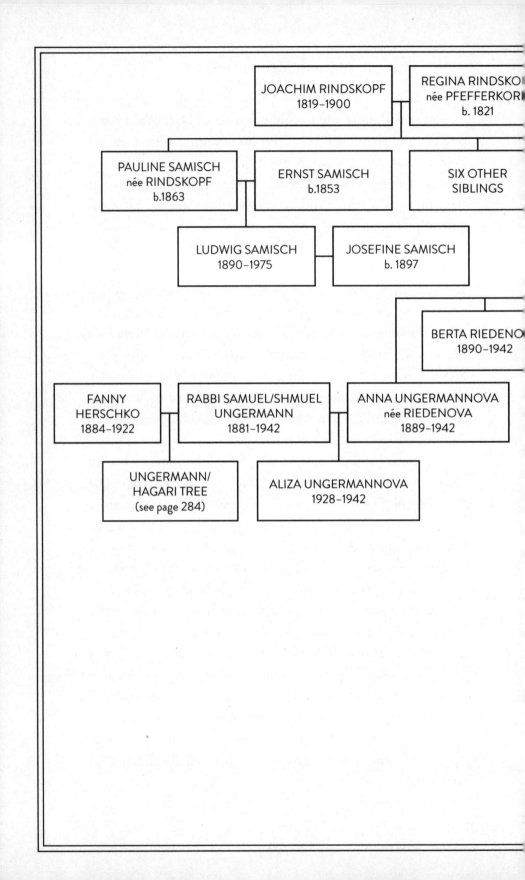

THE RINDSKOPF/RIEDEN FAMILY TREE

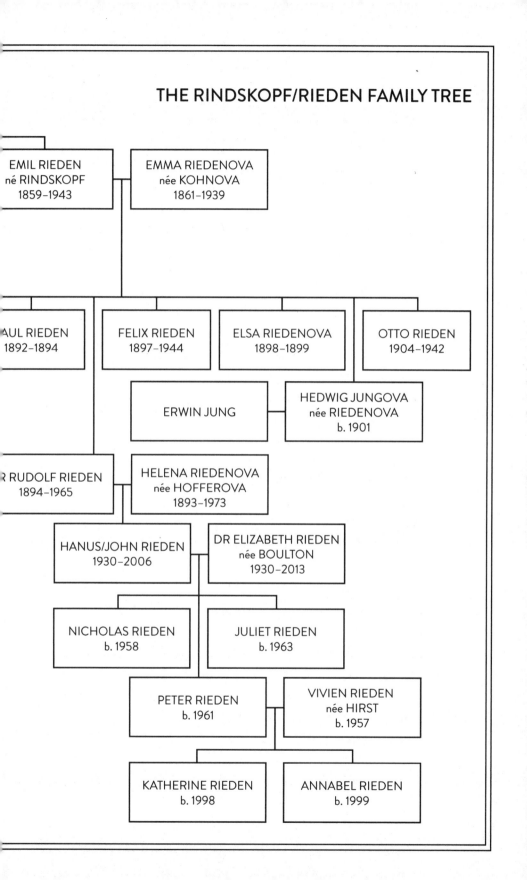

EMIL RIEDEN
né RINDSKOPF
1859–1943

EMMA RIEDENOVA
née KOHNOVA
1861–1939

AUL RIEDEN
1892–1894

FELIX RIEDEN
1897–1944

ELSA RIEDENOVA
1898–1899

OTTO RIEDEN
1904–1942

ERWIN JUNG

HEDWIG JUNGOVA
née RIEDENOVA
b. 1901

R RUDOLF RIEDEN
1894–1965

HELENA RIEDENOVA
née HOFFEROVA
1893–1973

HANUS/JOHN RIEDEN
1930–2006

DR ELIZABETH RIEDEN
née BOULTON
1930–2013

NICHOLAS RIEDEN
b. 1958

JULIET RIEDEN
b. 1963

PETER RIEDEN
b. 1961

VIVIEN RIEDEN
née HIRST
b. 1957

KATHERINE RIEDEN
b. 1998

ANNABEL RIEDEN
b. 1999

Emil and wife Emma had eight children. Their eldest son, Paul, died at the age of 14 months and their third daughter, Elsa, also died young at ten months, but there were six siblings, born between 1889 and 1904, who thrived.

Anna, the eldest, grew up to be an accountant. She married Samuel Ungermann (who I later discover was originally Hungarian, as his name suggests). Samuel was well known in Liberec's Jewish community. He was a cantor – a singer who leads the prayers – and religious teacher in the local synagogue between 1920 and 1923, and is proudly listed in its records.

The Temple was built in 1889 and was a very ornate, notable and expensive building in the style of the early Italian Renaissance, with a fabulous cupola (dome). This was a statement: the Jewish community was established and here to stay. Samuel and Anna married in the synagogue and Samuel's religious career prospered as he became Rabbi in the tiny Jewish community in nearby Bílina from 1922 to 1925.

But Liberec's beautiful synagogue could not withstand Hitler. It was burned down on 11 November 1938, when Kristallnacht destroyed Liberec and the city was overrun by the new Nazi occupiers. Jews in Bílina had already fled in advance of the Sudetenland takeover, abandoning their synagogue.

At this point in my research I had no clue what happened to Samuel and Anna. I couldn't find them in the Prague National Archives nor were they listed as victims of the Holocaust in the Czech database or in the transports to Theresienstadt. Could they have survived? I allow a glimmer of hope to shine for a moment and make a note to investigate further. For the time being this is welcome good news.

Berta, the next eldest in the Rieden family, worked as a seamstress. Then, nine months after Paul's death, my grandfather Rudolf was born and became the Rieden family's eldest son, who later became a war hero and a lawyer in the Czech government. I imagine they were pretty proud of him.

Felix, Rudolf's younger brother, worked in father Emil's business, and in 1928 there is a record in the archive file showing that Felix has passed his driving test and has a driving licence. It includes a rather serious but quite handsome photo of Felix and states that he owned his own Ford automobile. Daughter number four was Hedwig, a saleswoman who married a German gentile, Erwin Jung. And finally I come to the youngest, Otto, who became a clerk.

So Emil and Emma's children all had good jobs and most stayed living at home in the Liberec community. They were a significantly successful bunch.

Interestingly, as far as I can tell, only two of the siblings had their own children: Rudolf, who had a son, my father Hanus; and Anna, who I much later discover, had a daughter Aliza. I find this very surprising. Did my other relatives have illegitimate children who weren't registered, I wonder? Or perhaps the constant fear of persecution dulled the desire to bring more children into this uncertain world or literally affected their fertility?

But family was everything, and when the Riedens fled Liberec, it was to Rudolf they ran. Now Dr Rudolf Rieden, my grandfather was a successful married man and father, a doctor of law with a good job in the taxation department of the Czech government. He and Helena and their only child, my father Hanus, were living in an apartment in a nice Prague suburb, doing very well for themselves.

Documents from the Cabinet Council Presidium, the department in which Rudolf worked, reveal his employment record. I remember my father telling us that Grandpa was

JULIET RIEDEN

a civil servant working in finance or economics. In fact, he was a tax inspector for motor vehicles, working in the legal department. According to the records, he was exceptional at his job, putting 'all his energies' into discovering undeclared taxes and bringing those responsible to account. As I read this I can't help but laugh, for my father, Rudolf's son, also had an exceptional skill in this regard, only Dad was coming from the other side. Every year he would scrutinise his own tax assessment – with scrupulous honesty – and without fail would find errors in the government calculations that usually proved he had been overcharged and resulted in a rebate. In the genes, perhaps!

Rudolf had joined the Czech government's legal department in 1924 from his previous position working as a lawyer at the Prague law courts. He quickly proved to be doing '*velmi dobře*' (very well), and in 1927 was promoted to the next salary bracket and moved to the motor tax department, where he achieved impressive results.

Then, on 16 July 1933, something happened. Rudolf was the subject of a disciplinary hearing at Prague's Ministry of Finance. I have no idea what this was all about, as no details are recorded. My paranoia notes that it occurred a few months after Hitler came to power in Germany, though even the Führer's considerable powers wouldn't have stretched to the Czech government's staffing – not yet anyway. But with anti-Semitism spreading across Europe, it would be naive not to at least consider the possibility that Rudolf could have been the victim of a new groundswell of prejudice.

Grandpa's punishment was to have his salary level frozen for two years. This must have been extremely aggravating, but Rudolf refused to be bowed by the ruling and stuck with the job. By 1935 his assessment was back on track, he's declared

106

'*velmi dobře*' once more and it is also written that Dr Rieden '<u>fully deserves to be promoted</u>' – underlined! Accordingly, in 1936, Grandpa moves into the next salary bracket and a new job in the Ministry.

Then, on 6 October 1938, just five days after Nazis marched into the Sudetenland, Rudolf's parents – Emil, three weeks shy of his 80th birthday; and Emma, 77 – and his siblings – Berta, 48; Felix, 41; and Otto, 34 – were forced to flee Liberec. As Jews they were exiled from their home town, but as Germans they also had a fight on their hands to claim Czech citizenship so they could live in Prague. They left in a hurry, abandoning their jobs and everything they owned, and moved in with my father and his parents in Prague. So a city apartment for three was now stretched to accommodate eight. In the blink of an eye the Riedens were on the run.

Everyone knew it was only a matter of time before Hitler occupied the rest of Czechoslovakia, and it was at this point that the whole Rieden family started to explore emigration options.

I now know from my grandfather's application to The Barbican Mission to the Jews that with his war disability, his chances of being accepted as a refugee by other countries were next to nothing – most countries insisted on 'able-bodied' migrants who wouldn't be a drain on the health service; also I imagine the fact that Rudolf had obtained the disability fighting on the German side couldn't have helped his case. So he and Helena concentrated their efforts on finding refuge for their son Hanus, which they achieved a week before Hitler and his Nazi thugs marched into Prague on 15 March 1939. It's possible family resources were pooled to help fund Hanus's escape, and at the same time the brothers and sisters were exploring every possible avenue for their own way out.

From this moment on I can see that the family started to gather addresses, as they moved from pillar to post like scampering hunted creatures before ultimately being called up for transport to Theresienstadt. I know this because their addresses are listed on Civil Register residence cards. The last entry on each card is 'Transport', its finality ringing deafening alarm bells.

The cards have been stamped in the top right corner with a huge letter 'J' for Jew. It feels ugly and sinister on the hand-written record, and I suspect this was added post-Munich Agreement. This clumsy device to pick out those for perse-cution of course developed into the cloth yellow star, which from 1941 all Jews in the Protectorate were forced to wear stitched onto their clothes.

There is no card for Emil's wife, Dad's grandmother, Emma Riedenova, for on 19 October 1939, seven months after Hitler waved from the balcony of Prague Castle, she died. At the time of her death Emma was living just down the road from Rudolf and Helena. A couple of months after my father's escape, Emil and Emma and their offspring Berta, Felix and Otto had moved to a flat in the same street, which must have eased the crowding in my grandparents' home.

Emma was 77 when she died, and the family buried her in the New Jewish Cemetery in Prague. This graveyard was established in 1891 to solve the space problem in the Old Jewish Cemetery behind Pinkas Synagogue. It's a huge place located a little out of the centre, ten times the size of the old cemetery.

I don't know the cause of death. Emma's death certificate is not in the records, but I am certain the distress of her family's current plight would have been a major contributing factor. Reading of her death, I am comforted by the fact that she didn't have to go through the indignity of transport to Theresienstadt and the horror of watching her family picked off, one by one. And unlike the rest of her family, Emma would have had a loving and respectful departure from this world. When Dad left his home, Grandma Emma was very much part of the household. Did Rudolf write and tell his son of her passing?

On 30 June 1940, just over a year after he had organised my father's escape to England, Grandpa was sacked – or 'retired' as the documents record. He had been in the job 26 years, one month and 25 days. His termination was in accordance with Decree 136/1940, which excluded Jews from jobs in government, public administration, education, the law, health services and journalism. He must have seen it coming. Prague was changing every day for Jews in every stratum of society.

The days my father had remembered, spending afternoons in coffee houses, going for walks in the park, football in the yard, were no longer possible in the new Protectorate. Jews were excluded from all professions, and even menial work was heavily controlled. After war broke out in 1939, a curfew was introduced and Jews were forbidden to leave their homes after 8 pm. Soon they were banned from cinemas, restaurants, public swimming pools and theatres.

In 1939, Jewish children were thrown out of German public and private schools, and later Jewish schools were closed altogether. There were restricted shopping hours for Jews and many stores simply refused to serve them at all. These diktats also spread to the food Jews could buy, with fresh fruit and vegetables and a whole list of other goods only available to Gentiles. Property and businesses were seized and withdrawals from bank accounts restricted. By 1941, strolling in parks and forests were added to the *'verboten'* list, and some

Jews were even too scared to walk on the footpaths. Raids were frequent and punishment instant and brutal.

Control was wielded by systematic and compulsory registration of all Jews. And the next dossiers I find in my archival search are filled with cards. These, found in the Occupation Prison and Penitentiary files, bring more ominous overtones. They are obviously from a series of card indexes, the likes of which you'd more usually find in libraries.

There are various different types, on green and pink cards, and they all relate in some way to Theresienstadt. The cards have been pre-printed with specific named columns and boxes to fill out, which I find a little chilling. This was an impeccably organised system involving a great deal of thought and preparation. The Nazis knew exactly what they were doing, and every step was planned and catalogued.

The green card I suspect was created by Prague's JKG (Jüdische Kultusgemeinde: Jewish Community in Prague) for the 'Central Office for the Regulation of the Jewish Question in Bohemia and Moravia'. The 'Central Office' answered ultimately to the highest echelons of the SS, including Heinrich Himmler and Adolf Eichmann, and was responsible for what happened to all the Jews in the Protectorate. The JKG had to register Jews in the now German-controlled Protectorate of Bohemia and Moravia. Every Jew must be accounted for, and it was from here that the transport lists were made up. These green cards, one per individual, recorded personal details and the number of that initial transport from Prague. This was the first step on a road that for the vast majority led to certain death.

The card is in German, and the top line has boxes for surname, first name and transport number. Underneath is place and date of birth, and under that current home town and, most important of all (although redundant given the capital 'J' stamped on most of the cards), religion. Then marital status, job, address and identity card number, and finally details of spouse or, on the back, of wider family, listed with their transport number next to their names.

The pink card is specifically for Theresienstadt inmates and is in Czech. I suspect this was created on arrival at the concentration camp, when futures hung in the balance and decisions were often arbitrarily made regarding life and death. A new registration number is listed for each inmate on this card and then there are details of various barracks' locations within the camp. In my grandparents' case there is a long list of addresses, as they were moved around a lot, but for my other relatives there is the date and destination of transport East – to a specific death camp.

As I study the green cards I see there is one for my father, which literally sends a shiver down my spine. Obviously, the intention was to round him up with his parents. His registration number is 34135. His mother's is 34136, his father's 34138 and his uncle Felix's 34134. The Riedens were obviously all listed together, even though they were transported at different times. Dad's address, I think, is wrong. I don't recognise it among those where Rudolf and Helena lived. Perhaps my grandparents listed a fake address so that when the Nazis came to round them up they wouldn't find him. Studying the cards further, I think they were added to over time, recording new information as it happened, and further down on my father's card is a note that says he has moved away.

It doesn't bear thinking about.

This card cuts me to the core as I realise how close my father was to being a Holocaust statistic. But there are more documents to get through. In the General Register files from the Prague Police Headquarters are a number of passport applications from Rudolf, as a single man and then with his family on the passport. One from 1934 has a very sweet photo of my father, aged three, in a smart little white cap and coat. And then there is a solo application for Hanus using that passport photo I have already seen in his Barbican Mission files. This was lodged on 5 December 1938 and approved on 13 December. Just three months later Dad was using it to escape to England.

Other documents here show Rudolf's father and siblings trying to establish their state citizenship in Prague. They plead that they are of good character and do not own property, and you can sense the desperation behind their words.

And finally, there are documents from after the war. These are from the archives of the Repatriation Department of the Ministry of Labour and Social Welfare. Rudolf is now back in Prague and seeking help in compensation for three years spent in Theresienstadt. He is unwell and is granted recuperation in Teplice-Šanov, a spa town where the waters were used for healing. He is there for three weeks – one week for each year of incarceration!

———

I was now itching to get back to Czechoslovakia. I wanted to see where the family lived, what their houses were like. I wanted to walk in their footsteps and find out exactly how my smart, adaptable, independent relatives were reduced to fatal cogs in the Nazi bid for world domination. I was still hopeful that some had managed to break free and slipped away to a new life where their kin now prospered, waiting for me to find them. For even though this family seems to have spent generations running from persecution, the one thing they had so far achieved was survival.

As part of my trip I planned to visit Theresienstadt. I spoke to the historian there, Tomáš Fedorovič, who agreed to help with access to the archives to unearth information about my family, and offered to guide me around the former camp personally. This was fantastic news. Tomáš had been working at the memorial for the concentration camp for more than 18 years. If anyone could uncover what happened to my family there, Tomáš was the man.

I also planned a trip to Auschwitz with a specialist guide from Prague whose father was interned there. I now knew that at least one and possibly more of my relatives were murdered in the Polish death camp and, however harrowing, I needed to see this place for myself.

My other urgent search was for my grandmother Helena's clan, the Hoffers. At that moment I only knew that she was one of eleven children and she was born in Žlutice, in the Karlovy Vary district, a beautiful part of Bohemia. I knew Helena's sister Ida was close to my father from the photos we had in the family album and the postcard she wrote to him not long after his arrival in England, which he kept all his life.

I quickly realised that to find the Hoffers I would need to venture back into Prague's National Archives, but with so many people to track down and very little basic information as yet, I didn't have the necessary pointers to give a government archivist to narrow down the search for documents. The task would be too huge. Instead I decided to visit the archives and delve into the records in person, which could take some time. So in my increasingly busy Prague schedule I locked in an appointment with Národní Archiv.

Meanwhile, in England my brothers were sifting through boxes looking for any scrap of information that might help me on my journey of discovery.

From my work to date, I'd become painfully aware that my woeful attempts at the Czech language were starting to really slow me down, so I decided to hire a Czech researcher and found the brilliant Julius Müller, who specialises in Jewish genealogy. In addition to interpreting and searching out material from a range of archives, Julius would take me to Liberec to see where the Riedens came from and around Prague to find the family homes.

I was finally ready.

PART II
THE HORROR

CHAPTER SEVEN
THE HOFFER MASSACRE

It is late May when I arrive in Prague, and the city is basking in unseasonably hot weather. I am staying in a garret room in the Hotel Paris, a historic Prague landmark in the Art Nouveau style, built in 1904. This unique, handsome edifice is right in the centre of Old Prague, in the shadow of the Powder Tower (one of the original city gates), and with its walls lined with art, an elegant coffee house and a dazzling fine dining restaurant with gold and turquoise mosaic-tiles, the hotel encapsulates the culture and beauty of the Prague Hitler couldn't wait to get his hands on.

From my fifth-floor window I look straight into neighbouring Smetana Hall, where classical music concerts play nightly. After a day immersing myself in times of trouble, I open the windows and watch the orchestra, instruments in hand, climbing the stairs inside the grand building next door to take their seats for the performance. Down on the cobbles, strains of Mozart and Vivaldi waft through the streets. There has been so much water under the Charles Bridge, so much blood shed, and yet in other ways nothing has changed.

Hearing the music makes me imagine Dad wandering around his home town.

My father's passion for classical music was intense. 'Pop music', as he disparagingly called it, was heavily discouraged in our family home; my father couldn't stand it and my mother concurred. I used to go to my friend Mandy's to watch the seminal TV show *Top of the Pops*, compulsory viewing for all British teenagers in the 1970s, because if I tried to watch at home, it would send Dad berserk.

My father's classical music collection was comprehensive and specialist, and increased every birthday and Christmas. Music was the only gift that truly made him smile, but not just any music. He would seek out unique recordings and mostly bought from a Czech former conductor who ran a music store in central London. Dad would compile lists from which we would obediently order. I'm not sure how Dad found this man, but they formed quite a musical rapport, which I'm certain had a lot to do with their shared Czech-ness. Before his death, my father made us promise that we would never sell off his collection but that it would stay in the family. As it turned out, my brothers and I actually battled over the music, which is now split pretty evenly between us. Dad would have been proud!

It's no wonder, then, that here in Prague, the city that launched Dvořák, inspired Janáček and Smetana and nurtured Mozart, I can feel Dad. As a boy he must have been in musical heaven, and even though he left so young, I'm in no doubt that this is where his musical heart belonged. It feels as if he's with me as I start on this journey to find his past.

On my first afternoon I meet my researcher Julius in the hotel's elegant cafe. Julius is dapper and kind, and with his grey hair looks a little like my father. His English is very good, and as we settle down in the corner of the cafe I sense that same gentle, self-deprecating but fiercely intelligent humour I knew so well from Dad and his fellow Czechs. Over coffee and apple strudel, Julius outlines his plan for our search. He then tells me he has found the Hoffers in his initial research and he is very sorry, but all except two were definitely killed during Shoah. These two are Friedrich, who died in 1933, aged 31, from tuberculosis; and Josef, the youngest of Helena's siblings, who is for the moment unaccounted for.

It's a terrible blow. A whole generation wiped out. It was a massacre. My head is swimming.

Julius tells me that only three of the eleven Hoffer siblings were married, and that aside from my grandma Helena, only Anna had a child. Anna married Max Kohn on 25 December 1919 and their daughter Johanna was born on 11 August 1920. I start counting. This means Anna must have been pregnant when she wed. The head of the family, Moritz Hoffer, was Žlutice's Rabbi, and I can't imagine a pregnant bride would have been well received, bringing scandal on this religious family.

But when I talk further to Julius, he explains that Moritz Hoffer's rabbinic status, especially as a countryside rabbi, though respected, would not have awarded him especially high social status. In addition to places of worship, synagogues were places of education, where Jewish youngsters were taught not just religion but general education. The role of a rabbi was often more one of a community teacher. 'He may have only been paid in eggs,' notes Julius. As for Anna's pre-wedding pregnancy, Julius suggests there was a more tolerant attitude to sex and love at the time, and my assumptions regarding family dishonour are overstated. Of course, sex before marriage wasn't ideal, but 'it happens', he adds with a nonchalance I come to realise is something of a Czech trait.

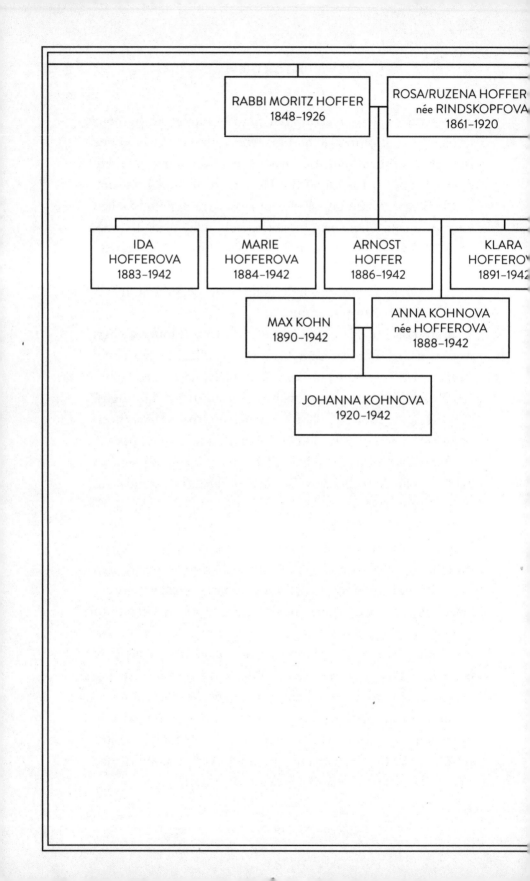

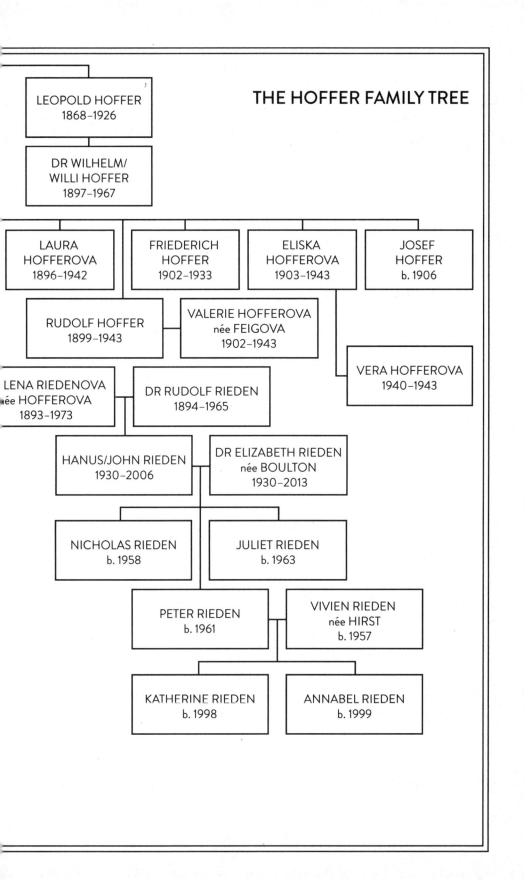

THE HOFFER FAMILY TREE

LEOPOLD HOFFER
1868–1926

DR WILHELM/
WILLI HOFFER
1897–1967

LAURA
HOFFEROVA
1896–1942

FRIEDERICH
HOFFER
1902–1933

ELISKA
HOFFEROVA
1903–1943

JOSEF
HOFFER
b. 1906

RUDOLF HOFFER
1899–1943

VALERIE HOFFEROVA
née FEIGOVA
1902–1943

VERA HOFFEROVA
1940–1943

LENA RIEDENOVA
née HOFFEROVA
1893–1973

DR RUDOLF RIEDEN
1894–1965

HANUS/JOHN RIEDEN
1930–2006

DR ELIZABETH RIEDEN
née BOULTON
1930–2013

NICHOLAS RIEDEN
b. 1958

JULIET RIEDEN
b. 1963

PETER RIEDEN
b. 1961

VIVIEN RIEDEN
née HIRST
b. 1957

KATHERINE RIEDEN
b. 1998

ANNABEL RIEDEN
b. 1999

There is a quiet stoicism in the Czech nature, perhaps informed by the nation's tortured adolescence. It was also part of my father's personality and makes me think of US poet Longfellow's famous line 'into each life some rain must fall'. That rain may well have been more of a dark horrendous storm for the Czechs, but their reaction was steely, always keeping sight of the long game. Enjoying the good things – music, food, coffee, conversation, love, family, intellectual debate – and developing a pragmatic, rational mechanism to deal with the bad seems to me to be part of the national psyche.

Looking at the few details Julius has discovered about the Hoffers, I am, however, still surprised by the lack of marriages and offspring among the Hoffer siblings. It echoes the Riedens, and I am starting to think a pattern is emerging. I had always thought Jews were typically family-centric, and the bigger that family the better. Certainly, this was upheld in my father's grandparents' generation, where the Riedens had eight children and the Hoffers eleven. Is it therefore significant that their children were en masse not following suit? I can't ignore the fact that from the 17 adults spread across one generation on both sides of my father's family, only six married, with just three children between them.

Have I stumbled upon another family cover-up? I start to imagine secret children or spouses, hidden from official registration because the family was protecting them from further persecution.

Again, Julius thinks I am leaping to conclusions too swiftly and misjudging the sophistication of the Czech Jewish community in the 1920s and 1930s. 'Jews were called, besides other things, a demographic avant-garde,' he advises. 'They stopped having more than one child way ahead of Christian families.' Julius believes my relatives simply chose to stay single and pursue careers. This was a new generation for whom following in their parents' footsteps and having big families was simply not in their life plan. 'I sometimes see that in Jewish families of the era,' he says.

Julius does have good news. He has traced home addresses for the Riedens in Liberec and Prague, and suggests a grand tour of the family dwellings, which we fix for a few days' time.

Before I do this, though, I must find out what happened to the Hoffers: how was it that this rabbi's family from a sleepy country town ended up slaughtered in its prime? Armed with the names and birth dates Julius has uncovered, I update my request with the National Archives, hoping this new information will help them locate specific dossiers that I can look through myself at my appointment.

In the meantime, I feel the need to go back to the Pinkas Synagogue the next morning. This is where my journey first started, and having discovered more family members I want to see if the Hoffers are there on the wall. I still don't want to believe that they were wiped out, hoping that Julius has made a mistake. The writing on the wall will be my confirmation.

A cantor is singing prayers over a loudspeaker, his voice soaring around the vaulted ceilings as I head straight for the lower floor. First, I need to check that the Riedens are still there. Unlike before, now I know more about these family members, my kin, I feel comfort in seeing them there. They take form on this wall, they exist once more, proof that not even Hitler can erase my family without a trace. I take a moment to read through their details again. I now know what some of them looked like from the few photos I gathered from the archives, and I am starting to feel a part of this family.

I then begin looking for the Hoffers, scanning the H's around the walls. When I find them, the shock is just as powerful as the first time.

I focus in on the vast towering expanse of painted letters, longing to find them, but feeling more and more anxious as I search. Way above are stained-glass windows, featuring a beautiful, harmonious abstract design in shades of soft green and blue. One of the panes is open, letting the fresh air in, the sorrow out, and shafts of sunlight dapple the wall with a rich glow. I'm not generally prone to bouts of spirituality, but at this moment it does feel as if something, someone is trying to make this easier for me, showing there is beauty and calm in the most surprising places. I take a breath and start running through the alphabet on the wall once more. And then . . . oh. There are so many. It's hard to take in. The Hoffers take up two lines. As I try to follow them, the letters flow into one another. It takes a while and some composure to read each one.

In total there are 17 Hoffers listed here. I later discover eight are Helena's brothers and sisters, a further two are from my father's generation, his cousins, and the other seven may well be more distant relatives.

It's strange to think that 18 months ago I was here staring at the Riedens, incredulous that there were four names etched onto the wall related to me, and all the time there were ten more behind me on the opposite wall, tapping on my shoulder. I think back and remember that strange sense I had that someone was behind me. It turns out I was right. It was the Hoffer family.

As I read through the names, there is one in particular that stands out. Vera Hoffer, 17/III 1940 – 18/XII 1943. Just three years nine months old. This is the youngest relative I have come across, just a toddler when she was killed. Vera isn't in the list of names Julius gave me. Could she be the daughter of one of Helena's single sisters, born illegitimately, or the unregistered child of one of her brothers?

I wonder if Helena and Rudolf ever came to Pinkas when they settled back into Prague life following their wartime ordeal. The memorial was first created in the late 1950s and stayed open until 1968 before the Soviets arrived on the scene. Would this have been a place of solace or trauma for my grandparents?

This time I notice how much security there is here. I understand – you see it around synagogues the world over – but it bothers me. It's as if the Jews are still having to watch their backs, as if nothing has been learned. Looking again at the walls I am filled with fear and doubt. The impact is incredible; this memorial is making a powerful statement, but the Jews in Bohemia and Moravia are still lined up in lists – beautiful lists that make me think of Moses tablets, but lists of names and numbers nevertheless. Is it the grouping together that feeds the prejudice, I wonder? Are we really tribes, or individuals seeking our own path?

The Czech National Archives are located in an industrial estate a little way out from central Prague. Since time was an issue I jumped in a taxi to get there, although I later realised the train would have been quicker. There's no place for sentiment and spirituality here; this is about order, files in boxes catalogued with a series of numbers, dots and dashes, under sections and subsections.

Like all archives around the world, there are strict rules and regulations. I have ordered my files and they are there waiting for me, along with a pair of white gloves to handle the paperwork. Since the Hoffer family is so large, the files are numerous, and I must take them one box at a time, signing each one in and out as I go. I am allowed to take photographs, as long as no flash is involved, and since the documents are largely in Czech I decide to photograph each file and then study it later, with help from my researcher Julius.

Some of this material, though, I recognise immediately. There are the same registration cards I saw in the Rieden files. In the civil registry I see an abundance of addresses – this family moved around a lot. But unlike the Riedens, their files do not have the Jewish 'J' stamped on the documentation.

On first glance my eye stops at Rabbi Moritz's wife Ruzena – also known as Rosa – Hofferova, the matriarch of the family, born in 1861. While I don't have any cards for her, she is listed on those of her children, and Rosa's maiden name is Rindskopf, the Rieden family's real name. Is it just a bizarre coincidence or is there more to it?

Julius later tells me that yes, it is highly likely that Rosa was from some branch of the Rindskopfs. Indeed, my grandparents Rudolf and Helena may well have first met through a relative of Rosa's. Julius adds that intermarrying between cousins and the like within the relatively small Jewish communities of Bohemia was very common.

Rosa had her first child – Ida, the aunt to whom my father was close – at 22, and her eleventh child, Josef, 23 years later. Between them were Marie, Arnost, Anna, Klara, my grandmother Helena, Laura, Rudolf, Friedrich and Eliska. It must have been exhausting giving birth roughly every other year. No wonder her children chose not to follow suit and have big families of their own.

Later, from the Žlutice archives, I discover that Moritz was the town's first rabbi in the local synagogue, which was built in 1883, a position he held until his death in 1926.

As in Liberec, Jews endured a tough time here historically, and going back a few centuries were thrown out of the town and not allowed to live there. This changed in 1864, when the December Constitution gave Jews the same rights as the Christian majority, and in 1875 Žlutice's Jewish *qahal* (assembly) was founded. It had 89 members.

The synagogue was modest, a conversion of an existing house amid a row of houses, and in the 1920s the Jewish community numbered 79, although not all of these lived in Žlutice itself. I'm unsure at the time if this number denotes families or individuals; if individuals, 13 of the 79 would have been Moritz Hoffer's family.

At the same time that Moritz was rabbi, the leader of the Žlutice Jewish community was a man called Leopold Hoffer. Clearly Moritz and Leopold are related, but how I am unsure. I have photos of them and they look very much like brothers. When I delve deeper, I discover that Leopold's only son is Willi Hoffer, the relative who later studied under Sigmund Freud in Vienna and fled to London before the war, the 'Uncle' Willi my father knew in England. I had always wondered how Willi was related to Dad. Finally I have found out.

My father wouldn't have known his Hoffer grandparents. Both Rosa and Moritz died before he was born. Rosa died age 59 in 1920, just 14 years after her last baby was born. Rabbi Moritz Hoffer died six years later, a couple of months shy of his 79th birthday. I am relieved that neither of them lived to witness the fate of their eleven children, or had to experience any of the horror Hitler wrought on their homeland.

Every now and again, amid the officious forms and handwritten missives, I come across a photograph. These are the most affecting, as I see my great-aunt or great-uncle staring back at me, flesh and blood, each with their own unique personality. In the men there is a strong resemblance to my brothers and father. There is no doubt these are our relatives.

As I go through the files with the help of Julius, a deeply disturbing picture starts to build. The Hoffers have become refugees in their own country. Thrown out of their home town of Žlutice, which is sucked into Hitler's Third Reich along with the rest of the Sudetenland following the mandate laid out in the 1938 Munich Agreement, they are stateless. The paperwork charts their fevered battles to register for citizenship in Prague and the pettiness of the authorities who stand in the way of granting these siblings settlement rights. A brutal game of bureaucratic cat and mouse ensues, and I can feel the terror building in my family as they try to hold their nerve while fighting for their lives.

There is a big file on Arnost Hoffer, whose full name is Ernst Ludwig Israel Hoffer. The 'Israel' may well have been added to comply with the 1938 edict that required German Jews whose first name had a 'non-Jewish' origin to add 'Israel' for men or 'Sara' for women to their names so that they could be more readily identified as Jewish.

On 16 May 1939, Arnost applied for a passport. His photo shows a studious-looking gentleman with round glasses in a smart suit and tie, and his profession is printer. Many of the documents in his file show how Arnost was forced to apply for a re-evaluation of his state citizenship. A letter from the Prague Land Committee demands Arnost present his citizen certificate, which he cannot do because he hasn't been granted one. This is typical of much of the paperwork in the Hoffers' files as the net closes around my family.

In one application, made on 16 June 1940, Arnost applies

to the police for permission to migrate to Shanghai. Whether the application was turned down by the Protectorate or the Chinese authorities didn't grant his entry, I will never know. What I do know is that Arnost never made it out.

In Rudolf Hoffer's file, I can sense the authorities are chasing him and they won't give up. Rudolf was a corn merchant, a middleman who sold grain, and after marrying Valerie Feig, moved to her home town of Vroutek, just 30 kilometres down the road from Žlutice and also in the Sudetenland.

In the documents Rudolf is asked to explain why and when he left Vroutek, and the suggestion seems to be he and his family don't have the right to live in Prague. In his defence, Rudolf says he received a 'military call-up' and while he was away advised his wife to pack up their household – including his in-laws – to move to Prague. Their life in Vroutek has now become unsustainable. By 28 September 1938 the family is ready to go and their belongings have been left in a removal company's storage facility.

The 'call-up' draft was a nationwide initiative by the Czech government to man the hastily built bunkers along the Czech/German borders in the face of increased Nazi pressure. The Czechs could see what Hitler was up to and they wanted to put up a fight. But all mobilised men were later ordered to withdraw, which at the time was a source of huge national frustration. The people felt betrayed by both the Czech government and their supposed allies – France and Britain. That betrayal was complete when the Allies signed over the Sudetenland to Hitler in the Munich Agreement on 30 September without the Czechoslovakian government even invited to the conference.

In the documentation, Rudolf claims that in Vroutek his life was threatened, which I believe was most likely to have been by the Sudeten militia, Germans who had long wanted the Jews out of the territory. He says he has witness statements as proof. But now, under the new Third Reich annexation, Rudolf and his family no longer have the right to live in Vroutek anyway, and although he had the nous to gather his things a week in advance, he arrived in Prague in a hurry, desperate, and it seems without the correct paperwork in place.

He states that he and his wife Valerie moved in temporarily with relatives – I think this may have been with his sister Ida – before they rented a flat in Prague with Valerie's parents. His mother-in-law, Anna Feig, who was almost 80 years old, was very sick, unable to move and in need of constant help. Their plan was to emigrate to the United States, and they had registered with the American Consulate in Prague on 10 October 1938. They have an affidavit to testify to this while they await their emigration permit. But the Consulate is waiting to process all the Jewish applications together, so they have not yet been given a departure date and are now playing a waiting game. Rudolf and Valerie are trapped. They have only been granted the right to live in Prague until 29 May 1939, and the authorities are closing in on them.

Certainly, in these early years when Hitler was trying to deal with the Jews in Czechoslovakia, the ideal for the Nazi regime was for Jews to emigrate, and exit visas were approved. But there were severe caveats, and after July 1939 all applicants had to go through the Central Office for Jewish Emigration in Prague. The head of security police ran this body, answering direct to the notorious Adolf Eichmann, who had set up a similar body in Vienna, Austria. Jews couldn't just leave and take their livelihoods with them. They had to sign over their property and much of their jewellery, assets and bank accounts to the war machine. It was a diabolical process, with reams of paperwork that had to be presented and sifted through in offices controlled by brutal SS guards. The experience was reportedly humiliating and frightening.

Meanwhile the countries taking in refugees had their own rigid entry requirements. While Czech Jews waded through the bureaucracy and pondered the best moves to make, the emigration door was starting to close. The number of Jews who managed to emigrate legally from the Czech Protectorate was 26,093; a few thousand also fled illegally and it is generally felt that around 30,000 Czech Jews emigrated during occupation. This was from the 118,310 Jews living in the territory. Then, in October 1941, emigration options stopped altogether, and the 'Final Solution' of concentration camps and the annihilation of the Jewish race became the preferred Nazi answer to the 'Jewish Question'.

The situation proved just as impossible for Ida, who was hounded by the police. Her dossier tells me that she moved to Prague on 16 March 1939 – the day after the Nazis occupied. She must have been terrified, clutching her suitcases as soldiers in tanks clanked through the cobbled streets shouting allegiance to Hitler.

In the documentation it's obvious that Ida has to defend herself repeatedly, stating time and time again that she fulfils her civic duties, that there are no complaints against her 'neither moral nor political', that she has never been prosecuted and that she does not even go out much. It breaks your heart to read.

I discover that Ida worked as a bank clerk in Prague. In one particularly chilling document, stamped 26 July 1939, Ida is summoned to present herself within the next three days to her district police station to 'door no 29 on the third floor' for 'interrogation'. She must bring all her personal identification papers with her.

Then a curious thing happens. The land office starts searching for Ida, sending an officer around to her flat on 1 September 1939, and a Mrs Subortova, who I think is her landlady, claims that Ida has never lived there. Was Mrs Subortova covering up to protect Ida, or did she simply not want to be implicated as someone who rented their flats out to Jews? In any case, Ida stayed living in the flat until she was deported in 1942.

There is no file on Vera, but there is a deportation card. From this I can see that her address is the same as Eliska Hofferova's, and that she is sent to Theresienstadt in the same transport detail on 2 July 1942. Eliska is number 214. Vera is number 215. On 18 December 1943, Eliska and Vera are transported to Auschwitz, numbers 1109 and 1111. They *must* be mother and daughter. Vera must be Eliska's illegitimate child. My father's cousin.

The deportation cards also tell me that sisters Ida, Klara and Laura were deported to Theresienstadt and then to Maly Trostinec (in what was then called White Russia, now Maly Trostenets in Belarus), together, while Marie, the second eldest, was deported to Theresienstadt and then to Riga on her own. It paints a daunting picture.

The file on Josef Hoffer charts a terrible journey that ended in Dachau. Josef was my only hope of a survivor, but here it seems to say he was murdered. I check the dates again, feeling a sense of despair, and then as I start to read I realise this is not actually my Josef, the youngest of the Hoffers – the birth date is different. This is another Josef Hoffer. I feel guilty as a selfish sense of relief washes through me. This poor man may well have been a more distant Hoffer relative, but for the moment my Josef is still alive. There is still a glimmer of hope.

I put in a second application for *my* Josef Hoffer and ask Julius to return when the documents are ready since my schedule is already packed. When I hear what he discovers I wish I had been there myself to see it.

=====

On 23 September 1938 in advance of the Kristallnacht attacks, Josef, Helena's little brother, came to live with the Riedens in Prague. Josef would have been 32; Helena was 13 years older and I imagine felt protective of her youngest sibling. I wonder what brother and sister talked about in those months before Hitler marched in. In a couple of weeks, Emil, Emma, Berta, Felix and Otto Rieden arrived. Now my eight-year-old father had six of his extended family living with him. I had previously thought there were eight living in this flat designed for three, but there were actually nine, and Josef is another relative my father would have known intimately. All were still there when Dad was put on that plane to England. It would have been an even more emotional send-off for little Hanus than I had imagined.

Then seven months later, on 20 October 1939, Helena faced another goodbye. Josef left for Palestine. Everyone in the family had been furiously trying to emigrate, with applications for a host of different countries stalled by bureaucracy and what proved a fatal tardiness by the world's nations to recognise the gravity of the Jewish situation. So for Josef to make it out is glorious news. This means that he and Helena were the only wartime survivors from Rabbi Moritz Hoffer's family of eleven children.

On his passport application it says that Josef is leaving with a group called 'Neo-Zion'. While I can't find any reference to this group, the name does suggest Josef could have been part of the Zionist movement, which is highly credible considering his father was a rabbi. It would also have been easier to obtain refugee status in Israel as part of a Jewish faction. Whatever it took, Josef at least was safe from the Nazis.

How much he knew about what was happening to his family while he was in Palestine I don't know, but the files do reveal that Josef returned to Czechoslovakia pretty swiftly after the war ended, and I am sure this was to find his brothers and sisters. He arrived back in Prague on 12 November 1945 and lived with Helena and Rudolf. This was six months after my grandparents had been liberated from Theresienstadt and one month after they had written to Reverend and Mrs Davidson. In that letter they said that they were too sick to have their son Hanus back with them since Helena had only just come home from hospital. So to have Josef return would have been a huge help for the mentally and physically traumatised Helena and Rudolf.

Nine months later, Josef returned to Žlutice. I wonder if he was looking for the family home and maybe even his siblings. It would no doubt have taken some time to trace what had happened to his brothers and sisters, and maybe Josef was hoping he and Helena were not the only survivors. He stayed eleven months, came back to Prague for a month and then returned to Žlutice. No doubt he came to report back to Helena on what he found in their home town. A grim conversation for sure.

CHAPTER EIGHT

WALKING IN MY ANCESTORS' FOOTSTEPS

After the gruelling revelations from the National Archives, Julius promises to take me to a happier place, to Liberec, where the Rindskopf/Riedens grew up. As we leave the environs of Prague and drive up into the mountains I can feel the city stresses fall away. It's a sunny day, and urban sprawl is quickly replaced by green pastures dotted with wildflowers. Julius tells me he used to come up here for family weekends skiing in the mountains.

My father adored lakes and mountains, and we spent many European family holidays amid such landscapes in Italy, Austria and Switzerland. I realise now that there was something primordial about the way he gravitated to this scenery. He was going home.

I don't know if Dad ever went to Liberec as a child. Rudolf left as a young man, but I imagine it's highly likely my grandfather took his wife and son there in the holidays so he could get to know his grandparents, aunts and uncles, especially since I now realise Dad was one of only two grandchildren for Emil and Emma.

Today, Liberec is a thriving spa city, one foot in the past
with its traditional square, Neo-Renaissance buildings and
ornate town hall, and one firmly in the future with its glass-
fronted Technical University specialising in nanomaterials and
new technologies, vast concrete sports arena and thoroughly
modern shopping and entertainment park. The city boasts a
uniquely picturesque position in a natural basin between the
Jizera Mountains and a jutting ridge near the German–Polish
border. The air up here is clean and fresh, and there is a
sense of prosperous relaxation in the coffee houses and cafes
dotted around the city. I can immediately picture this place
in the winter, coated in snow, the Bohemian coloured houses
set against the whitewash. This is how I always imagined
Czechoslovakia to be.

The elaborate synagogue where my great-uncle Samuel
Ungermann was a cantor, burned down in the Kristallnacht
attacks, has been replaced by a 'reconciliation building', a
public research library that includes a synagogue sitting on
the same spot as the original. Incorporated in this contempo-
rary glass and steel structure is a triangular space dedicated to
the Jewish community. It represents half of the Star of David
and around the synagogue's internal stone walls is a passage
from the Torah. Outside, patterned paving stones trace the
lines of the original synagogue, showing that even though
nearly all the Jews from that time were murdered, they have
not been forgotten.

That said, it took a while to do the right thing. This
place wasn't conceived until 1995 and opened in November
2000. It was a collaborative project between the then Czech
and German presidents, Václav Havel and Roman Herzog,
symbolic of a long-overdue healing process between the
two nations in this city where Jews had been so viciously

persecuted. Of course Czechs as well as Germans were complicit in the atrocities, and here the two came together.

There is a Hebrew-language lesson going on when I visit, and as I watch the young Jewish leader talking to a small group of adolescents, I think of Samuel teaching here back in the 1920s when he met Anna, Rudolf's sister, and then of the couple marrying on this spot. It would have been almost 100 years ago now. I am still hopeful that I will find descendants of the couple. I want to believe that they managed to emigrate, that they didn't end up in a death camp. And, so far, their names have not appeared on any lists I have uncovered.

In the pavements around the city are burnished 'Stolpersteine', another sign that Liberec is atoning. These brass plaques set in concrete squares are memorials – there are also many in Prague – for victims of the Holocaust. They are sunk into the pathway outside the last place of residency, or sometimes their place of work, where this member of the community was still in charge of their own destiny, before the Nazis arrived. In the case of those in Liberec, this would have been before they were either killed in the Kristallnacht attacks, or forced out to Prague and ultimately deportation.

The project was the idea of German artist Gunter Demnig and started in 1990. These shiny tablets, each inscribed with the name and details of a different individual, are now also in the streets of Austria, Belgium and the Netherlands, as well as Germany.

Stolpersteine literally translated means 'stumbling stone'. But it had a colloquial usage. Nazis would curse 'Stolpersteine' when they tripped on a protruding cobblestone, complaining 'a Jew must be buried here'; and in German its vernacular use is for a 'potential problem'. Demnig wanted to invoke both the historic anti-Semitic insult and the idea that society had a serious problem it needed to address. The fact that the 'stumbling stone' is now a gleaming smooth jewel also speaks volumes.

Julius says the plaques are often laid by family members, and suggests my brothers and I might like to consider our own memorials around Liberec, Žlutice and Prague. It's a nice idea that makes me smile – mostly because I can hear my parents whispering 'definitely not' rather loudly in my ear. Mum and Dad were far too pragmatic to sanction spending money on things like gravestones and memorials when, in their view, it should be spent on the living. I can't imagine either approving such an expense, especially considering the huge number of brass plaques we'd need to lay. They always looked to the future, not the past, and certainly for Dad I'm realising this was a mindset that helped him survive.

While I ponder this, we start looking for the family properties. En route we'd stopped at the Liberec archives – a much smaller place than the Czech archives – to ensure we had all the correct addresses, but even with all this detail the homes are not easy to find. Street names and numbering changed at various times over the decades in Liberec: both after the war, and then in the Communist era, and then of course the city has expanded, with new roads built.

We have seven homes to visit where the Rindskopf turned Riedens lived as a family. Emil and Emma moved to Liberec on 31 October 1859. In 1869 records show that there were 314 adult Jews living in Liberec, making up one per cent of the total population, and by 1930 this had grown to 1392, which was three per cent of the population. I can't find any documentation showing that the family owned property here; they rented and they moved around as they became more prosperous. Emil ran his specialist glass-bead jewellery shop and all the children grew up to develop their own careers.

Armed with a map, we head off to find the family's homes. The streets are narrow and cobbled, and while we can find houses nearby that would have been very similar to those my family lived in, a rather amusing pattern emerges – every time we locate the exact address, the house has been knocked down and replaced with a car park. Progress!

The houses in the areas where they lived are pretty, solid and traditional, and I can imagine the Riedens being very comfortable here. Indeed, the last one from which they fled in 1938 hasn't been subsumed into a car park, and is huge and very nice indeed, a real family home.

Baby Paul Rindskopf died at just 16 months old in 1894 and Elsa died at almost nine months in 1899, so we head to Liberec's Jewish cemetery to see if we can find their graves. The cemetery is nestled in a leafy suburban street and closed today, but the lady who is looking after it lets us in. This place is beautifully cared for, with clipped lawns, flowers and proud gravestones. But I can't find Paul or Elsa. I know they are probably here somewhere, but the stones are weathered and difficult to read.

Emil and Emma's youngest daughter, Hedwig, with whom I coincidentally share a birthdate, albeit 62 years apart, moved in January 1931 to live with her German Gentile husband, Erwin Jung, in the nearby village of Vratislavice nad Nisou, now a suburb of Liberec. On Hedwig's registration cards she does not list her faith as Jewish. Instead it says she has no religion and is a citizen of the German Reich.

My grandfather Rudolf and his sister Hedwig were the only Rieden siblings to survive Theresienstadt concentration camp. Hedwig actually evaded deportation until 1945, then spent just three months in Theresienstadt before the camp was liberated by the Russians. Hedwig was lucky. Her marriage to a non-Jew protected her from being called for transport for the majority of the war, which ultimately saved her life. But I imagine that staying under the radar in Vratislavice nad Nisou would have been a challenge following occupation in 1938. She would have been constantly trying to hide and separate herself from the rest of the Rieden family who had fled to Prague. I wonder if they remained in contact at all or if this was too dangerous. While the rest of the family was together, Hedwig was isolated.

I have tried to look for Hedwig's husband Erwin and can find no trace of him during the war. He was probably interned in a labour camp, as was the fate of many Germans who married Jews, or if he renounced Hedwig and divorced her, he may have been drafted to fight. But there are no divorce papers in Hedwig's archival files, so I think this would have been unlikely. Still, I can't find any reference to him after the war either. I later discover that following her liberation from Theresienstadt, Hedwig probably moved back to Vratislavice nad Nisou, where she lived alone. So . . . it seems highly likely that Erwin was another family victim of either the Holocaust or war.

My grandfather Rudolf, Emil's eldest son following the death in infancy of Paul, left Liberec family life in 1913 to study law at the German-speaking branch of Charles University. There were two parts of the historic Charles University at this time: Czech-speaking and German-speaking. Unsurprisingly, the latter ceased to exist after 1945, but this was Grandpa's alma mater. Even though he was studying in Prague, Rudolf seems to have stayed living in Liberec. I suspect he commuted to and from Prague. I'm sure Emil was incredibly proud when his son won a prestigious place at university to study law. To have a lawyer in the family is the archetypal Jewish dream.

But just a year later war broke out and Rudolf's life was to change forever.

My grandfather's file in the Austrian Army military archives is pretty comprehensive and very revealing. The First World War was a brutal war for everybody, and while Rudolf proved to be a hero, he paid dearly for his service to Emperor and country.

Rudolf was drafted on 26 October 1914. He was not quite 20. He spent six months being trained at Benátky nad Jizerou, a town in central Bohemia. Then, on 1 April 1915, he was sent straight to the front line to fight in Russia, as part of an Austrian Army infantry field battalion. This was fighting on foot with guns fixed with bayonets. It was bloody, exhausting and terrifying. Rudolf was slight, just 172 centimetres tall, which may have helped his nimbleness in battle, and he was courageous. On 23 March 1916 he was awarded a silver medal for bravery.

Then, 14 months later, in June 1916, Rudolf was shot and critically wounded in Sieniawa in Poland. This would have been at the beginning of what has become known as the 'Brusilov Offensive', named after Russia's General Alexei Brusilov. It lasted four months and is considered one of the most lethal attacks in world war history.

The Austro-Hungarian Army was decimated and never really recovered, with somewhere between 200,000 and 567,000 dead or wounded. Rudolf was felled in the first month, no doubt in one of the barrages of gunfire, accompanied by cavalry wielding swords, that broke through the Austro-Hungarian lines like a hot knife through butter. It's a little ironic that here Rudolf was pitched against the very army that almost 20 years later were the liberating forces freeing him, his wife Helena and sister Hedwig from Theresienstadt camp.

Rudolf's wounds were very serious. He was taken from the battlefield to a military hospital, where the only possible option was to amputate his right leg. The records show that after the operation, he was sent back to the hospital in his home town Liberec for rehabilitation. Emil and Emma must have been distraught to see their eldest son so badly maimed, but he was back with them and away from the terror of the front line.

On 1 September 1916, with the war still raging, Rudolf was retired from active service and declared 80 per cent invalid. He served the rest of the war behind a desk in administration and also received treatment to fit a prosthesis, the first of several the army doctors made for him. Of course, Rudolf was lucky to be alive, but his injury was considerable. In May 1918 at 24, he was made Oberleutnant – the highest-ranking lieutenant officer in the Austrian Armed Forces.

On Rudolf's military card from the official registry there is a '*Jude*' (Jew) added in pencil, and again lower down on the card it is noted he is 'a Jew'. The prejudice is there in black and white. Even on the records of a decorated war hero, *Jude* cast an ominous shadow. Was the pencil annotation added later, I wonder, when the Nazis were looking at the files and needed to know exactly who they were dealing with? Or was the anti-Semitism always hovering, waiting to strike?

In any case, Rudolf's record as a soldier was pretty flawless. He underwent several further operations on his leg, paid for by the military, and received compensation as well as a war pension. Despite his traumatic experience on the battlefield, Rudolf's commitment to serve continued, and in May 1919 he reapplied to return to the army. His army dossier notes that his last place of work was in the Hospital for Reservists in Liberec. In 1920, following the postwar establishment of an independent Czechoslovakia, Rudolf was duly drafted to the Czechoslovak Army. Interestingly, in the box that asks if he swears loyalty to the Czech Republic, Rudolf answers 'nein' – no! I can only assume from this that after putting his life on the line for the Austro-Hungarian Empire, Rudolf's loyalty remained resolutely with Austria. Later I suspect he revised that opinion.

Also of interest in Rudolf's file is that it continually states he is German-speaking and that his Czech is 'not sufficient'. I note that he must have improved on this; as we have seen, in his government work records for his position with the Ministry of Finance some years later, it states more than once that Rudolf's command of Czech was 'good'.

In 1920 Rudolf returned to his studies at the German University in Prague. At first, he lived in a recuperation home for injured First World War veterans. The building is still there, and is the first stop on my tour around Rudolf's homes in Prague. It is a very beautiful, vast, slightly eerie building in the Karlín district of Prague, which in recent years has transformed into a trendy, highly sought-after neighbourhood. The building is currently unused but I think is about to be redeveloped, hopefully with its elegant shell intact. The 'Invalidovna', as it was called, is surrounded by overgrown green lawns and trees, and I can imagine Rudolf relaxing here and learning to come to terms with his significant war wound.

By April 1921, he had moved to a quaint bachelor pad in the cobbled streets near Prague Castle, and then in 1923 he moved to the very nice residential area of Vinohrady. By this time he had graduated as a Doctor of Law and was working.

On 10 May 1927, Rudolf and Helena married at the Prague Town Hall and later that year (also on my birthdate of 18 October) they moved into a smart apartment in

Sudoměřská 28 in the Vinohrady district. This was a young couple's dream, a 1920s new build, and it was here, less than three years later, that my father Hanus was born. This was the home he left in 1939, never to return. At that time six other relatives were also living there, having been thrown out of their homes in Liberec and Žlutice. This place, more than any other I have seen today, is at the heart of my father's family's story.

It is pouring with rain as we arrive at the apartment, but I quickly realise that I have seen it before. It is the home my father brought me and my mother to when we visited in 1990, the one he instantly recognised. This time I am determined to try to see inside the apartment. I need to understand what it must have been like for eight adults and one little boy to live together here as their world disintegrated into chaos around them.

My researcher Julius is sure he can make it happen. He scans down the names on the doorbells and chooses the most Czech-sounding, in the hope they will appreciate a request coming from the daughter of a fellow countryman. Julius rings the intercom and an elderly lady, I will call her Mrs Z, answers. At first, she is warm and chatty. She says she has lived in her apartment from birth in 1934 and sounds proud to be still there in the family home. This is great news; surely Mrs Z will remember the Riedens.

Julius explains that I have come from Australia to see where my father and his parents lived and to trace the story of what happened to my relatives. He tells Mrs Z: 'You must have known the family. You would have been four or five when Hanus left, and at that time many others in the family had joined Rudolf and Helena Rieden, who had been living there for more than a decade. Then, in January 1940, Helena and Rudolf were moved on because they were Jews and ultimately deported to Theresienstadt. Is there any way Juliet might come up and see your apartment, to give her an idea of the sort of home where her father and grandparents lived?'

Mrs Z becomes rather agitated at this request. She says she knew all the names of those who lived there and in the block there weren't any Riedens. She says she knows this because there was only one Jewish family back then and her family helped them. They were called Brandeis.

Julius pleads some more, explaining that we are sure this is the apartment building, as we have found it listed in the archival records. But Mrs Z is having none of it. Julius says, 'Okay, but can Juliet at least come in?'

'No.' Mrs Z is adamant she doesn't want me in her apartment, and she shuts off the intercom. Julius rings once more, but she won't answer.

It is an astonishing reaction that stops me in my tracks. The name Brandeis is famous in Czechoslovakia. It is one of the best known dynastic Jewish families, so if one were trying to pluck a Czech Jewish name from the ether this would be it. I discuss the incident with Julius and he agrees Mrs Z was bluffing. He is not surprised; he thinks she believes I am either here to claim back the family property or to create trouble and ask difficult questions. This is a common response to relatives of Jews lost in the Holocaust looking for their family homes. More and more, these families are seeking compensation and restitution for property, valuables and bank accounts appropriated by both the Third Reich and non-Jewish Czechs, and those who are connected with this time often clam up.

In some ways I can understand Mrs Z's reticence. She was a child and can't be held responsible for what went on. And perhaps I am being naive when I find her knee-jerk suspicion and lack of empathy pretty shocking. It is also not lost on me that here we are, 80 years later, and in a very small way I am witnessing firsthand the sort of treatment my grandparents and the rest of the Riedens and the Hoffers must have experienced every day.

I hang around on the pavement for a while, in the rain, hoping Mrs Z may realise my pain and ask me up. Now I know so much about what happened to my family in this apartment block, I long to see inside, to have a visual idea of how they lived. Maybe even to see the sort of bedroom my father would have slept in. She doesn't. Julius is, I think, a little embarrassed by his compatriot and we resolve to let it go.

Rudolf's parents, Emil and Emma, and his siblings Berta, Felix and Otto stayed here with them in number 28 for seven months and then moved down the road to number 10, where Emma died. On 24 February 1941, Emil and his three children were forced to move again, downtown to the much less salubrious Michalská 3 and deported soon after, one after the other.

Rudolf and Helena were transferred from their flat in January 1940, first for four months to a smaller place in another suburb. They then moved in with the rest of the Riedens at Sudoměřská 10, just down from their own place (from which they had been so cruelly evicted), for two months until they were moved on again and then rounded up for deportation to Theresienstadt. The forced departures were intended to humiliate and engender fear, which I am sure was achieved. Also, with every new abode, the family lost more possessions. Prague was becoming almost impossible for Jews to live in, as the usual rights of everyday life were stripped away. Again, the only comfort for Rudolf and Helena would have been the knowledge that their son had escaped and was safe in England.

Meanwhile, elsewhere in the city, Helena's siblings were facing the same indignities as they ran for their lives. I'm sure they were all in contact, and together were trying to pursue every possible chance of escape, but hitting a brick wall time and time again.

Having fled Žlutice, the Hoffer family had left their home empty. I would have expected it to have been confiscated by the Nazis, as was the case for most Jewish property in the Sudetenland, but when I track down the house deeds in the cadastre (land and real estate) records I find a different story.

On 25 November 1900, Rabbi Moritz Hoffer and his wife Rosa bought the family home in Žlutice – number 148 on the Main Square. It's a pretty painted house in the traditional style flanking a central green, and these days sits next to the local post office at the heart of community life.

Following Moritz's death in 1926, ownership of the house passed to eight of the Hoffer children – my grandmother Helena and her siblings Ida, Marie, Klara, Laura, Rudolf, Eliska and Josef. Then on 10 March 1942, five-eighths of the house is sold 'at the drop of a hammer' to a man called Franz Trochler. At this time Marie Hoffer had already been killed, while the other Hoffers who owned the house were in Prague, months away from being deported to Theresienstadt. None of them was able to go back to Žlutice because of the expulsion of Jews following the Nazi occupation, so they certainly wouldn't have been present for the sale. When I talk to Julius he thinks that these shares may well have been sold in a desperate bid for money, maybe to pay off a bank loan or raise some capital. At this time all the family would have been out of work, their jobs taken from them, trying to emigrate, and exit and entry visas were expensive. Then there were food and lodgings to pay for. It is a theory but it makes sense. I am hoping that

Franz Trochler may have been a friend who helped them out while the world around them was slipping away.

The other three-eighths of the home still belonged to Helena, Josef and Laura Hoffer, and after the war the land registry notes in 1947 that Josef came back to live there for a while. This is a relief. So Josef did make it back to the Hoffer home as I'd hoped. He was the only one in the family to return to their home town. In 1949 the files again show that three-eighths of the house was still owned by Helena, Josef and Laura – the rest by Franz Trochler. But Laura was now dead. She was murdered following transport to Maly Trostinec.

As for Helena, after the war she and Rudolf faced a difficult time. They didn't return to their lovely flat in Sudoměřská 28. At first, directly after liberation, when I now know they were in very poor health, they were repatriated by the Czech government and housed in the impressive Vršovická building, which is now a chic hotel school but at that time was used for Czechs returning from the war who had no homes to go to. They stayed here for a little over a month.

I don't know if Rudolf and Helena tried to go back to their home in Sudoměřská 28, and when I check with the property registry I see that they were tenants not owners, so it's unlikely they would have had a significant claim. Instead, their national registration cards show that on 9 July 1945 they moved to another address. I visit the place and it is not nearly as nice as their pre-war apartment. And then, on 28 November 1951, Rudolf and Helena move into the home they stayed in for the rest of their lives. While the neighbourhood is verdant with a park, the apartment block is not especially attractive. One of the occupants, one half of a young couple with a baby, kindly allows me in to see their apartment, which is clean and basic, if a little small.

This is not really where I imagined Rudolf and Helena spending their last days, but this is where both Rudolf and Helena were living before they both died, years apart, in hospital. Rudolf never saw his son again. But after her husband's death in 1965 Helena finally came to England to be reunited with her son, my father. Why did she then come back here, to be alone in this rather bleak flat? I find the distressing answer to this question later in my journey.

CHAPTER NINE

THERESIENSTADT: SURVIVAL AND MURDER

Ever since I can remember I have lived with an idea of Theresienstadt. Even though the Holocaust was never discussed in detail in our house, the name of what I naively believed to be a benign concentration camp, where my grandparents had spent the war, was a point of reference for me as a child. At school we regularly touched on Hitler's invasion of Europe in our history lessons, and I would proudly announce that my family was not only witness to it, but we managed to survive.

I believed that the camp – the 'ghetto', as Dad called it – was somewhere my grandparents lived alongside other Jews who had been rounded up. I imagined that the accommodation was communal to a point (Rudolf and Helena would have had their own designated rooms together, I thought) and basic, the like of which you might get at a fusty old boarding school, but much more crowded, with strict rules, hard beds and limited food and supplies.

As I grew older I realised Theresienstadt was more like a mini-city in size and population, and was also a prison where conditions were extremely harsh and inmates died every day from sickness and hard labour.

Then, as an adult, I began to understand that my grand-father, Dr Rudolf Rieden, and my grandmother, Helena Riedenova, suffered a great deal in the camp, not just physi-cally but mentally. Somehow Rudolf and Helena's names were continually pulled from the transport lists and they made it to liberation. When I asked about this, my mother said she thought it had something to do with grandpa's war wound, that having a prosthetic leg somehow protected him from being transported. Nazi propaganda had painted Theresienstadt as a place where the disabled as well as the elderly were looked after, so perhaps there was some truth in this.

But secretly I wondered if my grandparents had collabo-rated in some way to save their skin, though I would never have voiced this out loud to my parents. As it turned out Mum was right, only not in the way I had imagined.

One thing I was never aware of – and I now realise my father certainly knew, and I'm sure he told my mother – was that Rudolf and Helena were not the only members of his family in Theresienstadt. This place was the centre of everything, the transit 'lounge' that decided the fate of 19 members of Dad's immediate family and many more of his extended family.

My father never visited Theresienstadt. It wasn't even a consideration for him. I think when he returned to Prague and later to the Czech mountains more than 50 years after he had been hurriedly hustled out of his homeland, it was to find the happy places, reconnect with the life he lost, not dwell on the agonising genocide that kicked in following his departure. It was a common reaction from those who lost family to the Holocaust. A corner of Dad's brain simply closed down; somewhere in that grey matter was a locked room where he just couldn't venture, and I fully appreciate that this was how he survived the horror of what happened.

But I now know I have to go there. I want to. I am just beginning to know my relatives, to learn about their lives and understand a little bit about who they were. I need to follow through on their journey to Theresienstadt and discover what happened to each and every one: Emil and his high-achieving family including my grandpa the war hero; Rabbi Hoffer's feisty girls and determined sons, including his two grand-daughters. Having only just found my family, I'm not ready to lose them.

The Riedens and Hoffers would have travelled to Theresienstadt by train, crammed into second-class carriages, scared, uncomfortable, hugging their belongings and totally unaware of what lay ahead. They then would have faced the long trudge from Bohušovice train station to the ghetto. From 1943, trains rode directly to Terezín thanks to a new railway track siding that had been constructed (by the prisoners). It was designed to increase the efficiency of transports, as Nazi extermination of the Jews shifted up a gear and speed and volume became a key factor in the transportation planning. Only Grandpa's youngest sister, Hedwig, would have arrived at the siding, though some of the family certainly departed from it.

———

I ride to Theresienstadt with my partner Katie in a taxi, quickly leaving behind Prague's grandeur for lush green, undulating hills. It is brilliant sunshine and very warm, which feels at odds with my visit here. I am apprehensive about what I will find in Theresienstadt but also excited to be finally walking in my grandparents' footsteps. Wild poppies blotch red smudges through the surrounding fields and hedgerows all along the route, an immediate symbol in my mind for fallen servicemen. Only the casualties I am about to uncover did not die in combat; they were murdered, defenceless victims of the worst war crimes the world has ever seen.

I spot signs of industry here and there on the skyline as we drive, and I am reminded that Czechoslovakia was considered the engine room of the Third Reich. It played a crucial role in the production of Hitler's armaments, possibly one of the reasons it was largely protected from heavy bombing.

I find the town of Terezín – as it is now called, rightly reclaiming the original Czech name, as opposed to the German Theresienstadt the Nazis designated for *Juden* – to be a curious place. Calm, quiet, contemplative and very spread out; not at all what I expected.

The countryside around here is gentle and quite beautiful. The Elbe river flows peacefully into the Ohře, and all around are meadows filled with wildflowers, the petals of which, at this time of year, flutter with visitations from butterflies, below the soft bluey-purple of a mountain backdrop. Set into this scene of pastoral harmony was the eighteenth-century fortress, many of whose ancient buildings still stand. This star-shaped twelve-pointed military city with high ramparts was originally surrounded by a moat, had six gates and was Emperor Joseph II's pride and joy. In addition, a civilian town of typically Czech painted stone houses with the usual town square and other buildings fill out Terezín. Around 7000 lived here before the war, half of whom were soldiers.

At the height of its Theresienstadt use, there were 58,491 inmates. At first it was for Jews from the recently declared Protectorate of Bohemia and Moravia, and then also those from Germany, Austria, the Netherlands, Denmark, Slovakia and Hungary.

Nazi propaganda tricked some of the elderly wealthy Austrian and German Jews into believing that Theresienstadt was actually a health resort with all sorts of facilities – coffee houses, theatres, spa treatments. Eager for a piece of paradise amid the chaos of war, the Jews paid to go, thinking this would be a holiday away from the trouble. They packed their best dresses and suits, smart shoes, jewels, furs and resort-wear – all of which was confiscated as soon as they arrived.

Now this place also has the rather sinister feeling of a ghost town, which of course it is, on this day for me especially, as I contemplate the ghosts of the 35,088 who died here when it was a concentration camp, and the further 84,000 who left here and were killed following deportation to the East. It is a lot to process, and very quickly I start to understand why my father didn't want to come here.

The taxi driver drops us off at the end of the long tree-lined cobbled drive that leads to what is known as the Small Fortress. As the car drives away we are left alone in the deathly quiet. The grass is shiny green, trees are in full leaf and flowers are pushing up through the soil, but I can feel the pall of suffering here hanging in the air around every building, clinging to the ramparts. Along one side of the drive is the Terezín National Cemetery, with row upon row of 2000 gravestones set into a well-kept lawn beside a memorial rose garden.

Before the crematorium was built at Theresienstadt, those who died in the camp were buried in graves in the nearby Bohušovice basin. In less than a year, around 9000 inmates were buried there – 1250 in individual graves and the rest in 217 mass graves.

Immediately after the war, survivors pushed to have the corpses of their fellow prisoners exhumed. After all they had endured, they wanted the deaths they had witnessed day in, day out, to be respected, their bodies properly buried with the humane dignity that had been absent for the past five years in this nation.

And so this cemetery was created. In 1975, symbolic uniform headstones were erected and a central granite memorial in the shape of a seven-branched candelabrum – a Jewish menorah – added. Standing over it all is a Star of David and a cross.

Even though none of my relatives are remembered here, I do feel some connection with the graves. And later, when I look back at the cemetery at the end of my visit, a day of dark, dark discoveries, I wish that the Riedens and Hoffers had ended their days here rather than meet the terrible fates they faced when they were deported from Theresienstadt.

Ahead, beyond the graves, I walk towards the ominous black-and-white painted arched opening in the brick ramparts leading to the ghastly Small Fortress. Any sense that Theresienstadt was an easy camp is wiped out by this place.

Built and used as a prison under the Austro-Hungarian regime, the fortress was seized upon by the Nazis as the perfect location to incarcerate political prisoners. Here, members of resistance groups, mostly Communists from Czechoslovakia but also from elsewhere in Europe, along with Jews who broke anti-Semitic laws and homosexuals who were considered criminals in the Third Reich, were interned and used as slave labour, building an underground munitions factory in nearby Litoměřice. Any trouble makers from the camp would also find themselves interned here. Symbols on their black prison shirts denoted each inmate's 'crime'. Political prisoners wore red triangles, homosexuals pink triangles and Jews the yellow star.

The statistics are chilling, and the structure itself, now kept as a memorial bearing witness to what went on here, feels like a medieval torture chamber. Prisoners wore clogs and all men had their heads shaved bald; there was no heating and water had to be re-used.

This is the first place I have seen that fallacious Nazi edict 'Arbeit Macht Frei' (work makes you free) painted over the entrance. In five years from 1940, 32,000 men and women passed through the gates of this fortress. Of these, a third were sent to concentration camps, where they were most likely to have been murdered, while just under a quarter were tried in the courts, the majority found guilty. Approximately 2600 died here.

Executions were carried out, and more than 250 were shot in a courtyard with other prisoners forced to watch. Their corpses were then piled on top of one another in a mortuary inside one of the fortress's many tunnels, and some were buried in shallow graves before the opening of the crematorium that served the Fortress, Theresienstadt camp and the Flossenbürg work camp in nearby Bavaria.

The ovens in the crematorium were alight 24 hours a day to cope with the sheer volume of human flesh. According to records, some 30,000 bodies were burned here, the urns containing ashes then stored in the columbarium in the fortress ramparts.

Towards the end of our tour of the fortress, I leave claustrophobic Katie to enter the 500-metre section of tunnel. This was the route to execution for condemned prisoners. The tunnel is cold, dark and constantly winding, punctuated by individual prisoner cells. There are slits in the thick stone walls through which shafts of sunlight help to light your way. It is utterly terrifying to walk through, unbearably claustrophobic . . . and then, when I finally reach the end, by which time my heart is pumping out of my chest, I am greeted by the execution ground, where prisoners were shot, and around the corner, a wooden gallows where a small number were hanged.

It is some small comfort that I have no reason to believe any of my relatives came to the fortress, but I can see how this place would have played its part in quashing opposition, insurrection or any escape attempts within the camp.

From here I meet up with Katie and cross the river and walk to the town and the site of Theresienstadt itself. Some parts of Terezín stand as a permanent memorial to the horrors that took place, but what initially I find incomprehensible is that most of the buildings where Theresienstadt inmates were packed together, crammed into rooms like sardines – including those where my grandparents Helena and Rudolf lived – have since been renovated into Czech homes where families live today. After all that had happened here, I am surprised that anybody would choose to live here.

The civilians who had lived in the town before the war were thrown out by the Nazis in 1942 so they could devote the entire garrison and its environs to their 'concentration' of Jews. These original Terezín homeowners would have received some sort of recompense back then, but it's likely that if they survived the war, some returned to reclaim their property and their descendants may be among the current occupants. But today there are also newcomers living in the town, which is after all well situated, easily accessible from Prague. Life indeed goes on, however shocking that feels to me.

It is extremely hot and a little windy on the day we visit; the light is piercing and bright white, and the streets are dry and dusty. We are to meet Tomáš Fedorovič at his office in the memorial museum building, which in the camp served as home number L417, for boys aged ten to 15. This was one of the more uplifting places in the 'ghetto', for it was here in the attics that secret lessons were held and these lads were able to learn and live a little. The teachers were also prisoners, who fortuitously included some of Czechoslovakia's leading figures in the arts, academia, culture and politics. Even though they were incarcerated and sadly very few survived, the boys were receiving a privileged and inspirational education. In the gym here, clandestine artistic performances were staged, including one of *The Bartered Bride* – the comic opera by Czech composer Smetana – which many survivors have recalled fondly.

And it was here that Petr Ginz, age 14, created the trailblazing *Vedem*, one of the world's most famous underground magazines. It was the most impressive of a few student publications written in the camp. Petr was an extraordinarily gifted young man, a writer, poet, artist and, for two years in Theresienstadt, a media editor. Through the magazine, Petr mobilised the incarcerated children to write articles, poems and prose, and create drawings, to express their inner thoughts and chart life inside the camp as well as have a little bit of fun. Petr was ultimately transported to his death in Auschwitz in 1944, age 16, but his legacy was felt by many, if only for a short period of their short lives. As a fellow journalist, I had known about Petr before I came to Theresienstadt, so I was thrilled that I was meeting Tomáš here in the place Petr worked.

The permanent exhibition in the museum was a hub of activity as we arrived, with groups of international schoolchildren as well as a few curious tourists. More of the drawings by the Theresienstadt children that we had seen at the Pinkas Synagogue decorated the walls, and inside was a comprehensive exhibition about what went on in Theresienstadt.

I stop at a poem on the wall. It was written by Teddy who lived in L410 in 1943 and sums up what life was like here. It talks of sleeping on a dirty floor, of flies carrying disease, having to eat black potatoes and finishes: 'Here in Terezín, life is hell. And when I'll go home again, I can't yet tell.'

It makes me think of Dad. He was safe in a British boarding school in 1943 speaking English, being awarded 'excellent' by his scripture teacher on his school report. But I am sure, like Teddy, he was wondering if he would ever go home again.

One installation in the museum shows a wall of transport lists, name after name typed on pieces of yellowing paper, some annotated with handwritten comments, next to a sculpture made from brown leather suitcases, marked in white paint with transport numbers identifying their owners. Behind is an evocative black-and-white drawing of queues of Jewish prisoners arriving – or are they leaving? – wrapped up against the cold, weighed down with makeshift sacks bulging with possessions, and with a faceless Nazi standing guard in his tin helmet, army greatcoat and jackboots, holding a gun.

I am immediately drawn to the lists and start scouring them for Riedens and Hoffers. It's a habit I can't kick as I walk around, scrutinising every photograph and official document. Is there anything left of my kin here?

———

There isn't in the exhibition, but Tomáš has much to impart. Having been talking to Tomáš for months via email I have built up a picture of him in my head that I discover is completely at odds with the round, bearded, gently smiling man before me. He actually bears a striking similarity to my brother Peter, which makes me realise that many of the men I have seen around Prague look like my brothers, who in turn look a lot like our dad. This gives me a feeling of belonging and also somehow of coming home. I am meant to be here.

We follow Tomáš to his rather chaotic office at the end of

a corridor. Pasted to the wall are photos of his young children watching over his work, and next to them are some of their drawings, a poignant echo of the work of Theresienstadt's children created here more than 75 years earlier. And as I talk to this sensitive father and historian who has devoted the past 18 years of his life to uncovering and documenting what happened in Theresienstadt, I know Tomáš Fedorovič will find my relatives.

We start with Rudolf and Helena, and my burning question of how my grandparents managed to survive when their siblings did not. I feel anxious and break into a sweat as I posit my theories and present my bulging document of archival papers. Tomáš flicks on his computer and starts to access a database of information. I ask about the names of those in the Theresienstadt Ältestenrat – the Jewish Council of Elders – hoping that this will be an easy question to answer.

'Is it possible that Rudolf, being a war hero, a doctor of law, and having worked for the Czech government's Ministry of Finance, might have been on the council?' I ask.

Ever since I started this pilgrimage, I have been searching everywhere for the list of those on the council. But while the key leaders are widely known, finding out the names of others on the council and then those who worked in the different departments of the self-administration is much more difficult. Many of these lists were destroyed, of course, along with much of the documentation attesting to what went on inside Theresienstadt. But there is more to it than that. It would be an overstatement to suggest a cover-up, but I have become increasingly aware of the extreme sensitivity around identifying those who decided the fate of the inmates in the camp, and this is one of many instances when I feel the camp secrets are being protected. I do understand.

This question of exactly what the Elders knew about the East is a sticky one and has never been fully resolved. Some believe they knew more than they shared, but didn't want to incite fear and panic. The 'company' line was that the transports were to labour camps, where Jews would be used as workhorses. Whether Theresienstadt's inmates swallowed this lie is unclear, but one thing is certain: everyone was afraid of the transport and nobody wanted to go. There was a perceived finality to it that sent shudders of terror through the camp. So choosing those who would fill the railway cattle trucks was a hideous task, and families would use all possible powers of persuasion to influence the judgements.

Those in the self-administration also had power: they decided which jobs people had and where they lived, how much food they received and other privileges. And while ultimately few of them survived, these people had a better chance of protecting themselves and their loved ones from transport.

There were three Jewish Elder leaders who governed one after another at Theresienstadt, and only the last survived. The first, Jakob Edelstein, was the camp Elder from 4 December 1941. It is thought Edelstein believed that in Theresienstadt he could help prepare Czech Jews for an ultimate move to Israel after the war and that he had no clue about the gas chambers in the East. It was Edelstein who decided that the camp's children should receive greater food allowances and be secretly educated, especially in Hebrew. These children were the future; through them they would all survive. Edelstein was arrested for having corrupted transport lists and later sent with his family to Auschwitz, where he was found guilty at trial. On 20 June 1944, he was forced to watch as his wife and son were shot in the head and then faced the same fate himself.

Next was Dr Paul Eppstein who took over in January 1944 but was also arrested, for allowing inmates to form self-defence units within the camp. He wasn't awarded a trial and was executed at Theresienstadt on 7 September 1944.

The last, Dr Benjamin Murmelstein, is a more controversial figure. He ruled from 5 December 1944 until the Red Cross took over on 5 May 1945, and dealt very closely – some say too closely – with Adolf Eichmann. Tomáš tells me that Murmelstein had 'the worst reputation' but adds that it may have been because he favoured German and Austrian Jews, which the Czech Jews were well aware of. They accused him of collaborating with the Nazis – especially in helping to create a false impression of the camp when the Red Cross came to inspect, with the laughable beautification project that was also filmed in the documentary.

When I ask about the others on the council, Tomáš says there is a list of some of those who were in the Jewish self-administration, but it's difficult because it only exists for a certain period of time. What he can say for sure though is that Rudolf was not an Elder nor was he part of the self-administration staff. A key indicator would have been where he lived in Theresienstadt. The Magdeburg Barracks was the seat of the self-administration and Rudolf did not live there. Nor did Helena or any Riedens or Hoffers.

Rudolf's registration card lists all the different places he lived, and it is here that we finally find the answer to my question. Rudolf lived first of all in what was called the 'Engineer Barracks', which was specifically for the sick and elderly. After a month there – probably recuperating from the journey to Theresienstadt – he was moved to Bahnhofstrasse, numbers 33, 35 and 37. 'These three barracks were specifically for war veterans who endured the First World War. They were put together so they could be cared for,' says Tomáš. This is very important, for as a decorated war hero and an officer, Rudolf was protected from deportation East and that protection also extended to his wife.

This respect for Rudolf's service initially takes me by surprise. When I think of the seeming ease with which the Nazis committed atrocities and treated Jewish people and other minorities as subhuman, I am amazed that my grandfather would be afforded this small scrap of decency. But as I come to examine the Nazi psyche more, it does make a warped sense. Duty, honour and military prowess were at the heart of the Third Reich, and Rudolf had risked his life playing his part for his nation, as it was at the time. Unfortunately, he was also a Jew, which posed a dilemma for Hitler, so this was the rather cack-handed salute the Nazis afforded Rudolf.

It seems that losing his leg in that horrific battle while fighting for the Austro-Hungarian Empire actually saved Rudolf and Helena's life, and the fact that he had a very visible war wound also helped. If anyone in a decision-making position was unaware and hadn't acquainted themselves with the records supporting his protected status, they could see that Rudolf had one leg and from his age – which was 47 going on 48 when he first arrived in Theresienstadt – they would immediately realise that he was a war veteran.

Unfortunately, that protection did not cover his siblings, Tomáš explains. 'Rudolf had no power to say, "Hey, that's my brother, please let him stay here with me." But Rudolf was definitely protected by his war decoration, no question.'

Although Helena was also protected, she was not permitted to stay in the same barracks as her husband, so her association with a protected spouse would not have been immediately evident. So when my grandmother told my mother that she had been pulled from queues for transport, it is likely that until either Rudolf came to her aid or the records were checked properly she may have been listed erroneously, which would have been terrifying.

The protection however didn't ease the conditions, which were the same for everyone. Helena's card shows that she was moved around regularly, living in eight different lodgings in her three years in Theresienstadt. This was a specific technique to disarm prisoners, to prevent them from feeling settled and from forming alliances. The idea was to uphold a reign of terror, which the Nazis hoped would thwart any organised dissent or uprisings, and, on many levels, it worked.

As an '*Invalide*', which was listed as his profession on one of his cards, Rudolf didn't have to work, but Tomáš says he would have wanted to, because this was the only way to increase your meagre food allowance. Workers were sorted into different categories, each with a designated food portion. The higher the category, the greater the amount of food. And since food meant life, there was a lot of competition for the best jobs.

'There were three or four categories for food, and the portion for every category was settled by the Self-Administration Council' says Tomáš. 'So, the rich men in Theresienstadt were the cooks and those who worked in food. After them those who were in the council since they fixed the portions.'

On his second card, Rudolf's profession is listed as 'finance adviser' rather than '*Invalide*'. I wonder if he managed to secure an office or administration position inside the camp. If he did, I imagine this would have made his days a little more comfortable, since Tomáš says disabled and elderly inmates would often have had jobs such as 'staying guard outside toilets or policing the amount of water people used'.

On her cards, Helena at first listed her profession as 'house-wife', but then it was changed to 'seamstress' on a later card. Tomáš said she would have done this deliberately so she was seen to have useful skills. As a seamstress she could be put to work, mending, making clothes, sewing sacks and so on. And this might have helped both her food allowance and her usefulness to the camp. Even though everyone dreamed of freedom, the longer you stayed in the camp as a useful member of the workforce, the more chance you had to escape deportation East. For the Jewish Council, it was far easier to put newcomers straight onto transport lists than to upset the status quo, however callous that might have been.

Word of who had arrived in the Schleuse with each trans-port did spread around the camp, and family members often tried to visit, even though this was a little risky. Then, if they discovered one of their newly arrived family was on a trans-port list, they could put in an appeal to the Council of Elders. In Rudolf's case, though, Tomáš can't find any clues that might suggest he knew anyone on the council. In fact quite the opposite; he thinks it's highly likely he didn't, considering the annihilation of his and Helena's siblings, and the speed at which it happened.

There is some joy on these registration cards, though, for on 20 January 1945, Rudolf and Helena were reunited, living under the same roof. Tomáš says they wouldn't have been able to live in the same room, but at least they would have been near each other for the precarious last four months in the camp.

I can't imagine what physical state they would have been in, and perhaps being together helped them last through to the end. By this time, they would have witnessed so much. Rudolf's father Emil died just a few months after they arrived, and then over the next three years, 16 of their siblings came to Theresienstadt and only one, Rudolf's sister Hedwig, made it to liberation with them. It's highly possible that Helena and Rudolf didn't even realise some of these brothers and sisters had been there, since some were loaded off to death camps with terrifying efficiency.

As I sit beside him, Tomáš and I now go through the archive database together, and one by one I trace exactly what happened to those siblings. Even though I already knew they hadn't survived, I was totally unprepared for what I heard next.

====

Felix Rieden, then 44, was the first of my family to arrive in Theresienstadt and also among the first couple of groups of prisoners to arrive in the camp. He left Prague on 4 December 1941, number 936 in a group of 1000 called Transport J. This was a special transport of single young men, the second batch of a 'working command' chosen to help prepare the camp for future inmates. They worked hard bringing in supplies, building equipment and furniture, shifting rubble and cleaning. They carried coal and food supplies, and fixed machinery. It was tough physical work, and over the next three years when numbers ebbed and flowed, they would be brought in to clean out barracks ready for the next wave of prisoners.

As part of Transport J, Felix would have received good food rations and was protected from deportation, since this group of men were far too useful to the camp. And the tragedy of Felix is that he so nearly made it through. But while Transport J had saved him, it was also his destruction. Transport J knew too much. They knew everything that had happened inside Theresienstadt, and as the war started to falter for the Germans, they eliminated those who could bear witness to the atrocities. Transport J's young men weren't the only ones; members of the Jewish administration and their families also had their protected status lifted.

On 28 October 1944, Felix was number 360 on Transport Ev of 2038 Theresienstadt prisoners – men, women and children – bound for Auschwitz. It was the last ever transport to leave Theresienstadt, and the list was drawn up personally by SS officers; camp commander Karl Rahm; Ernst Möhs, one of Adolf Eichmann's chief aides; and Hans Günther, head of the Office of the Settlement of the Jewish Question in Prague, who was personally responsible for the deportation of Czech Jews to death camps throughout the war. Günther was killed by Czech partisans in 1945, but not in time for Felix, who was 47 when he was sent to his death.

The train took two days to reach Auschwitz. The prisoners were crammed into cattle cars, standing room only, with one bucket of water and one bucket for a toilet between every 50 people. According to one account of the transport, Günther himself ordered that the windows be sealed with tin so no light could get it. It was pitch-black inside the carriages.

H.G. Adler's exhaustive study *Theresienstadt 1941–1945* recounts that having left from the camp siding, the train stopped just three kilometres down the line at Bohušovice station, where 20 men were taken off the train and ordered to work at the columbarium. This was the vault where the urns containing the ashes of those who had died in the camp were stored. The men were told to toss the ashes from 22,000 cremations into the Ohře river, and a further 3000 were buried. Karl Rahm didn't want any evidence of the high death rate in Theresienstadt. These men were then incarcerated in the grotesque Small Fortress prison, where no doubt they died. I hope Felix wasn't one of these men, for among those urns would have been his father Emil's ashes.

In a testimony in Israel's Yad Vashem archives, Ada Levy, who was one of the lucky 171 who survived Transport Ev, says that many died en route to Auschwitz, their bodies propped upright between the living on the hellish journey. The train arrived at Birkenau on 30 October. Historian Danuta Czech reports that 132 men and some women from this transport were sent on to labour camps, and a further 217 proceeded through the registration process at Birkenau. The rest were sent to the gas chambers.

There is no mention of Felix in the Auschwitz archives, except that he was part of this terrible transport, and he wasn't among those who were liberated in January 1945 just three months later.

Marie Hoffer, 57, was the next to arrive in Theresienstadt, just two weeks after Felix on 17 December 1941. She was number 279 in a group of 1000 called Transport N. Marie lasted barely a month in the camp before she was called up again for deportation, bound for a concentration camp in Riga in the then Soviet Union (now in Latvia).

Marie was number 258 of 1000 on Transport P. This was in the first phase of transports out of Theresienstadt. The oldest on the transport was aged 64 and the youngest seven. The journey was reportedly in crowded passenger cars, their windows shut, with no food or water provided, and would have taken five days. But on arrival SS officers forced the Jews out into the snow, leaving their luggage on the train. Around 80 of the young men were marched to a sub-camp of the Riga complex, and the remaining prisoners – no doubt including Marie – were taken into the forest and shot. Fifteen Jews survived this transport, but Marie was not one of them.

Marie's sister, **Anna Kohnova**, 53, with her husband **Max Kohn**, 51, and their daughter **Johanna Kohnova**, 21, arrived in Theresienstadt probably around the same time Marie was being shot in a forest in Riga.

They were on Transport S, rounded up in their home town of Pilsen in West Bohemia and marched through the town onto a train bound for Theresienstadt on 22 January 1942. Max was number 103, Anna number 104 and Johanna number 629 of 1000 deportees.

They lasted only seven weeks in the camp before they were all deported together, numbers 906, 907 and 908 in a group of approximately 1000 Jews (some reports say there were 1080) deported on Transport Ab to Izbica, a transit camp south-east of Lublin in Poland. This was just the fourth transport to leave Theresienstadt, and 710 of the deportees were women. It was a gruelling three-day journey in cattle cars.

It is unclear how many of those on the transport ended up in the Izbica camp. Some were also sent further east to Krasiczyn and Gorzków in Poland, and possibly to Bełżec, one of the deadliest extermination camps. It had started as a labour camp but the gas chambers began operating on 17 March 1942, the same day the Kohn family had been deported from Theresienstadt. Anna, Max and Johanna could have died of starvation and sickness in the camps, or if they were sent to Bełżec they would have been gassed.

Arnost Hoffer, 56, the second eldest of the siblings, was deported with the youngest of his sisters, Eliska Hofferova, 39, and a 15-month-old baby, Vera Hofferova, on Transport AAl from Prague to Theresienstadt on 2 July 1942. Arnost was number 483 in a group of 1005, with Eliska and Vera numbers 214 and 215. The numbers often denote connections between the deportees, with those living in the same house having consecutive numbers. Eliska was not married, but Theresienstadt historian Tomáš Fedorovič comes to the same conclusion as I did when I saw Eliska's registration card, which listed Vera living at her address. Vera must have been Eliska's illegitimate daughter.

Once they arrived at Theresienstadt, Arnost and Eliska parted ways. For just over three weeks later, on 28 July 1942, Arnost is off again, deported as number 74 on Transport AAy carrying 1867 Jews to Baranowicze, then in Poland (now Baranavichy in Belarus). With such a huge number of prisoners, this three-day journey would have been hellish.

Testimonies and research about this particular transport suggest that it may have originally been bound for Maly Trostinec, near Minsk, but an official order demanded that the train stop at Baranowicze. It is possible that this was to prevent Arnost and his fellow prisoners arriving in Minsk at the same time other deportees were being 'liquidated' there. In essence, there was a bit of bottleneck.

In any case, the end result was no different for Arnost.

Despite a partisan attack blowing up part of the train track, reports say that on arrival at Baranowicze, the SS chose 100 fit men for a work detail and then ordered the rest of the Theresienstadt deportees to board waiting trucks with their eating utensils. These trucks were in fact specially fitted gas vans, killing the prisoners as they drove along. Jews were crammed into an airtight compartment into which exhaust gas was pumped. The carbon monoxide would suffocate the prisoners as they stood, and the tangled mass of limp bodies would then be driven, usually to a pit, for a group burial. Because of the number of people on the transport, the gassing took several journeys, the trucks constantly reloading. So to speed things up, the local Gestapo was ordered to shoot any deportees who had not been killed in the trucks. These bodies were buried at the Haj grove near the village of Kolpenice. The Czech guards who had accompanied the deportees were also shot, even though they pleaded that they were not Jewish.

It's unclear where the bodies of those killed in the trucks were dumped, but in early 1945, the mass graves at the Haj grove were uncovered. The monument that was put up to mark this atrocity was almost immediately vandalised, and it took 30 years for a new gravestone to be erected.

Although 37 survived Transport AAy, I can find no trace of Arnost, who on Holocaust files is listed as murdered.

Eliska and **Vera Hofferova** spent almost a year and a half in Theresienstadt. There is no reference to where they lived, but I am hoping that Rudolf and Helena managed to spend a little time with their niece, who left the camp age three years and nine months.

My father never got to meet his cousin. Indeed, I wonder if he knew about her at all. She was a war baby, born a year after Hitler had occupied Czechoslovakia. Poor Vera didn't stand a chance.

Mother and daughter were deported to Auschwitz-II Birkenau on 18 December 1943 on Transport Ds. They were numbers 1109 and 1111 of a huge transport of 2503. The transport order was issued on the morning of 17 December: 'Appeal was impossible.' The destination was not revealed; instead it said the trains would go into the Reich territory.

Eliska was now 40. She and Vera would have made their way to the Schleuse with their one suitcase of permissible luggage plus one bag of hand luggage. The suitcase was loaded separately onto the train, and I can't imagine Eliska ever saw it again. They left direct from Theresienstadt station from the new railway sidings that were now fully operational. Snow would have been thick on the ground, with temperatures well below freezing.

But this transport was different from earlier deportations to Auschwitz-II Birkenau. On arrival, the agonising selection process others had faced, which would decide an instant fate in the gas chambers or life in the camp, didn't happen. And some records say that those on this transport were allowed to keep their own clothes and may not have their heads shaved, though other reports conflict with this. Certainly, mother and daughter would still have had new identification numbers tattooed on their arms and all the other indignities of the arrival process. They would have then been sent to a fenced-off area of Birkenau known as 'Familienlager BIIb'. It was the Family Camp.

The inmates here, who had arrived a couple of months before, received special privileges. The children spent their days in the children's block, where they had teachers and were entertained, and at night Vera may have been allowed to sleep in barracks with her mother. And while the food was still woefully inadequate and inmates were freezing and ill, the mortality rate was much lower than elsewhere in the camp. Best of all, these prisoners were not selected for the gas chambers.

But this lucky state was not to last. Those who had arrived in September disappeared exactly six months into their stay. They were told they were going to the Heydebreck labour camp. Instead they were sent straight to the Auschwitz gas chambers. Witnesses recall them singing anthems of resistance as they were stripped naked and sent to their deaths. From this moment on, selections were reinstated, and Eliska would certainly have been terrified, for inside Auschwitz everyone knew what was happening to Jews in the gas chambers. The thick smoke from the bodies being cremated could not be ignored.

There are no records that chart exactly what happened to my great-aunt and little Vera. The Nazis destroyed most of the paperwork from Auschwitz-II Birkenau. Some of the Family Camp occupants were sent to other concentration camps to work before they were ultimately killed, but I think it's more likely that Eliska and Vera were among the 6000–7000 prisoners who were sent to the gas chambers between 10 and 12 July 1944. Thinking of Eliska holding on to her toddler as they walked naked to their death is unbearable. In just six months' time they would have been liberated.

The exact purpose of the Family Camp is unclear. Some think that a visit from the Red Cross similar to that made to Theresienstadt was on the horizon, and that the camp was established as an illusion to hide the genocide that was really going on. But the Head of Research at the Auschwitz Museum, Dr Piotr Setkiewicz, says that the SS would never have allowed international Red Cross inspectors into Birkenau, and that the Family Camp was created as the nerve centre for a periodic 'letter writing campaign' to reassure Jews back in Theresienstadt about the fate of their deported relatives. Ultimately, the Family Camp inmates' privileges were removed, and they faced the inevitable fate of so many here.

A couple of days before she and Vera were gassed, Eliska would have been forced to write a postdated postcard back to her relatives in Theresienstadt saying that she was alive and well. This was part of a letter propaganda campaign called 'Briefaktion'. The contents of the missive were censored, and the intention was to dispel any rumours that were starting to spread about Auschwitz, to quell fears. Would this card have been sent to Helena and Rudolf? Probably. Only when they received it, Eliska and Vera would already have been murdered.

Emil Rieden, Dad's grandfather, was 82 when he was deported from Prague on 20 July 1942 and sent to Theresienstadt, number 181 of 1000 Czech Jews on Transport AAs. He made the journey on his own. Inside the camp at that time would have been his son Felix, and then a couple of months later Rudolf and Helena arrived.

Emil lasted just over five months before his body gave up on 8 January 1943. By this time his son Otto and daughter Berta were already dead, but Emil probably didn't know this. Emil's cause of death was 'marasmus-senilis', a general term for old age that covered a multitude of potential failings. Death was an hourly occurrence in Theresienstadt, treated with little regard, and autopsies were carried out infrequently.

At this time in particular, the city was full to bursting, as more and more transports arrived. Overcrowding, contaminated water, filthy toilets, freezing conditions, vermin-fed diseases and infection, starvation and contaminated food hastened death. Several typhoid epidemics seized the camp as well as scarlet fever, but the most common causes of death were gastroenteritis, malnutrition and pneumonia. Every day, dead bodies appeared in front of the houses, the corpses laid out with their heads covered and their feet protruding. Bodies that were cremated would have been placed in the incinerator out of their coffin, lying only on the thin wooden baseboard it was attached to. This was so coffins could be recycled – again and again and again . . .

It's possible Rudolf and Felix would have staged a hasty funeral for their father; sometimes relatives were permitted to say their goodbyes in the central morgue, but not always.

Emil was cremated on 12 January 1943 in oven number IV at 10.30 am. By 11.05 am Emil was reduced to ashes. His body took 35 minutes to burn. I know this because we have the record sheet I found in the Prague National Archives. Emil was one of 28 burned in oven IV that day.

Jewish prisoners tasked with working in the crematorium, who numbered as many as 18 in peak times, tried to separate each individual's ashes. But first they had to sift through to find any gold from tooth fillings or dentures that didn't burn, to hand over to the SS.

The remains were then put into individual marked urns, originally made from wood but then replaced with paper bags so as not to waste the wood. The urn was annotated with Emil's vital information, copied from the identification card that had been attached to his foot before his body went into the oven. This included his name and some of those numbers the Nazis loved so much – his transport number and a new one, his cremation number. Emil's ashes would then have been placed in the columbarium.

Today commemoration plaques line the walls of the columbarium, but I don't want to put one here for Emil. I don't want this to be the place that future generations of Riedens remember him.

Sisters **Ida Hofferova**, 59, **Klara Hofferova**, 50, and **Laura Hofferova**, 46, arrived in Theresienstadt on 23 July 1942. They had been deported from Prague together, numbers 864,

865 and 866 on Transport AAt. They also left Theresienstadt together, just over a fortnight later. Tomáš tells me it was unlikely the trio left the Schleuse while in Theresienstadt, as there are no card entries for their accommodation within the camp, and that their time in this squalid holding area would have been pretty unpleasant. At least they would have had each other. Their brother Arnost would also have been in the Schleuse for the first five days they were there, before he was deported East. Did they all meet up? I hope so.

These three women were deported on 4 August 1942, on Transport AAz of 1000 Jews bound for the village of Maly Trostinec. They were numbers 328, 329 and 330. They were told they were going East, and the first part of the journey was in passenger carriages. On 6 August the train arrived in Wołkowysk (then in Poland, now Vawkavysk in south-west Belarus) and the prisoners were moved into freight cars. In the village of Maly Trostinec, on the outskirts of Minsk, was a Nazi extermination camp that operated between July 1942 and October 1943. This was the destination for the three sisters. A newly opened railway siding meant that trains of deportees could drive right up to the village. Earlier transports had arrived in Minsk and then had to be transported by truck, which according to reports from the time proved to be an expensive drain on petrol. This was much more efficient.

On arrival at the camp, the three sisters were told to hand over their valuables and property while a selection process took place. Somewhere between 20 and 50 fit young men were selected to be used for hard labour. Ida, Klara and Laura, along with their fellow deportees, were then taken to Blagovshchina forest, where they had to undress to their underwear then line up on the edge of vast recently dug pits. SS officers lined up behind them. They shot Ida, Laura and Klara in the back of their necks so their bodies would fall into the pits. It was a lengthy operation, and it is highly likely not all three sisters were shot at once. I can't imagine how petrified they would have been. Reports note that some prisoners tried to run, but they didn't get very far. Tractors then flattened the ground. It is unknown exactly how many were killed here. In Maly Trostinec itself, the death toll was around 65,000 with a further 200,000 murdered in the surrounding area. In October 1943, Sonderkommando 1005 arrived at the camp. This special unit was made up mostly of Jewish prisoners, and their task was to cover up Nazi mass murder. These forced labourers were commanded to dig up the mass graves in the forest and burn the decomposing corpses.

As Tomáš tells me about Maly Trostinec and what happened to my Dad's aunts, my mind is taken back to the photos I have of Ida and the postcard she sent to my father asking him to remember their time together.

While Ida, Klara and Laura were being murdered in Maly Trostinec, their brother **Rudolf Hoffer**, 42, his wife **Valerie Hofferova**, 40, and **Otto Rieden**, 38, were arriving on Transport Ba from Prague to Theresienstadt on 10 August 1942. There were 1460 on this deportation. Otto was number 508, Rudolf number 691 and Valerie number 1274.

Otto would have witnessed first his brother Felix, and then his father Emil, being called up and deported. They all lived together in Prague. Now it was his turn, leaving only his sister Berta at their rented lodgings and my grandparents who they all had earlier lodged with. The Riedens were being rounded up like sheep.

But it's unlikely Otto even managed to see his father and brother in the camp, for he was deported three weeks later on 1 September 1942 on Transport Be. This transport of 1000 was rumoured to be headed for labour camps in Riga in Latvia. The Baltic states were now being used by Hitler to speed up the 'Final Solution'. The Nazi plan was hampered by the sheer numbers involved, and Nazi henchman Adolf Eichmann made the decision to send seven transports to the camps in the Baltic states. Otto's transport was one of these. The journey was in passenger cars, and although it was crowded with men, women and children on the transport, Otto would have had a seat. They were also able to look out of the windows as they chugged through the countryside. Many thought they had escaped the sickness and squalor of Theresienstadt and would be out in the fresh air working. Considering what happened next, there is some comfort in thinking that Otto at least had a reasonable journey, his head filled, I hope, with positive thoughts.

When they reached Riga, the train reportedly stopped for several hours. It was then rerouted and a day later arrived in Raasiku in Estonia. Here everyone was forced off the train and panic and chaos ensued. According to testimonies from survivors, selections were made by German guards of around 100–150 of the younger women and 60–80 men. Everyone else was forced onto buses and driven to the Kalevi-Liiva sand dunes.

Since Otto was 38 and had only recently been deported, he would have been in relatively good health, so there's a slim chance he was one of the men selected for hard labour. But statistically he was more likely to have been taken to the coastal dunes with the majority. Both paths led to despicable ways to die.

On the sand dunes, the Jews were forced to put their valuables in their suitcases and strip naked. Then a squad of Estonian police shot them. Reportedly, Russian political prisoners who had been incarcerated in nearby Jägala concentration camp had earlier prepared pits for the bodies in the sand.

Those not killed here were used as forced labour at the Jägala camp and most likely murdered before the end of the war.

Today there are two memorial stones erected on the Kalevi-Liiva sand dunes for the Jews and Romani (gypsies) murdered here. Current estimates put the Jewish death toll at around 1750.

Husband and wife **Rudolf Hoffer** and **Valerie Hofferova** stayed in Theresienstadt for 16 months until they were selected for Transport Dr to Auschwitz on 15 December 1943. This was a big deportation of 2504, and Rudolf and Valerie were numbers 895 and 896. Like Rudolf's sister Eliska and her baby daughter Vera, who followed them just three days later, this was one of those 'privileged' transports that was most likely bound for the Family Camp.

The journey to Auschwitz would have been horrific – the travellers packed into cattle cars, with one bucket for men, women and children to defecate into. A memoir by Judith Jaegermann, a survivor from this transport who was then a child with her parents, recounts the moment her father realised their fate:

As we neared the murderous death machine called Auschwitz, and the train slowed down, I overheard Papa speak through a tiny opening to a railway employee. Papa asked him if transports went on to other destinations. The employee replied, with a raised thumb, 'Yes, up there, through the chimney, which burns 24 hours a day, that's where the transports go.'

I sent research requests to the official Auschwitz archives for all five of my relatives who were deported there, and while all appear on the incoming transport lists, only Rudolf Hoffer has additional paperwork. The records cite that Rudolf arrived 'at KL [Konzentrationslager (concentration camp)] Auschwitz on December 16, 1943 from Theresienstadt'. He was registered with prisoner number 168444 tattooed on his arm, and then two weeks after his arrival, 'on December 30 1943, he is mentioned in the prisoner's infirmary in the part BIIb in Birkenau,' the archivist tells me, adding, 'Unfortunately, there is no information about his further fate.'

This sets off immediate alarm bells. Either Rudolf was sick or he was being used for the notorious experimentation that went on, which included sterilisation for men and women. Either way, his most likely path would have been to the gas chambers, and I imagine Vera also was sent there. I am hoping that Valerie at least would have had the chance to meet up with Eliska and Vera, if only for a few months.

Dr Rudolf Rieden and **Helena Riedenova** arrived in Theresienstadt on 12 September 1942. They were identified as numbers 614 and 615 on Transport Bg. Also on that transport was Rudolf's elder sister **Berta Riedenova**, who was number 259. Now Hedwig was the only Rieden sibling not to have been deported to Theresienstadt. But while Rudolf and Helena managed to cling on to their protected status thanks to Rudolf's war record, Berta, 52, was selected for transport out of Theresienstadt just ten days after she had arrived.

Berta was number 778 on Transport Bn, which she was told was headed East. In fact, it was bound for Maly Trostinec, where the Hoffer sisters had been murdered a month before, and Berta's fate would have been exactly the same. She was taken to the Blagovshchina forest and shot in her underwear in front of the pits that became mass graves.

Hedwig Jungova, 43, was the last to arrive in the concentration camp. She was one of just 20, number 13 on Transport XIX/12 rounded up in Ústí nad Labem, where she lived, and deported to Theresienstadt on 2 March 1945. By this time her mixed-marriage status could protect her no longer. Inside the camp, Hedwig ended up living in the same barracks house as her sister-in-law Helena Riedenova, my grandmother. I can't imagine what state Hedwig found Helena and her brother Rudolf in.

Hedwig would have heard of the death of her father two years earlier. How much any of them knew about what had happened to the other 15 relatives who had passed through Theresienstadt is unclear. It's likely they knew nothing and that barbaric discovery was awaiting them on liberation.

══

A pall of silence comes over me as we come to the end of our searches. I had come here to Theresienstadt for answers, and now I have them the horror is numbing. Having found so many more relatives than I could ever dream of, I now realise why my father never spoke of them. But something inside me wants to go on, and hope takes hold of me.

As I look at my family tree and consider all I have heard, I realise there are still two of my grandparents' siblings – a Rieden and a Hoffer – who are not listed in the Theresienstadt archives, who weren't transported here and whom I can't find recorded elsewhere in the concentration camp archives or Holocaust victim archives. They are Anna Ungermannova (née Riedenova), who married Rabbi Samuel Ungermann;

and Josef Hoffer, the youngest of the Hoffer children. Even as I'm heading back to Prague, I can't stop myself desperately googling their names . . .

On that drive back to Prague, my head swirls with nightmarish visions of my relatives: on trains; shivering, starving and frightened in the Theresienstadt barracks; lined up in front of a pit naked, waiting to be shot. The beauty of the countryside and glamour of the old city don't feel apt or possible.

Later that night at a pizza restaurant in a pretty square near the hotel, Katie and I can't talk about what we have seen. Instead we imagine my dad as a little lad running around these cobbled streets, where we both now know he truly belonged.

CHAPTER TEN

THE TERRIBLE TRUTH ABOUT 'THE EAST'

I'd never believed I would make the journey to Auschwitz. This place wasn't part of my story, or so I thought. My grandparents had been 'safe' in Theresienstadt. They were the lucky ones. But as soon as I discover that after so nearly making it to the end of the war, Felix Rieden, my father's uncle, had been sent to Auschwitz, I knew I had to go.

Then, as the truth about my family tumbles out of the archives in Prague, in Terezín, in Liberec and in Žlutice, and again and again 'Osvětim' – the Czech name for Auschwitz – appears with a deafening finality on dossier after dossier, I realise how intrinsic this dark, dark town in Poland is to our family footprint.

From my day in Terezín, I now know that two of my father's uncles, two of his aunts and a young cousin had been deported to Auschwitz. But the thing about the records is that there are no absolutes. In the wake of the Nazi destruction of much of their obsessive cataloguing was a painful jigsaw puzzle of partial information without closure. Lives that in all likelihood were callously struck down were left hanging in the balance for those looking for them. While I have traced the journey of each and every transport that deported my relatives, scouring the official reports and the archival testimonies from survivors and uncovering incredibly bleak outcomes, I still harbour a sliver of hope. Could any of these five have escaped the inevitable somehow?

I hope in Auschwitz I might find some definitive answers, even a miracle perhaps.

I wear white – I don't want to mourn, but to triumph that finally I have found my relatives, that they haven't been forgotten by us, the Rieden family heirs; and to show them that their little Hansi, my father, became their secret weapon against the Nazis. While the Third Reich may have tried to wipe out a generation of Riedens and Hoffers, Dad was the beacon of light ripping through his school tests, climbing to the top of his class, out of Hitler's grasp.

My guide for the visit is Vida Neuwirthová, a Czech whose father, a doctor, had been deported to Auschwitz but had managed to escape with a medical unit, but not before the tuberculosis in his leg had been experimented on by the notorious Dr Josef Mengele. Vida is one of the tour guides for Wittman Tours. I chose this small experienced Prague-based company because it specialises in Jewish history and especially post-Holocaust trauma, and Vida because of her intimate knowledge of Auschwitz. When not working as a tour guide, the stylish and flamboyant Vida runs a leading children's theatre within Prague's Jewish community, and is passionate about bringing Jewish life back to the synagogues destroyed by the Nazis.

Vida didn't actually know she was Jewish until she was a teenager. After all that had happened to him, her father wanted to protect his offspring from anti-Semitism. And for a long time after the war he felt he had to hide his Jewishness, to keep a low profile, so much so that even his daughter and son didn't know. When she found out, Vida was filled with a need to claim the Judaism of which she had been robbed, even though her family urged caution.

It's a story I have heard again and again from the Jewish descendants of the survivors of the Holocaust in Prague, and it makes me rethink my own reaction to my grandparents' decision to leave my father in England rather than collect him after the war. For me, my mother and my brothers, this action had always seemed inexplicable, cruel even. My mother especially had never understood why Helena didn't reclaim her son with open arms. As a mother she felt her mother-in-law had let her only child down. She really couldn't forgive her actions. And thinking about it now, I wonder also if Mum's passionate reaction had meant that even though Dad had never spoken to us about that moment when he heard that he wasn't going to be reunited with his parents, he did talk to his wife about it. And yes, of course it hurt.

But here, as I make my own way to Auschwitz, with the tortured journeys that my grandparents and their brothers and sisters had endured throughout their years of persecution chasing around my brain, I start to appreciate my grandparents' situation. Just like Vida's father, they too must have been fearful about what lay ahead, and even though the Third Reich had been defeated and was no longer in their homeland, they couldn't trust that another wave of tyranny wasn't waiting to pounce. No doubt the establishment of Communist rule in Czechoslovakia in February 1948 would only have heightened their notions of insecurity. In short, they had lost all faith in humanity, and who can blame them?

It takes five hours to drive with Vida to KL Auschwitz from Prague – it took my relatives at least two days, possibly more, crammed into cattle trucks, locked in with no fresh air or sunlight, desperately trying to peek through any gaps in the wooden planks to get some idea of where they were headed. This was the dreaded journey 'East' that everyone had feared. On the day I go it is stiflingly hot, with a powerful side wind that feels as if you're standing in front of a hair dryer. I always pictured Auschwitz coated in thick snow, the mud paths hard with ice, but now I realise the summers must have been just as punishing.

I barely notice as we pass into Poland. There are no borders now, no checkpoints, no guards. As we approach the small city of Oświęcim, where today around 40,000 people live, I can't help but notice the normalcy of life here. A home store sells sofas and side tables, a bar advertises Polish beer, and a stone's throw from the perimeter of the most pernicious site in Eastern Europe, locals are carrying on with life. Some even live in the same houses that Nazi officers occupied – including Camp Commander Rudolf Höss – while they embarked on the systematic murder of hundreds of thousands in the gas chambers. Others live in the homes where non-Jewish Polish villagers then lived, trying to ignore the thick smoke and constant glow on the horizon. The two million tourists who flood in every year would certainly boost the economy of Oświęcim and if you ignore Auschwitz I and Auschwitz-II Birkenau, this rural setting with lakes and fields is a very pretty part of the country. But how can you ignore these sites, which reach into your soul?

For me, there is also definitely something extremely unsettling about being among the coachloads lining up in the car park. Holocaust tourism has a tainted, grisly feel, especially when you see people clamouring to pose for photos in front of key landmarks – the watchtower, the gas chambers, the famous 'Arbeit Macht Frei' sign ... But very soon that uneasiness turns into shock, horror and utter disbelief. The other visitors fade into the background as I take in the 'sites' of this permanent memorial, walking in the final footsteps of Felix, Rudolf, Valerie, Eliska and Vera. This is now about finding my family, about refusing to let them be just numbers on a list of those presumed dead. I want answers. Vida provides a staccato commentary of what went on here, and with each monstrous anecdote the faces of my lost relatives appear before my eyes. I trace their experiences around the camp, and the more I discover about their deaths, the more they become vital and alive.

We start at Auschwitz-II Birkenau, the second part of this enormous death camp complex with its multiple sites, and the place where my relatives would have arrived and in all likelihood been killed.

With all the films, the documentaries, the books and the plays, you think you know about Auschwitz and what went on here, but you don't. I didn't.

As in Terezín, the first things I notice are the trees rustling in the feverish wind, fresh with new bright-green leaves, the birds singing brazenly, loud and melodious, and the wildflowers – white and bluebells – peeking through the long grass. What must these plants have seen? Nature seems oblivious and it feels wrong.

The scale of this place is mind-blowing, and the sheer manpower needed to conceive it, build it, operate it and keep all of it hidden from the world unconscionable. This was not the work of one evil despot or even of a group of deluded amoral individuals. So, so many would have been involved in these barbaric acts. What had humanity come to, and how had so many been persuaded that this was the right and just course of action? Even with everything we now know about the Nazi rationale, hatred on such a monumental scale is utterly bewildering – though even as I think on this I realise tragically it still goes on for Jews, for Muslims, for homosexuals.

Walking under and into the central watchtower, which stands almost 15 metres high, the tallest building in the camp, I imagine the SS officers, pistols cocked, sitting up there crowing over their domain, a city of suffering that included at least five of my relatives. They had a large bedroom, toilets and offices in their comfortable observation post, as well as a transformer station connected to the camp fence wires, which were of course electrified to prevent escape. From up here you can see the extent of this camp – it goes on forever. The scale is obscene. With the sun beating down and the sky bright, bright blue, even with the evidence laid out in front of me, I still can't believe it.

Unlike Auschwitz I, a short ride away, which like Terezín was established in existing pre-war barracks, Auschwitz-II Birkenau was completely built for purpose on the site of Brzezinka, a Polish village. The local population was expelled, the houses demolished and 10,000 Soviet prisoners of war brought in to build this city of extermination on 140 hectares of land.

By the time Rudolf Hoffer and his wife Valerie, his sister Eliska and her daughter Vera arrived in December 1943, this place was all set up, with around 300 barracks surrounded by 16 kilometres of barbed-wire fencing. The four gigantic gas chambers were also fully operational, with crematoria attached and fired up, so bodies could be swiftly reduced to dust. The efficiency was breathtaking. This was a killing machine on a scale never before conceived. Arriving here would have felt like drawing up to Jerusalem's valley of Gehenna, the Biblical destination of the wicked, only these internees had done nothing wrong.

The first barracks I see are in a long row, bleak wooden buildings with no openings in the side walls and a row of windows just below the roof line – essentially horse barns, which would have been quick to construct and offered little protection from weather extremes. Behind them is a wilderness of brick chimneys as far as the eye can see, which are all that remain of most of the other barracks on the north side of Birkenau, burned by the Nazis along with much of the camp in an attempt to hide the truth.

Inside each barn are wooden bunks in stacks of three running down both sides, and in the centre a brick stove. In a separate toilet block, rows of holes have been cut into slabs of concrete set above the ground. There was nowhere for the faeces to go but to drop on the floor below and prisoners had to clean out the latrines. The stench would have been powerful. These barracks were, I'm told, for quarantining newly arrived male prisoners, and Vida explains they were really to terrorise prisoners and teach them camp discipline. Here inmates also gained an early introduction to the complete lack of privacy and dignity that drove the psychology of concentration camp ethos.

Later, on the far side of the camp, I discover other sorts of accommodation – brick barracks with bunk beds set into the icy walls, the bottom rung literally on the floor – and I hear that the children in their barracks, with a seemingly charming painting of happy tots on the wall, were actually all eventually murdered. Indeed, this was the fate of the vast majority of all human beings here; the only question was when and how.

At the Family Camp, which from my research I believe is where Eliska and Vera, and probably Rudolf Hoffer – before he was sent to the hospital – and his wife Valerie lived, I hoped to find a little comfort. But it turns out to be a wooden structure similar to the quarantine block, with little to suggest they faced anything other than horror inside.

Through the middle of the camp the train lines scar the ground, a reminder of the constant arrival of more and more prisoners. As an example, a simple railway cart has been positioned, testimony to the conditions the deportees endured. Here, people were treated like animals, which is exactly how the Nazis saw Jews. Originally, trains arrived at the train station in Oświeçim and deportees walked from there to the camp. But these extra train tracks, specially constructed to deliver prisoners direct to the camp, opened in the spring of 1944. Felix would have arrived here, but the rest of my family had walked from the town.

On arrival, deportees were told to leave all their personal belongings on the ramp beside the train. These were collected and stored in a series of warehouses called 'Canada', which Vida tells me was probably a slightly ironic moniker, since Canada was seen as a place of plenty, and here were the riches of an entire race ... Naturally, jobs in 'Canada' were highly sought after, she adds. The property was sorted and much of it sent to the interior of Germany to support the war effort or appropriated by the Nazi officers. Some ended up on an internal black market. At the end of the war, when the Soviet Army liberated Auschwitz, they found warehouses stuffed with hundreds of thousands of men's suits, pieces of children's clothing, more than 800,000 women's outfits and 14,000 pounds of human hair, bundled into batches ready to be sent to textile companies to make carpets and fabric.

The selection process on arrival has been well documented: the commotion, the terror, the brutality and then the finality of being directed to the left or the right by an SS officer, with the power of life and death in one hand gesture. Those loaded onto the trucks hoped they were being shipped out of Birkenau, maybe to the labour camps they had been told they were being sent to. But the trucks took victims straight to the gas chambers. Their fate was sealed.

Those who stayed were marched to the 'Sauna' building. This complex opened in December 1943, and my relatives were probably among those to have passed through here. As deportees on the transports from Theresienstadt that were bound for the Birkenau Family Camp, some of my family would have been spared selection and may have been allowed to keep some of their own clothes. But they wouldn't have escaped the 'Sauna'.

Every part of the Auschwitz journey was designed to degrade, to humiliate and to dehumanise. Tens of thousands arrived at the 'Sauna' to queue up for the Birkenau induction, often waiting for hours in bitter cold or, as I experienced, searing heat.

First the new arrivals would have had their heads shaved. Reports conflict over whether those in the Family Camp had their heads shaved, but if Felix, who arrived in 1944, survived selection, he would certainly have had his head shaved. With bald heads, prisoners would be recognised immediately if they tried to escape, and it also helped prevent head lice. Camp barbers used blunt instruments and worked quickly, so prisoners were often left with painful bloody cuts all over their heads.

Next, the deportees were stripped naked and herded into shower rooms, where disinfectant rained down. Today the 'Sauna' remains as a memorial, with an exhibition space that includes the huge steam ovens that disinfected clothes. It takes a while for me to grasp that this was the very room where in all likelihood my family stood, naked and wet on the concrete floor, exposed to drafts, as they waited, often for several hours, for their clothing. It's unlikely that Rudolf and Valerie, husband and wife, were together, but I am hoping Eliska was holding her daughter Vera tight as they passed through this purgatorial waiting room.

Registration followed and – the final insult – the camp number that would now replace their name was tattooed on their arm. Originally a metal stamp with numbers made up of a series of needles was used. This was stamped into the prisoner's chest and then ink rubbed into the bloody wound. But later a single needle device replaced the stamp, and I think this would have been in use when my family arrived. Also, by this time tattoos were usually made on either the outer side of the left forearm or the inner side of the left upper arm. I wonder if three-year-old Vera would have been tattooed, and later, when I search through reports, I come across the famous photograph of children liberated from Auschwitz holding up their tattooed arms. Yes, Vera was murdered with a tattoo on her little arm.

As I file out of this hovel of humiliation, I stop at walls of beautiful photographs, mementoes from the luggage of the Auschwitz victims. Here are families dressed up in their finest: proud, vital, happy and very much alive. I stare into their eyes, these vibrant groups shining with vivacity, studying each photo intently. Is my family here? Eventually I have to stop. I'm not even sure I would recognise them. While I had found passport photographs of Rudolf and Valerie in the National Archives, I have no idea what Eliska or Vera looked like. Somehow, though, I feel certain I could pick them out ... I long to catch sight of them, something to show they had been here, that they couldn't just disintegrate into thin air without a trace.

Next stop is the gas chambers. I have been steeling myself for this. Again, the fact is much more horrific than the myth, and even as I write this in my calm study at home overlooking our patio garden currently blooming with peace lilies, I am reeling from the memory of what I saw. The chambers were destroyed by the Nazis on 20 January 1945, blown up with dynamite a week before the Soviet Army liberated all of Auschwitz, and what remains is rubble, but enough to build a picture. A chillingly comprehensive floor plan on a sign in front of one of the chambers, plus the detailed model in part of an exhibition in Auschwitz I and a full description from Vida, builds up a picture I can never erase.

Most of those who came here were straight off the transport — filthy, smelly, their legs coated in urine, exhausted, sick and terrified, clinging to each other. A large number of these people had arrived on trucks. They had been told that they were going to labour camps outside Birkenau, and here they would first be disinfected and could wash. It was of course a lie. Others arrived on foot, either marched under guard from transports or selected from inside the camp.

The chambers were underground. This I wasn't prepared for. Victims would queue up, walking down a stone staircase into a subterranean network of chambers. There they were told to remove all of their clothes. In some cases, the disrobing was done outside, and queues of naked people huddled in lines under the command of SS officers, crowding the entrance.

Next, they were told they were going to have a shower, and to add credence they were given soap and a towel. They would carry on walking, thousands herded like sheep, and eventually end up in the gas chambers. Many broke down and started to panic, and screaming could often be heard by those in the barracks and surrounding houses.

In the chambers they could see the pipes above on the ceiling. Some who had heard rumours feared gas would come out of them. Others believed they would be showered with water, some relief after their tortuous journey. But the pipes were just for show. Vida says that the SS often told them to sing through their shower, which many did; this would have hastened their death as they breathed in the gas more swiftly. I can't decide if this was cruel or benevolent.

The doors were bolted shut, and then through hatches in the ceiling, granules of Zyklon B were dropped into metal mesh columns. On hitting the air, the pellets turned to suffocating gas. Usually it took a few minutes for everyone inside to die, the bodies piling on top of each other, and when the doors were opened they would tumble out in a mangled mess.

The Sonderkommando – a 'privileged' group of prisoners tasked with working in the gas chambers – then dragged the corpses out and set about the task of untangling them. They had to cut off the hair from those women who had come directly from the transport, to add to the camp supplies, and remove jewellery and metal dentures. Gold fillings were melted down in a crucible. The bodies were then either burned in the crematoria, which had been built next to the gas chambers for maximum efficiency, or on a pyre. Any bones that didn't burn were ground down into powder before they were added to the ashes. Even so, there was a great deal left of these human beings. The amount of ash produced was substantial and needed to be removed. Some was thrown in the rivers Soła and Vistula, some tossed into nearby ponds and some used to fertilise the surrounding fields or to level uneven ground.

The gas chambers, I'm told, were dismantled on 2 November 1944. When I hear this I immediately pull out my diary where I had recorded the details of the transports that brought my family here. I thought nothing more could shock me, but there it is in black and white. Felix would have been among the last Jews to have been gassed in Birkenau. The majority of the men on his transport of 2038 Jews were sent directly to the gas chambers. Without any other archival reference to Felix, I realise at this moment that my great-uncle's life ended here where I am standing, just two days before gassing ended altogether ...

As I take this in, nearby I am drawn to a series of standing gravestones next to one of the ponds where human ashes were dumped:

To the memory
of the men, women, and children
who fell victim to the Nazi genocide.
Here lie their ashes.
May their souls rest in peace.

I place a stone on top, to mourn Felix, Rudolf, Valerie, Eliska and Vera. Their ashes may have been in here or even under my feet. Even though I still can't pin down incontrovertible proof, in my heart I know that here was where their journey finished. I have found my relatives.

Walking around, not knowing where to turn, I come to another prominent memorial here called the International Monument to the Victims of Fascism in Auschwitz-Birkenau. This is a platform with steps at different levels set among the ruins of the gas chambers and crematoria, its form intended to reference tombs and sarcophagi. Here I lay another stone, reading in bold powerful capital letters:

FOR EVER LET THIS PLACE BE

A CRY OF DESPAIR

AND A WARNING TO HUMANITY,

WHERE THE NAZIS MURDERED

ABOUT ONE AND A HALF

MILLION

MEN, WOMEN, AND CHILDREN,

MAINLY JEWS

FROM VARIOUS COUNTRIES

OF EUROPE.

AUSCHWITZ–BIRKENAU

1940 – 1945

With a heavy heart we leave Auschwitz-II Birkenau and join the queues to visit the permanent exhibition at Auschwitz I.

Here in the former Polish Army garrison I learn of more atrocities, including the horrific experiments of Dr Mengele. I walk under the infamous 'Arbeit Macht Frei' inscription where the letter 'B' was attached upside down, which many believe was an act of resistance to warn prisoners of the duplicity of the slogan. The standing cells, measuring 90 by 90 centimetres, where prisoners who were being punished were incarcerated for five to ten nights and many died, are unspeakably cruel and still figure in my nightmares. And then there was an actual gas chamber and accompanying cremato-rium, the first of its kind in Auschwitz, where Zyklon B was tested and perfected. Many thousands of Jews were murdered here within hours of their arrival.

I stand before the displays of piles of shoes, of human hair woven into bolts of fabric, artificial limbs, suitcases, tin cups, spectacles, all piled up behind glass – horrific tableaux, each telling its own tale of a human life. And then I come to Block 27, and an exhibition dedicated specifically to the Jewish victims of the Holocaust, which was opened in 2013.

It includes a vast Book of Names, an art installation of huge white pages filled with the names of the Jews murdered by Hitler, not just here in Auschwitz, but in camps all over Europe. It feels like a religious book. Each name has the year and place of birth and the place of death. I leaf through the individual sheets, searching, searching and then slowly, as I find each name, here in Auschwitz, the information I had uncovered in Terezín is confirmed. I have found them, my family, all over again, and next to the names of Felix Rieden, Rudolf Hoffer, Valerie Hofferova, Eliska Hofferova and Vera Hofferova is written 'Murdered in Auschwitz Birkenau'. This is my proof.

At the end of the Book of Names are blank pages for victims still to be found.

As we drive back to Prague, I ponder this demonic blueprint for mass murder, the most effective episode of ethnic cleansing ever seen. Nearly six million Jews were annihilated in the Holocaust, 78,150 from the Nazi Protectorate of Bohemia and Moravia – which had been Czechoslovakia before the Nazis invaded. Today there are only around 3900 Jews in the Czech Republic and around 2600 in Slovakia.

In many ways it worked.

Except here I am . . .

And I still have high hopes for my great-uncle Josef Hoffer, my great-aunt Anna and her husband Samuel Ungermann. Their names were not on the list. The wartime Riedens and Hoffers were not completely extinguished.

PART III

NEW BEGINNINGS

CHAPTER ELEVEN

THE FORGOTTEN KINDERTRANSPORT

As I return to Prague filled with the horror of Auschwitz, I realise how resourceful and courageous my grandparents were in organising my father's escape. Aside from the difficulty of actually securing a place on this risky and controversial airlift with an organisation they knew nothing about, there was the paperwork to organise and pay for in a nation in freefall with Hitler banging on its door. Add to this the emotional anguish of waving goodbye to their only child, and I am starting to appreciate the gravity of their actions. But with that supreme sacrifice, Rudolf and Helena ensured the future of our family.

When I had told Tomáš Fedorovič, the historian in Terezín, about my father's remarkable journey with the BMJ his eyes lit up. Tomáš immediately recognised the 'Mission', but he said he had only just heard about it in the past few weeks. Before that he'd had no idea the BMJ even existed and certainly no clue that the organisation flew Jewish children out of Czechoslovakia. This, he said, was a 'kindertransport' that was hidden, a secret mission that no one in his world – that is the world of Czech Holocaust history – knew about.

Here at last was a benevolent transport, and talking about it lifted our moods on that difficult day in Tomáš's office in Terezín. The story of Reverend Davidson's rescue had been uncovered in a brand-new documentary film that had only just aired on Czech national television. It was called *Barbican: A Forgotten Mission* and was all about the flights that included Dad's escape. Tomáš had been astonished by the film and was fascinated to hear that my father was one of those children. He told me the name of the documentary maker was Jiří František Potužník, a former journalist, and that the film followed Jiří's journey as he tracked down some of those children as adults and interviewed them about their memories of the airlift.

As I sit in my hotel room in Prague I know I have to find this filmmaker and I start making enquiries. In the end I speak to two Jiřís – father and son, both with the same names, who had both worked on the film, although it was Jiří senior who conceived the film and wrote it. Miraculously, his office is in central Prague, just a short walk from my hotel. He agrees to meet me and fortuitously he speaks perfect English. If I believed in a god, I would suspect some divine intervention was at play at this juncture.

Jiří's office is in one of the grand old buildings of Prague in a beautiful square. There has just been a blackout when I visit, plunging the dusty rooms into complete darkness. Everyone is leaving, so Jiří and I agree to meet later in a restaurant nearer to his home. Jiří is a very busy man, currently working on a government expo. He spent five years making the film and tells me it was something of a hobby. He's charming and intelligent, and was clearly utterly consumed and affected by his discovery of the BMJ transport. He says finding the children was incredibly difficult, and although he had amassed a great deal of material from a range of sources in Israel, Prague, Canada and the UK, which included the records of my father, Hanus Rieden, he hadn't managed to trace my brothers and me. So he is very excited to hear what I can tell him about my father's experience. He had, however, managed to talk to Aunt Annalisa for the film at her home in North London. And, as it happens, our meeting is mutually beneficial, since he has also uncovered some fascinating information about the airlift that fills in a lot of the gaps in my research.

Jiří had originally stumbled upon the story when he was working on a book about Prague's national airport. The facility had been seized by the Luftwaffe during Hitler's occupation of Prague and was turned into a Nazi military base. Consequently, while there were books of records of the incoming and outgoing flights up to 1938, there was very little information from the period of occupation. This material was either destroyed or taken away by the Third Reich. But one photograph that dropped out of the files captivated Jiří.

It was a black-and-white photo with a date of 12 January 1939 written on the back, taken just two months before Hitler occupied Czechoslovakia, and was one of very few photos of the airport from this era. Staring out of the photo was of a small boy, very young, in a striped cap and thick coat, in the arms of a foreign pilot with a second pilot standing in the background. The lad looked lost, anxious and vulnerable, but the pilot was smiling and caring. Jiří was intrigued – what was going on here?

As he investigated further, Jiří realised that this little boy was actually known the world over. He was the same child who had appeared in a famous photo of Sir Nicholas Winton, used to illustrate the Englishman's lauded 'Kindertransport' mission from Czechoslovakia. The assumption was always that this child was part of Winton's exodus, which involved transporting Czech Jewish children by train out of the Nazi Protectorate of Bohemia and Moravia before war broke out, to the safety of foster homes in the UK, where they were granted temporary residence as refugees.

When Jiří compared his photo from the file with the famous photo of Nicholas Winton holding the little boy, he realised they were taken at the same time. And when I compare Jiří's photo with the one I have of my father walking up the aeroplane steps to leave Prague, I can see that the second pilot in the shot is the same man. Although Dad's flight left in March and this was January, they clearly involved the same team of people.

In Prague especially, Sir Nicholas Winton is a hero. In 2014 he was awarded the highest Czech state decoration, the order of the White Lion. When he died, aged 106, in 2015, mourners paid their respects with a vigil of thousands of candles laid by the memorial statue of him at the main railway station. It depicts a young Winton with a child in his arms and a young girl by his side.

But what was Nicholas Winton doing at Prague airport that day? Could he also have been involved in Reverend Davidson's BMJ evacuation?

This was the starting point for Jiří's film, which then developed into a full-blown investigation into the BMJ. He flew to England to talk to Nicholas Winton, scoring a rare interview some months before his death. Sir Nicholas said he had very little memory of the incident and confirmed that this was nothing to do with his own 'Kindertransport', underlining that in January he still had no authority to bring Czech children to the UK.

But when I later catch up with his daughter Barbara Winton, she tells me that this photograph was taken during the time her stockbroker father was in Prague over the Christmas period in 1938–39. It was then that he had first realised the desperate need to save Jewish children from Hitler. He had started looking into what he could to do to help, and this was probably when he came across the BMJ team.

'On January 12, my father had been in Prague for two weeks and he'd been seeing all the different organisations and what they were trying to do, and what I understood was that he was helping in some way – either because he was working with the British Committee for Refugees from Czechoslovakia or just because he'd been at various committees over the city,' explains Barbara. 'So he was helping with the logistics of these children and families going to the airport and getting on the planes. He never really explained what that entailed and he was always rather vague about it, but I was assuming that he just offered to help in a personal capacity, which meant that he was somehow at the airport when all this filming took place.'

I suspect the 'vagueness' Barbara Winton is referring to may have had something to do with the religious nature of the BMJ. Sir Nicholas was always very clear that he had no hand in converting any of the Jewish children he saved, that this was never part of his intention. In an interview with him in the United States Holocaust Memorial Museum archive, Sir Nicholas says he only found out later that the BMJ was in existence 'merely to convert good Jews into good Christians', adding that 'it didn't really alarm me very much because after all they were saved. And I thought the most important thing was to save the children rather than save the religion.'

In a scrapbook of Sir Nicholas Winton's notes and letters on his website I find Winton's description of the exodus, which gives more explanation of his own involvement. It is from a diary note made on 12 January 1939:

The first party of children today left Prague. This was fixed up by the Barbican Mission to the Jews in London and transport was arranged by us. Being the first lot of kids to leave Czechoslovakia it aroused much attention and cinema men and journalists were much in evidence. I myself was photographed in different positions, holding, leading and helping the children. From the K.L.M. office in Prague the entire convoy was taken out in several buses to the airport. Here for over 1½ hours there was a mixture of complete chaos, high excitement and passionate adieus. Every child seemed to have about 10 relations judging by the number of people there. They all wished to be near the children up to the very last moment and the scenes as the children finally left were heartrending . . . posing as a journalist, I was actually able to accompany the children onto the flight and into the plane. This of course the parents were not allowed to do, but the final adieus, being made at a distance of some 50 yards, were all the more pathetic. I did not see one of the kids crying. They were far too excited.

As Jiří tried to track down the origin of the photo he hit gold in the archives of the United States Holocaust Memorial Museum, based in Washington. Here he discovered a film of the BMJ's first airlift in January, complete with a note from the cameraman, Julius Jonak:

Today at the aerodrome at Ruzyne nearly 30 child refugees took leave of their parents. Two Dutch Douglas airplanes brought them to Rotterdam and from there to London. This is the charitable work of the Barbican Mission of London under the direction of Reverend Wallner. He intends to give 60 children altogether a new home in

London where they will remain until their 18th year. The youngest of these children is only two and a half years old. The eldest one, 11 years old. The leave taking was grievous, nobody was untouched seeing the tears of the remaining parents who will not see again their children for many long years. Before starting the pilot said: 'Never in my life have I had such a responsibility. My lord – 30 children!' Five hours later I get the news that airplanes are well landed in London.

Reverend Wallner was the Polish cleric who had helped Reverend Davidson organise the children's evacuation. The Mission must have notified the local press, which filmed the airlift, and when I look at my photographs of my father leaving, and of Rudolf and Helena with him on the bus that took them to the airport, I realise that these were also professional photos, probably taken by a news outlet.

After talking to Jiří, I conducted my own search in the Washington archive, where I scrutinised this film hoping there may be a second reel of my father's airlift. I drew a blank. But this original 80-year-old film stopped me in my tracks. With snow on the ground, the children all gather around the plane, largely bewildered but excited, about to embark on a thrilling journey. Their parents are frantically waving from behind a barrier. One desperately kisses her child goodbye; all are trying to keep their emotions in check and stay cheery and stoic. Inside the plane, the little faces stare out of the tiny windows and then they are gone, leaving their families stunned in a huddle, turning in circles as they leave for home, most never to see their children again.

In his documentary, Jiří talks to Inge Plitzka at her home in London. Inge was nine years old when she flew on that very plane with her older sister Helga. She was originally from

Vienna in Austria and talks about how, with her pretty blonde pigtails and snub nose, one minute she was the school favourite and then as soon as they discovered she had Jewish blood, no one would talk to her. Inge's grandfather in Prague had heard about 'an English religious organisation taking Jewish or half-Jewish children back to London'. Her mother immediately found the Mission and said, 'Will you please take my two little girls?' Inge says Reverend Davidson pointed out that 'we would be in a Christian environment, not a Jewish environment'.

Inge remembers arriving at the airport for the flight: 'We had one suitcase each,' she says, 'and we were all allowed one toy to put in the suitcase.' It has a horrible echo of the Nazi transports, only these children were reunited with their luggage and keepsakes.

I wonder what toy my father took with him.

The little boy in the photo that had started Jiří's journey was called Hansi Beck. He was the youngest to be evacuated and Inge remembers him well. 'Originally Hansi Beck's mother contacted Mr Davidson and said, "Will you take my child?" and he said "I can't do that" (because he was too young at not yet three years old). And then he said that "God had told him yes you can",' adds Inge. So Hansi was given a place on the plane.

People had queued for hours outside the Mission office in Prague. One of these, Jiří discovered, was the famous writer Ruth Bondy. Ruth was a 15-year-old and told Jiří that she had been sent by her family to queue up for a place on the transport, but eventually gave up and went home, lying to her mother that the doors had closed. It was a terrible mistake by Ruth, who did survive the Holocaust, but was sent to Theresienstadt and then to Bergen-Belsen, horrific experiences she describes in her books.

Inge has no memory at all of saying goodbye to her parents but says when she arrived at the Mission home in England and realised what had happened she 'cried and cried'. Slowly she got used to it and ended up a fervent Christian, which is very much part of who she is today, unlike many of the other Mission children I have met.

When the children's home, which was in Kent, on the flight path to London, was bombed by Nazi fighter planes, the children were lucky. Annalisa had already told me about this incident, which she recalls vividly: 'The Germans dropped two bombs together. The idea was to drop an oil bomb and then the incendiary would follow and make the oil catch fire. But what happened there was they dropped the oil bomb, which broke, spreading oil everywhere, but the incendiary bomb didn't go off. It dropped on the garage next to the house. If it had caught fire we would have burned with it. You can imagine what prayers we had that night.'

It was after this that the Mission decided they had to evacuate the children to a safer part of England, but finding another home during wartime was not easy. In Mrs Davidson's publication *For a Future and a Hope: The Story of the Houses of Refuge in Chislehurst*, she explains what happened next:

One terrible night the Girls' Home was struck by a bomb. We began to question the advisability of seeking refuge in the country. This looked an almost impossible proposition. It seemed that all the large houses had already been commandeered either by schools or for Government purposes and by the time that we were sure that such a move was really God's intention for us, to find anything that could meet our requirements appeared out of the question. We wrote to and visited many house agents and took many a fruitless journey, but always with the conviction that God had His plan and would guide us most surely in the right direction. 'Your Heavenly Father knoweth that ye have need of all these things'; how gloriously we have proved that, step by step in all the way, and in this also.

We had almost decided on one house which, though in no way to our liking, seemed the only possibility when another [Craddock House] was offered to us at a very moderate rent, beautifully situated in Devonshire. The decision had to be made very quickly and, as the owners were still in the house when we saw it and we were only permitted a very hurried inspection, we were not able to take in by any means all its points or to realise quite the state of dilapidation in which it was. Nevertheless we have never doubted that this refuge was indeed God's provision for us and in spite of difficulties that have at times seemed insurmountable our stay here has been wonderfully happy and blessed.

Prayer and faith in God powered the Davidsons throughout their extraordinary mission to save Jewish children, and in most cases it seemed to come through for them. In England, Jiří talked to a Mike Moore, who then worked for CWI, the organisation the BMJ later joined and which now stores the archives for the BMJ. Mr Moore explained that when Reverend Davidson decided he wanted to put his rescue plan together to save Jewish children in Prague, he was rightly concerned about how it would be funded. Then a Christian businessman came forward and offered to pay personally for 50 children to be brought over to England. It was donations like this, plus funds from Reverend Davidson's preaching, that paid for the airlift. But that wasn't the only cost.

I ask Jiří if he knew whether the parents of the children also donated money. He tells me there are no records to prove this, but it is possible. In order to enter the UK, each child needed to pay a £50 're-emigration surety' into a government fund. This was government policy for all Jewish refugee children arriving at that time, and was intended to pay for the child to be sent back to Czechoslovakia once the war was over. Jiří discovered in the CWI archive that there was one Australian called Sydney Jacobs (whom I have been unable to locate), who paid this bond for 50 of the children. He says there were also donations from volunteers, and adds that families may also have pooled their resources. One organisation that may have helped is the British Fund for Refugees from Czechoslovakia, with which Nicholas Winton worked closely.

Fifty pounds was a considerable amount at that time, equivalent to approximately £3000 today, and I wonder what happened to that money, which in almost every case was not used for re-emigration, since the parents of these children were murdered in the Holocaust. Despite searching the archives of the British refugee bodies, I can find no reference to this surety, nor can I find anything to suggest that my father received this money after the war.

═════

After talking to Jiří, I am excited by the prospect of my own imminent visit to the BMJ archives in the CWI offices in England. But before I leave Prague I want to pay my respects at the grave in the New Jewish Cemetery, where I have been told my great-grandmother Emma – who is listed in the cemetery records as Emilie – Rieden and her son, my grandfather Rudolf, are buried together. I thought that his wife, my grandmother, Helena must also be buried there, but apparently not.

The New Jewish Cemetery was established in 1891 to relieve the space problem at the Old Jewish Cemetery, next to the Pinkas Synagogue where my search for my family began. It is a huge place with space for around 100,000 graves, some of which are works of art and include the grave of famous Czech novelist Franz Kafka. Jews do not traditionally cremate their dead, so graveyard space is at a premium.

The site's management tells me that Dr Rudolf Rieden is in grave number 028 in row number 013, section number 026, and at the gate I am given a diagram denoting the layout. There is no elaborate tombstone for Emilie, I am informed, but she and Rudolf are in the same grave, and to help guide me I am sent a photo of a gravestone.

It's a daunting site and very overgrown in places, but after walking for half an hour through rows of graves I finally come to the place where my relatives' stone should be. I find the gravestone whose photo I was sent, but the name etched on the masonry is not Rudolf's but someone called Olga. Indeed, there is nothing here at all to say that my relatives are buried here. Exhausted and crestfallen, I message the management, who a couple of months later tell me they are sorry, the photo wasn't of the actual gravestone, just the site of the burial.

I later read that in the Czech Republic relatives rent graves – you can't just buy a plot for eternity – and that once the money stops, which would no doubt have happened when Helena died, the graves are sold to someone else. Bodies are exhumed and buried in mass graves, and often gravestones are dismantled. I can't find out if this happened to Emma and Rudolf; the cemetery management is keener to suggest that I might like to pay for a new headstone.

On the metro train back to the hotel, my afternoon gets worse when I am grabbed by two very officious guards who take my passport from me and pull me off the train. At the station I purchased a ticket and followed the directions of the ticket seller to the platform. It turns out I was also supposed to validate the ticket in a machine. The guard demands an on-the-spot fine, and when I don't have enough cash he grabs my arm and manhandles me to the ATM. My Australian card won't work in the machine, so the guard says he is calling the police to arrest me.

When, extremely distressed, I try to explain that I am here to find out what happened to my Jewish relatives who were killed in the Holocaust, he and his fellow guards start to laugh. And in that moment of knee-jerk anti-Semitism, I get a tiny taste of what my family endured. Eventually the guard relents and takes all the Czech money I have in my purse, which is a few cents short.

CHAPTER TWELVE

NOT IN OUR BACKYARD

The CWI offices are now located in a rather faceless industrial estate in Eynsham, just outside Oxford in England's south. I have an afternoon to go through the archives, and my brother Nick comes with me to help. He has already been sifting through our family photo albums and official documents, looking for any clues that may shine a light on our father's time with the Mission, especially addressing my question of how Helena and Rudolf may have funded both Dad's escape and his education. As the eldest, Nick is the keeper of all things official, but he has found no relevant paperwork in our own family files. We hope we might have more luck at the CWI.

On the way over, Nick and I discuss what I have uncovered so far. Nick, who like my mother is deeply practical and also a keen historian, is eager to be as useful as possible, and asks what exactly we are looking for. This is hard to pinpoint, since I have no idea what may be there, but I think a key aim is to find out how our father's schooling was funded and if our grandparents paid the Mission for his evacuation. I also want to get more of an idea of who these missionaries were and what sort of life Dad experienced there.

We are a little hampered by a minor car accident Nick has en route before he picks me up. A huge freight truck drives into the side of his rather swish car and while it's drivable, the insurance company keeps calling for extra details, which means by the time we arrive at the CWI we are slightly late and feeling pretty harassed.

The archives are essentially the contents of a storeroom at the back of a small network of offices. Following a fire, many of the early handwritten books of detailed minutes, which date back to 1891 when the BMJ was first formed, are both heavily charred and water-damaged, which means some of the history has been lost, but their contents still prove revelatory.

Here Nick and I hole up. We have free rein to search through the one box of files left that relate specifically to the Czech children who were brought over on the airlift, and the charity's Executive Committee minutes, publications and paperwork from that era.

The people who work here are kind and helpful and still dedicated to guiding Jews to Jesus. Not having had a great deal of exposure to missionaries, I wasn't sure what to expect, but I could see that whatever preconceptions I may have harboured, the staff were deeply committed to their vocation. Nevertheless, it does seem inconceivable to me that such an organisation can still exist, especially considering Jewish sensibilities following the Holocaust. But far from face oblivion, the group has expanded, with outlets thriving all over the world.

In its literature, the CWI talks of 'Hebrew Christians', who they believe are everywhere. These are Jews from all walks of life who 'are quickened by the Spirit of all grace, convinced of their sin and guilt. They are at the feet of Jesus, and enabled to say with every believer, "We have redemption through the atoning blood of Jesus, even the forgiveness of our sins".' Essentially, the Jews are being blamed for killing Jesus (himself a Jew, a fact that seems to escape them, as does the fact that Pilate was Roman) and the CWI is on hand to offer redemption.

It's a curious dogma, and this teaching still feels unconscionably inappropriate to me. From the archives, I discovered that I am not alone in my criticism of their work. Indeed, there has always been opposition and much of it quite forceful.

To be fair, the BMJ and now the CWI takes such hostility on the chin and hasn't shied away from recording it in its publications or fighting their corner. As far as they're concerned it's all part of God's test, and they are more than ready to rise to the challenge.

'To the world we appear fanatics, interfering with the religious conviction of others,' writes Mrs Davidson in her second publication [*Homes for Children*], talking about the organisation's rescue of the Czech Jewish refugees. '"So you entice Jews to become Gentiles," a gentleman sneeringly remarked to me the other day, while there is misunderstanding and something very like reproach from many so-called Christians . . . the way will never be smooth or easy . . . but we can and do praise God often,' Mrs Davidson continues.

In the BMJ's June 1939 edition of *Immanuel's Witness*, the organisation's monthly magazine, I come across a piece by Reverend Wallner. This was the cleric I had seen in the film footage of the first batch of Czech children flying out of Prague. Evidently Wallner ran the Polish BMJ office and also worked in the Czech office. In an editorial probably written just after Wallner had helped put my father on the final plane out of Prague in March that year, the Reverend is triumphant.

'"O sing unto the Lord a new song; for He hath done marvellous things." These words of praise that rejoiced the heart of the Psalmist, were the key words that marked out work during the past year,' he writes. 'We were brought in close touch with thousands of Jewish seeking souls, to whom we have delivered the message of salvation, the Holy Spirit bearing witness to the truth of the message. Vast numbers were convinced of the truth, and found grace in believing, and were saved through faith.'

There's something distasteful about the way Reverend Wallner was rubbing his hands with glee and crowing as terrified Jews flooded through his doors to convert. If God was working in mysterious ways, it almost feels as if he may have been colluding with the Nazis, bartering for Jewish souls who push their religious conviction to one side in the vain hope that going on the record as a Christian will save their skin. In the end, such conversions meant nothing, for it was Jewish blood Hitler was interested in eradicating, but it didn't stop the BMJ from proselytising.

And while he may have been away from prying eyes in Eastern Europe, Wallner's work was not going unnoticed by official Christian authorities. In the minutes from a BMJ Executive Committee meeting on 5 January 1939, I discover mention of a written complaint against Reverend Wallner from a Reverend R. Smith of the Church of Scotland, 'who accused Mr Wallner of Church irregularities and threatened exposure'.

The committee decided that an interview with the Bishop of Fulham should be sought 'at the earliest possible date' to try to mitigate the situation. This issue is picked up again in the 9 March 1939 minutes. It seems the BMJ was having issues being officially recognised by the Church of England.

What's more, following the meeting with the Bishop of Fulham, it transpired that Wallner was not actually a minister at all; he needed to 'apply direct to the Bishop of Fulham' for ordination.

The brazen hypocrisy of the BMJ's work seems to have been totally lost on Wallner, who naively reports his progress with unabashed pride and joy. In June 1937, he says, the Czech office baptised five converts, in November that year a further six, and in March 1938:

> Twenty Jewish men and women ... were baptised in the Name of the Lord Jesus. By the end of July that year fifty candidates were ready for baptism.
>
> But when the troubles came upon Czechoslovakia, and that unfortunate country had to cede the best part of her territory and give up the main sources of her wealth, we were by this time dealing with about 15,000 Jews who not only gladly listened to the message but were honestly seeking the Way of Salvation. It came upon us like a flood.

The numbers make for sobering reading. Czech Jews were in a high state of panic, and they were right to be.

The BMJ team certainly milked it, working day and night to get through the backlog of potential converts, but they didn't cut corners. Each candidate was made to attend lengthy instruction sessions and 'write the story of their conversion', which had to be approved by Wallner, one of his staff or Reverend Davidson himself. These men of God needed to be convinced that their newly minted born-again Christians 'were true believers in the Lord Jesus'.

Wallner went on to say that after seeing the light and joining their flock, many then went back to their homes in the provinces to 'spread the Gospel'. Of course, what they were really spreading was the idea that in converting with the BMJ, Jews might escape the anti-Semitic laws being introduced. 'As a result, we received many letters, vast numbers of people pleading with us that we should send them missionaries; that they too desire to be baptised.'

Wallner was especially satisfied when relatives of 'the famous Rabbi Low [sic], to whose memory there stands a statue in the City of Prague', walked through the door. This was a real trophy for the BMJ. Rabbi Loew, known as the Maharal of Prague in the 1600s, is considered the most important rabbi of all time for Czech Jews, and is buried at the Old Jewish Cemetery in a very impressive grave where Jews pay homage.

In the minutes of the BMJ's Executive Committee from a meeting in November 1938, Reverend Davidson describes the work in Czechoslovakia and reports on a Sunday-morning service when he addressed 'a congregation numbering between five and six hundred of the professional type of the people', adding that 'a large number of them are now doing their part in supporting the work financially by the Collection [money donated by parishioners] and gifts'. He adds that there were 'some 20,000 people, refugees and residents, who could muster a collective amount of a half million pounds and were anxious to leave the country if they could take their capital with them'.

This explains some of my questions about how the BMJ financed both the airlift itself and then the subsequent care of the children. The Jews knocking on their Prague office door were rich and prepared to pay for their 'salvation'.

The BMJ must also have sought help, and maybe even funds, from the various British refugee organisations. Since

Chamberlain all but handed over Czechoslovakia to Hitler, there was a knee-jerk reaction of guilt that manifested itself in relaxed British government refugee policy. The end result was that visas would be granted for Jewish and 'non-Aryan' (mostly Christian) children to seek refuge and education in Britain until such time as it was safe for them to return to their homeland. While quotas were vague, it seems around 10,000 were to be accommodated. Funds would come from official charities and religious organisations; these could work with the Children's Inter-Aid Committee (a charity supported by donations from private individuals, synagogues and the very active Women's Appeal for German and Austrian Women and Children), which had been authorised by the British government Home Office to issue the necessary passports, visas and paperwork.

Later, as the number of refugee organisations keen to help children facing Nazi persecution burgeoned, a new body called the Movement for the Care for Children from Germany was also set up to take over much of the increased weight of paperwork. Charities and bodies that sought to 'save' these children had to guarantee that they would be financially responsible for them until age 18, after which time the refugees would re-emigrate to rejoin their families. 'Transmigrants', as they were called, were not permitted to work in Britain, so local jobs would not be at risk. And in an additional measure to assuage opposition from the many Britons critical of opening their borders to a flood of refugees, from 1 March 1939, further government policy stipulated that a £50 bond must be raised against each child, which would be banked as a surety to fund later re-emigration.

This policy inevitably meant that most children who managed to get to Britain came from wealthy families with the means to find such a sum, although ultimately some were funded by donors or concerned refugee organisations. At no point did the British government consider that offering safe haven to whole families might be a more humanitarian option – an idea that still causes First World governments to shudder, even as they continue to lock would-be refugee parents in detention camps separate from their children, needlessly traumatising both parties.

When the first batch of refugee children was flown out of Prague in January 1939, Reverend Wallner says 'even the most noted journalists were at the aerodrome'. The photographs hit the daily newspapers and the film was played in America. 'Everybody talked about the Barbican Mission.' And while he notes that London Jewry showed 'opposition and jealousy', he adds that 'the Jews of Czechoslovakia are most thankful and grateful for all that is being done to rescue their children'.

The Executive Committee's handwritten minute books paint a picture of the BMJ battling against opposition from all sides – the Christian Church, British Jews, the local community in Chislehurst where the BMJ eventually managed to purchase two houses for children's homes, and the other refugee organisations.

On 5 January 1939, just seven days before the first group of children was due to arrive, Reverend Davidson reported that there was 'a certain amount of opposition by neighbours to the house being used for the purpose intended'. The issue had been submitted to the Town Planning Committee and 'consequently the purchase of the house has been held up ... Meanwhile, it was stated that arrangements had been made for the boys to be lodged in Christ Church Parish Room; some of the girls in Naomi Home, and the remainder in the Girls' Hostel.'

I follow this opposition later in the newspaper archive in the British Library reading room, where it was clear a huge 'NIMBY' (not in my backyard) battle ensued. This was not about the BMJ and their dubious religious conversions, but revealed an alarming degree of anti-Semitism on the ground in Kent at the time.

A letter printed in the *Chislehurst & Kentish Times* on 20 January 1939 was signed by 31 landlords and residents of Lubbock Road. This was where the BMJ was hoping to purchase the home of Seven Trees, adjacent to Christ Church, to house the Czech refugee children. The ugly statement had also been forwarded to the local council in advance of a Sunday public meeting that had been urgently called.

Dear Sir

Your readers in the locality affected will be interested in the following activity protesting against the invasion of foreigners.

'We the undersigned property-owners and ratepayers strongly protest to the Council against the proposed use of Seventrees [sic], Lubbock Road, as a home for foreign refugees.

It will greatly depreciate the sale value, amenities and rate-able value of all the property in Lubbock Road and adjoining neighbourhood. Both house and garden are wholely [sic] unsuitable for such a purpose and quite inadequate for the fifty children and requisite attendants.

. . . We, property-owners and ratepayers, claim the right of protection by the Council of our interest and consider that the residential district of Chislehurst is totally unsuitable for the purpose suggested.'

I am naturally one of the signatories and while I agree with the principle of giving shelter to selected foreigners from reigns of terror and cruelty, at the same time we must not forget our own children have the first right of protection and help in adversity . . . we cannot become a nursery for all the world's troubles and deplorable incidents . . .

We Britishers deserve and pay for the right to have and live in our homes in peace without foreign incursion that would not only ruin our amenities but jeopardise our hard-earned financial stake, represented in a little piece of English land, bricks and mortar.

Sandy Ridge, Lubbock Road, Chislehurst.

PS When these foreign children grow up it would give the dictator from their country of origin enough excuse to demand annexation of the country they reside in. That is how minorities occur, and this is not even fantastic in present-day foreign politics.

Unpleasant though this letter is, the Davidsons admirably held their nerve, appealing for help in the form of furniture and donations. This was supported by the Vicar at Christ Church, who pleaded, 'No work could be more important than saving these children, soul and body.' A great deal was made of the children being 'non-Aryan' and of them now being raised as Christians, as if this was somehow less problematic than if they had still been practising Jews.

By February 1939, Reverend Davidson was happy to report that the purchase of the house had gone through, and in the BMJ committee meeting announces that, a 'friend' had given the sum of £2250 (equivalent to approximately £143,000 today) to the Mission for the purchase of the house and that 'the local opposition broke down – 20 voting in favour of granting permission . . . three opposing'. But this wasn't the only battle for the BMJ. Mrs Davidson noted 'particular difficulties with which the work is now faced in regard to

the opposition of the Inter-aid Committee and their determination to remove all unbaptised children from the Homes'.

On 9 May 1939, Sir Charles Stead, the executive director of
the aforementioned Movement for the Care of Children from
Germany wrote a stern letter to the BMJ that was recorded
in the Executive Committee minutes. Water damage means
that some of the letter is illegible, but below is what I can
decipher, and it's pretty clear the committee has taken a very
dim view of the BMJ's plan to convert these Jewish refugees
to Christianity:

Dear Mr Davidson
Our discussion last Friday between both you and ourselves
to clear up the question of the Refugee children brought
over under our . . . and now in the care of the Barbican
Mission. As explained to you, my Committee decided . . .
we ought to remove the children who came . . . and had
not been baptized before arrival . . . glad to hear from you
when it is convenient . . . you to hand over these children.
I also explained to you that if . . . make arrangements that
only children . . . already been baptized are received . . . there
should be no further difficulties or misunderstandings . . .
Yours sincerely
C. Stead

Reverend Davidson was incensed by the command from
Stead. As far as the BMJ committee was concerned, these
children had been handed into their care by parents who
were fully aware that their children would now be raised
in a Christian environment, and that spiritual care was no
business of Stead's organisation. The movement Stead headed,
though well regarded, was not a government body, so had no

jurisdiction over the BMJ. While it may well have found the Mission's work reprehensible, it was not illegal.

This was the letter the BMJ sent back a week later:

Dear Sir Charles Stead,

My Committee has considered the subject matter of your letter of the 9th at a meeting this morning, specially called for the purpose, and regret they cannot comply with the request contained in the second paragraph of such letter.

Yours faithfully

I.E. Davidson

But the opposition didn't stop there. According to the 9 September 1939 committee meeting minutes, Mrs Winton (Nicholas Winton's mother, who was the chief organiser of her son's Kindertransports, and worked on the British Committee for the Care of Refugee Children from Czechoslovakia at Bloomsbury House in London) had apparently written to Sir Thomas Inskip, a former politician who at this time was the Lord Chancellor. She wrote that Winton's committee 'were not prepared to hand over any children to the Barbican Mission as they did not consider that institution suitable for the reception of refugee children'.

As I mentioned earlier, Aunt Annalisa and her brother Theo had actually arrived on one of Nicholas Winton's trains. Their mother, Eleonore, had a friend in England who knew of the BMJ and Reverend Davidson's work, and had specifically asked that her children be placed there. Eleonore was intending to follow her children to England, and when she managed to get her children a place on the Winton train she was also feverishly trying to arrange an exit visa with the newly arrived Nazi authorities. Eleonore didn't want her children raised by a foster family she didn't know, and felt they would be better served in the Mission. In Eleonore's application to the Mission in the BMJ archives, she wrote that she had already secured a position as a cook with a Mrs Edwards in Gloucestershire. Clearly, she was hoping to join Annalisa and Theo, and probably find a way for them all to live together as a family again. Tragically, Eleonore never made it over. She died in the Łódź concentration camp. From Mrs Winton's letter I imagine Annalisa and Theo were the last Kindertransport children placed with the Mission.

As far as Mrs Davidson was concerned, this lack of acceptance of the BMJ seriously hampered their work and prevented them from saving more Jewish children; but to anyone not in accord with her argument, the righteousness of the BMJ's tone is pretty stupefying, and could be seen as their own unique brand of anti-Semitism.

In the July 1939 issue of the organisation's magazine *Immanuel's Witness*, the editorial stated:

> Our numbers were recently enriched by nine more children, six boys and three girls ... At present we suffer from a powerful attack upon our work from the Jewish headquarters. For given reasons, we think it wiser not to publish details ... Meanwhile about 40 children are waiting out here, and anxious parents writing daily, asking when their children will be taken into safety. In one case, two Hebrew Christian children, both under 10 years of age. The parents were obliged to leave for South Africa, and on our promise to accept the children into our Home, left them in Prague. We have applied for permits, application forms accompanied by baptismal certificates. These applications were turned down, on account of our spiritual work. In our estimation, the Jews

should be the last people in the world either to persecute, or discriminate, yet their attitude towards those that differ from them is regrettable. We do invite earnest concentrated prayer for those that persecute our work, and the parents with children in Prague.

It seems the BMJ's access to entry permits was halted – probably as a result of Sir Christopher Stead's complaints – and my father's airlift was the last they organised, even though they had further plans. More children could definitely have been saved, but the organisation's unguarded opportunism ultimately proved its downfall. Lucy Davidson found the reaction of the authorities difficult to take, and she discussed it further in her publication *Homes for Children*:

> During the war years the great majority of the children were refugees. At the close of hostilities, the need for a place of refuge for orphaned or homeless Jewish children was as great or greater than ever; but by this time the authorities were thoroughly awake to the nature and aim of the work we were doing, and every avenue that we explored to reach either groups or individual children for whom our help was solicited, was successfully frustrated. This is one of the apparent victories of the Enemy of souls for which we can give no explanation now.

The 68 children the Reverend and Mrs Davidson and their disciples had saved were not handed over to the authorities, and from the rest of the minutes and reports, and from first-hand accounts, it seems the children were well looked after. Many were baptised, though in my father's case this baptism happened age 13, not 16 as promised.

Meanwhile, back in Czechoslovakia, Reverend Wallner continued his work. In the 6 July 1939 Executive Committee minutes, the director reports that 'Mr Wallner is still there' and the children are still queueing up. 'The Mission Hall had been closed ever since the Germans had entered Prague and meetings for Jews forbidden, but the work was being carried on in the Mission flat which has been secured for three months. It was decided to watch further developments.' Later in the same minutes, it notes that Reverend Davidson has had an interview with Sir Thomas Inskip to discuss further permits to bring children over but that the 'Jewish Authorities' were 'opposed to the work of the Mission'. While this reaction from Jewish elders is completely understandable, the sad truth is that the Mission could have saved the lives of more Jewish children.

I am unsure what happened to Reverend Wallner. In the minutes it states that the director is having extreme difficulty 'making contact with workers on the Continent'. The Mission meetings were eventually shut down by the Nazis in Prague and the landlord came around to collect the furniture. Meanwhile, Wallner, his family and staff were trying to organise visas to come to England.

═══

The next thing I turn to is the box of individual files that includes my father's. Of course, I have already seen the copy of this that John Ross sent me, but holding the documents – especially Dad's passport, the Christmas card he made as a young boy, his letters and Rudolf and Helena's letters – brings a sense of completion to my journey. I would love to take these home with us for the rest of our family to see and hold, but appreciate they belong here in the CWI historical archives.

Helena Hoffer, my bohemian
and stylish grandmother, in
August 1924, three years
before she married my
grandfather.

Dr Rudolf Rieden, my
grandfather, looking handsome
in his passport photo.

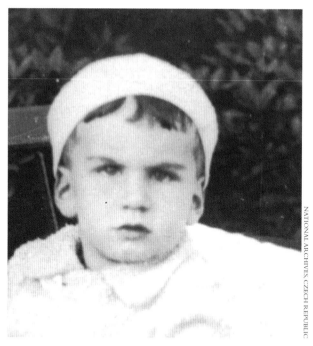

Dad as a toddler. This photo was attached to his father Rudolf's 1934 passport application.

Dad, aged six or seven, skiing in Königsstuhl, Germany.

Dad in his beloved mountains enjoying an alfresco lunch with his mum and Aunt Ida, June 1936.

Karlsbad macht Dich gesund!
Carlsbad restores your health!

Karlovy Vary Tě uzdraví!
Carlsbad rend la santé!

19 37

Dad's beautiful *Tante Ida* in Karlovy Vary. Ida sent this photo as a postcard to his new school in England. She never saw him again; she was murdered in 1942.

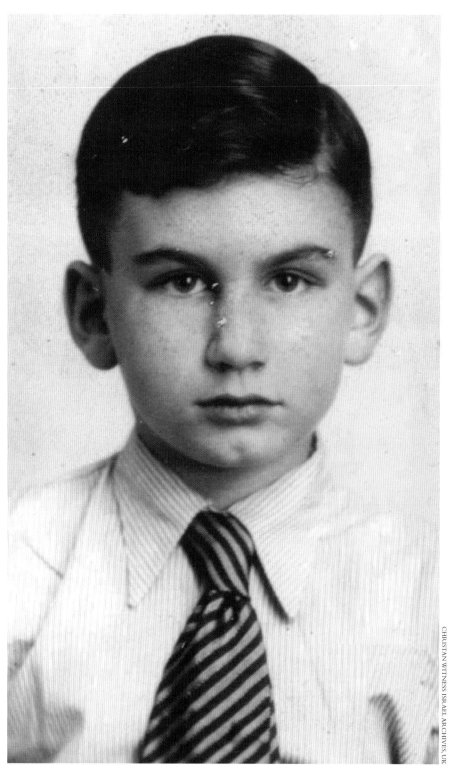

My father, Hanus Rieden, about to have his world turned upside down.

My grandparents paint on brave faces as they board the bus for the airport and the daring mission to send Dad to England. Rudolf never saw his son again.

8 March, 1939. This photo of my eight-year-old father boarding the plane to leave his parents and homeland – and Hitler – always makes me cry.

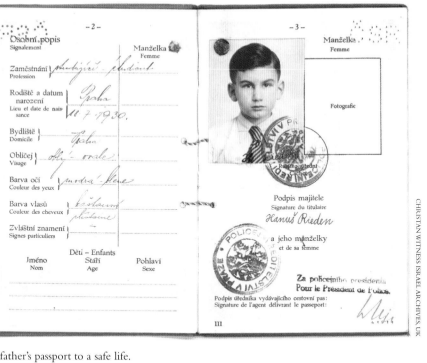

My father's passport to a safe life.

Seven Trees, The Mission's children's home that greeted my father when he arrived in England in 1939.

A rather sad and lost Dad sits in the front row, second from left, along with the other Czech refugee children who were on his flight from Prague. They are posing with their new mother figure, Mission leader Mrs Davidson (centre).

I found this incredibly poignant handmade card in Dad's private file in the Christian Witness Israel archives. Is this 'Christmas plane' flying my traumatised father away from danger or back home?

The Barbican Mission to the Jews' leaders Reverend and Mrs Davidson, whose courageous actions certainly saved my father's life.

with love your. Nov. 1946. mother

Having escaped Hitler, Helena sent this photo from Prague to Dad in England with the inscription: 'With love, your mother. Nov 1946.'

A shrunken, smiling Grandpa Rudolf in Prague, June 1951. He was one of just two Rieden siblings to survive the Holocaust.

Right: Triumphant news.
The letter that reveals Rudolf
and Helena have survived Hitler.

Below: Rudolf and Helena Rieden's
first letter to the Davidsons following
their liberation from Theresienstadt
reveals how much they have suffered.

Speedwell 8861

46, Norrice Lea,
N.2.

18th June 1945

The Rev. I.E. Davidson,
The Barbican Mission to the Jews,
Mount Zion,
Lubbock Road,
Chislehurst.

Dear Mr. Davidson,

I have just received word from
Prague that Hansi Rieden's father
and mother have returned there safe
and sound from the Concentration Camp
of Teresen.

I am giving you this very cheerful
news and would ask you to be good
enough to impress on Hansi to whom
I have written separately to write
at once in English and to post his
letter to me so that I can forward
it through the Czech Embassy to Prague
in the event of his not having written
yet

I think it would do a lot of good
if your goodself would address a few
lines to those poor sufferers in Prague.
I am glad to be at your disposal if
you require any assistance.
Wishing you all the best, I remain,

Dr. Rudolf Rieden,
Prague XII.,
Stalinova 138.
Czechoslovakia.

Prague. oktober 13 th 1945.

19 OCT 1945

Dear Reverend & Mrs. Davidson,

Don't worry please that our answer
will be late. Mrs Rieden left yesterday the hospital, where she
has been so many weeks in follows, of 3 years concentration camp
Terezin. Now she is not yet recovered and has still pains, it will
have a long time till she get back her strength.
We can't say, how thankful we are
for all you do our child, he found a second home, what we will
never forget. You saved him his life, you give him such a good
education, either you have'nt one but a hundred of children.
Just now we have learned how dread-
fully you have been bombed in 1940 - 1 and V - 1 and V - 2 and
how splendid did the English Nation under such horrid conditions.
We got a long letter from Hans, where
he describes his life and now his school during the last 6 years.
He enclosed 2 fotos where we see that he gets well and is a good
pupil. Please change his name " Hans " - in czech we call him
" Hanuš " in " John ".
When we have been deported we said
to take back our child at once we came home. Only 10 % of Jews
came back. Later we learned, not to do it, the conditions they are
here in the moment are not so well to take back our child. Hansi
has forgotten the czech language and it would be better for him
to stay in England to continue his studies. Please, should you tell
me it would be possible for Hansi to get the British Nationality?
Hansi writes that you will be so kind
to try to get for him a Stipendium. He prepares himself for a
Schoolmaster. What do you mean about it? Would not be better to
to become another studium , a technical an Engineur or Physician?
Sorry we ask you so many questions,
but we hardly need your advice.
We remain, dear Reverend & Mrs.

Davidson

yours thankfully

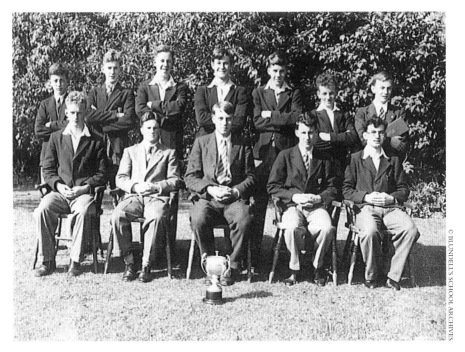

© BLUNDELL'S SCHOOL ARCHIVES

Dad, front row far right, every inch the perfect Englishman, as a key player with a batting average of 80 in the Francis House cricket team at Blundell's school.

© RIEDEN FAMILY ARCHIVE

2 August, 1958. Mum, left, in the blue silk wedding outfit she kept all her life, holds Dad's hand tight as they pose looking brilliantly happy at St Saviour's Church, London, surrounded by friends including The Mission's matriarch, Mrs Davidson, right, in a blue and white floral ensemble.

Mum and Dad on holiday in Europe in the late 1950s.

Two new Rieden arrivals – baby me and puppy Polly. Guess which my brothers Pete, far left, and Nick preferred in those early days?

Three generations of Riedens: proud Dad with his daughter, me, and his mother, Helena.

The heartbreaking letter that shows Dad asking, in vain, for help to bring his mother over from Prague to live with us in England.

25, Robins Bow,
Camberley,
Surrey.
September 20, 1965.

The Trustees,
Czech Refugee Trust Fund,
Rutland House,
Rutland Gardens, S.W.7.

Dear Sirs,

I am writing this letter about my mother, Mrs. Helena Riedenová. She is a Czech citizen, domiciled in Prague, and is now 72 years old. (J.U.Dr. Rudolf Rieden)

She and my father remained in Czechoslovakia during the Second World War, and spent 3 years together in Terezín. They probably owe their survival to the fact that my father served as an officer in the Austrian Army during the First World War, and lost one leg. After the last war he returned to his job as a civil servant (Finanční Rada) in the Ministry of Finance in Prague, and later he retired on full pension. In recent years he suffered from a gastric ulcer which could not be satisfactorily operated on, and my mother looked after him during the illness. He died in March of this year.

Both my parents came from large families, but almost every member was killed during the war. Apart from myself the only survivors are my mother's youngest brother, who lives in Israel, and an elderly sister-in-law, who lives alone in a village well away from Prague. I am the only child of my parents.

In effect father's death has left my mother entirely alone in Prague. She has a small flat and receives a state pension of about 1000 crowns per month, partly on her

Helena finally reunited with her son at our home in England, 26 years after they parted in desperate times. Dad is holding his mother's cigarettes, the only time I have ever seen him with cigarettes on his person!

Helena meets her Australian daughter-in-law (my mum) and three grandchildren for the first time. (I'm on the verge of a tantrum in Dad's arms.)

.IV 194? ✶ REISS ALBERT 22.XI 1913
4 ✶ AMÁLIE ? 1918–18.VIII 1943 ✶ BE
0.VIII 1906 ARNOŠT 14.VII 1929–30.IV1
EDŘICH 2.IX 1900 HELENA 23.III 1903
.X 1941 ✶ REITLER ANTONÍN 13.V1
–4.X 1944 ✶ LUDVÍK 22.IV 1887 ZDEŇKA
2–17.V 1942 ✶ MAX 9.VI 1891 VĚRA 11.IX
VIII 1942 ✶ RESCHOVSKÁ MAR
9.II 1941 ✶ ROBERT 10.X 1887 MARKÉT
RIEDEN EMIL 31.X 1859–8.I 194
VALD 1.VII 1880 MARTA 10.V 1890–2
.IV 1942 ✶ RIESNEROVÁ MARTA
LFRÉD 14.VIII 1920–6.IX 1943 ✶ ANTO
1912–13.V 1942 OSKAR 27.VIII 1886

My great-grandfather Emil Rieden is remembered on the walls of Pinkas Synagogue.

Ninth line down: my great-grandfather Emil's body took 35 minutes to be reduced to ashes in the crematorium ovens at Theresienstadt.

The blanket that my grandparents carried with them in Theresienstadt; the yellow Star of David all Jews were forced to wear by the Nazis.

Face to face with the tiny, cramped freight wagon on display in Auschwitz II–Birkenau. It was these windowless wagons that transported some of my relatives to their death in Auschwitz.

Unimaginable discoveries and sadness following my family's footsteps to the gates of Auschwitz.

Searching the Auschwitz death books for answers I feared I would – and did indeed – find.

A fitting end to my journey, sitting on the memorial bench dedicated to the couple – Reverend and Mrs Davidson – who saved my father's life.

There are also similar files on some – not all – of the other children, and the overriding sentiment from all is of loving parents grabbing on to a lifeline for their offspring. Most of the dossiers contain signed parental permissions for the BMJ to baptise the children when they are 16, should the child wish it, and to raise their child in the Christian faith. There are also many letters of thanks from parents clearly at their wits' end.

Dad's is the only file bulging with private school reports, and though I had hoped to find some reference here to who paid for his prep school education and how he achieved his scholarship to Blundell's, there are no receipts or mention of money at all. From these records it seems as if he was the only child from the Czech refugees in the Mission's care to be sent to fee-paying schools. While I can see from his academic reports the educational benefit, I also know from the few conversations we had on the topic that being sent away to school set him apart from the other children, and I fear he was very lonely both at school and in the Mission. For Dad there was no one place where he really belonged as a child or adolescent. He didn't find that until he purchased his own family home many years later and put all this behind him. As I said, he also nurtured an abhorrence of private boarding schools, and sent me and my brothers to the local state schools.

━━

Having been mesmerised by little Hansi Beck, the two-and-a-half-year-old in the pilot's arms in the film of the first exodus from Prague, I am especially keen to find out more about the youngest of the Mission's refugees. In his file, I see that Hans was the son of Dr Max Beck, a medic from Teplitz-Schönau (now Teplice-Šanov) in north-west Bohemia, part of the Sudetenland that was handed over to the Third Reich, and Rita Beck who was originally from Vienna in Austria. In Rita's January 1939 notes to the Davidsons, she advises that her son 'is a bad eater' but is 'a very lively child and wanting fondness. He loves being with other children.' She adds that she is 'so grateful for all you will do for my child . . . and thank you from all my heart'.

But just a week after he arrived, Hansi began to complain of severe earache. At this time the boys were still sleeping in the church hall, and Mrs Davidson, increasingly worried about the little boy, writes about it at length:

> He was still finding everything very strange and missing his mother sadly, while the strange language greatly added to his troubles. We immediately consulted a doctor about the ear, who saw that there had been previous severe trouble and that there was now an abscess in the inner ear. Little Hans was very ill and needed much care and nursing. The conditions of life in the parish hall naturally made this far more difficult.

The first doctor called had said Hans needed to go to hospital, but Mrs Davidson knew this was not possible. Hans was 'extremely nervous . . . and just beginning to know and to cling to us and to find our faces and voices at least familiar. I felt that removal to hospital with more strange faces and, with perhaps no one at all to speak his language, would be more than he would be able to bear,' she writes.

Instead Mrs Davidson opted to nurse Hansi herself, with the help of a couple of BMJ helpers, an option that was not so unusual in those days. When a lady doctor visited that evening, she agreed that Hansi was too anxious to be moved and that

Mrs Davidson had probably saved his life. 'The doctor came twice daily to treat little Hans and finally brought another doctor to assist her while she opened the abscess which was very deep and difficult to get at,' writes Mrs Davidson:

> This meant an anaesthetic and was not easy to carry out in the conditions under which we lived in the parish rooms . . . After the abscess was opened little Hans made a good and satisfactory, though slow recovery. The daily treatments were such a terror to him and as it was my lot to carry these out he regarded me for a considerable time with aversion and distrust. He was very slow to give his affection to anyone, never allowed himself to be kissed or petted as most little ones do, until he could honestly respond; so it was one of my happiest moments when weeks later he spontaneously threw his arms round my neck, and solemnly announced, 'I lull you!'

It's a beautifully told story, and Mrs Davidson has clearly fallen for little Hans who she continues to watch over. But in February 1940, his ear trouble flared up again, this time in his left ear. He was taken to Bromley and District Hospital, all the time crying: 'Take me home! Take me home!'

'From the first the surgeon who operated told me that there was no possible hope of our little treasure recovering, for he had discovered that Hans had a cerebral abscess as well as the mastoid infection,' she writes. Hansi rallied a little, but ultimately Mrs Davidson was called to his side: 'By the time I reached there the Good Shepherd had folded His lamb and little Hans had already entered the Heaven he longed for . . . At this time, April 1940, channels of communication were still open through Holland and Switzerland to people in Czechoslovakia and it was a terrible task to write to the stricken parents.'

Hans Beck died on 5 April 1940, aged four. On his death certificate, the cause of death is cited as 'Cerebral Abscess (left temporal lobe) and Left Mastoiditis Acute (after operation)'. Hans was the first child ever to die in BMJ care, and it hit the children and the Davidsons hard. Eighteen months after Max and Rita Beck received the news of their son's death, they were transported from Prague to Łódź concentration camp. Neither survived the Holocaust.

The funeral service was held in the Chapel at 'Mount Zion', the boys' home. Aunt Annalisa, who was 13 at the time, later tells me she remembers the funeral as a very sad occasion. The paperwork from the council tells me that Hans Beck was buried in Chislehurst cemetery.

—

After the war, the children started to go their separate ways. While a few, like Inge Plitzka, remained devoted Christians and some even worked for the BMJ for periods, Mrs Davidson was obviously rather peeved that more didn't see the light. The children clearly considered her and the Reverend as surrogate parents, and many – including my father for a while – continued to keep in touch. This excerpt from Mrs Davidson's writings sums up the matriarch's reaction:

It is of course, easy to keep in constant touch with those in whom our oneness in Christ makes a close bond of love and fellowship; but where this is not the case, it is often a problem to know how much time and energy should be spent in keeping up with those who have obviously decided to go their own way. Yet there are surprisingly many who appear to have no spiritual affinity with us any longer, and yet determinedly keep in touch either by correspondence or personal visits. These often amaze us by their obvious affection, instant response to any invitation, and even by confidences in regard to their private affairs and problems. We want them to feel that the door is always open and that there is always leisure to enter into these things with them, and however discouraging the outward life may appear we refuse to give up hope for any single one for whom we continue to pray.

I find Mrs Davidson's reaction rather cold. For these children, who were to all intents and purposes orphans (and some soon were in fact), she was a mother figure, and my father certainly must have retained some affection for her, since she was invited to his wedding in 1959 and may well have influenced my parents' decision to marry in a church when neither were practising Christians.

CHAPTER THIRTEEN

THE HOUSE OF REFUGE

The next stop on my journey is to visit Chislehurst and the sites of the BMJ children's homes. It takes barely half an hour by train from London's Charing Cross station, but I suddenly find myself in Kent countryside, the garden of England as it is known. This is the stockbroker belt, one of those Home Counties that hug London, where England's financiers and business folk raise their families in comfort away from the city grime and bustle. And as I walk up the hill from the pretty suburban station to Lubbock Road, where the children's homes used to be, I realise my father was really very lucky to find himself here back in 1939.

Chislehurst is more built up now than it would have been then, when I suspect it had more of a village-y feel, but it's still magnificently leafy, with rich canopies of ancient trees and patches of green space amid the private clipped lawns and English country gardens. It feels eminently familiar to me. This is just like Surrey, where my parents moved from their London flat in the 1960s to raise their three children, and where they remained for the rest of their lives. Even though

I now live in Sydney, this is the sort of landscape that will always conjure up home to me, and I suspect my father felt the same.

Seven Trees, the house that had been the subject of such bitter arguments and ended up being my father's first English home, is still standing in Lubbock Road, and thanks to Aunt Annalisa, I have spoken to the current owners, who are happy to show me around. It's hard to believe that this mansion, which housed 30–40 children and some staff, is now a family home for five. Annalisa, now in her nineties, has kept in touch with Amanda, the owner, to ensure the memorial bench she helped organise, which pays tribute to the Reverend and Mrs Davidson, is looked after. The bench is now the only reminder of what went on here.

This bench heralds my arrival at the road that became so much part of my father's childhood. It sits in front of the boundary fence of a residential property under a tree at the entrance to Lubbock Road. You can't miss it, and I find it heartening to think that everyone who comes this way will read about the 68 children rescued from central Europe in 1939 and wonder. I like the idea that the full story is not laid out here; it has a warm sense of joy and mystery that I hope will prompt locals to investigate further. It also reminds me of the reticence to talk about the Holocaust that has under-pinned my investigation from the start. Even here the facts are hidden, shaded, truths buried.

The houses in this road are all sizeable and well-to-do, and I hope that the residents' original opposition to the establish-ment of a children's home for Czech Jewish refugees in their midst dissipated as they got to know their new neighbours and understood a little more about the pain that had brought them here. These lost children posed no threat to the financial stability of little England, nor did they grow up to be Cold War spies or angry terrorists. Though the spy issue did pop up later in my research . . .

My father always expressed intense gratitude to England for saving his life, and completely assimilated into national life as an impeccably obedient – but meticulously exact – taxpayer. The only time he ever expressed Czech national fervour was when watching sport: especially the Football (soccer) World Cup, and Martina Navratilova winning Wimbledon – again and again and again!

The book *Secret Chislehurst*, by local historians Joanna Friel and Adam Swaine, talks about the conversion of one Lubbock Road gentleman. The leader of the BMJ Executive Council described this man as 'our most bitter opponent' when the BMJ purchase of Seven Trees was being opposed, but once the children moved in, he admitted they were 'the best behaved he had ever met'. Not long after, when Seven Trees ultimately proved too small for the number of refugees Reverend and Mrs Davidson needed to house, and the BMJ put in a further application to purchase another big home in the same road, this man happily signed the petition in favour. This house, which is no longer standing, the BMJ renamed Mount Zion; it became the boys' home and Seven Trees ultimately the girls' home. Mount Zion also had its own chapel, which was used by the boys for twice-daily prayer.

At the heart of Lubbock Road is Christ Church, approached by a smart gravel drive and set in a beautiful thicket of trees and lawns. This is a typical chocolate-box English church, with a bell tower and Gothic arches, straight out of an Agatha Christie Miss Marple mystery. It was here the Mission children attended church services on Sunday, the girls walking from Seven Trees next door and the boys from Mount Zion just down the road. And it was here they first heard that war had broken out. While some were too young to appreciate the implications, others, like Annalisa, knew this would change their lives forever.

Today Christ Church still plays an active part in this community, with evangelical services I suspect Reverend Davidson would have wholly endorsed. It's a very handsome building from the outside, but when I try to go inside to see where my father spent his first night away from his Prague home, I am told the church is closed for the afternoon so the local schoolchildren can practise a performance. I explain why I have come, but the schoolteacher is adamant . . . Some things haven't changed at all in Chislehurst!

As the church bells strike two o'clock, I walk up to the gates of Seven Trees. It's strange but also rather comforting to think that Dad would have heard these bells too. Amanda welcomes me at the door of what is a very beautiful home. Currently there are a total of 12 bedrooms linked by four flights of stairs, with a stunning attic conversion in the rafters. Mother-of-three Amanda is a former dancer who is now a Pilates instructor and runs private sessions from her specially kitted-out studio in Seven Trees. She's a sensitive and thoughtful woman, and there's an immediate sense of calm here in her home. And even though the interior is far removed from its layout when the children were here, I can see why those BMJ refugees I have spoken to felt so warmly about this place.

The floor tiles and many of the original features of this Victorian house, which Amanda tells me was built in 1880, have been retained, including some curious Tudor-inspired detail on panes of stained glass, and as I wander about I try to picture my father as a little boy running around here.

Surrounded by England's pleasant land, here was safety and comfort and an ordered life, which though strict and bound by religious instruction was nurturing and loving.

The garden at Seven Trees was on three levels, and Annalisa tells me that 'the bottom and more shady one was mainly used for rough tennis and croquet'. My father recalled playing football in a courtyard or field around here – perhaps it was the church courtyard. But as we walk outside Amanda tells me that fields used to run all the way down where houses now sit, so this was probably where Hanus and the boys kicked a ball around.

'There was a large garage attached to the house on the Christ Church side, its roof covered in a vine bearing delicious fruit. It looked very tempting but we were not allowed to climb up and retrieve it,' remembers the still very independent Annalisa, who I strongly suspect broke those rules. 'The long room at the rear on the left was the dining room and one of the front rooms was "the quiet room", though I suspect it wasn't always quiet. It was nicely furnished, and I particularly remember two deckchair-style chairs covered in green velvet.'

Like my father, Annalisa says she doesn't remember learning English as such, only that very quickly they all spoke it. She says that both children's homes were staffed by a team of pious women and a few men. 'We called the senior one, a buxom lady with a fine singing voice, "Mother", but having left my own mother behind it took me a while to call her that. The other staff were aunties.'

Annalisa's brother Theo, who lived at Mount Zion until they were evacuated to Devon, remembers the air raids that would keep them awake at night. 'We were right in the path to London and the planes came over every night. If the planes were intercepted they dropped their bombs wherever they were, so quite a lot of bombs fell on Chislehurst. But we were very near a golf course and fortuitously a lot of the bombs fell onto the golf course. Luckily Mount Zion never got hit, but I believe it may have been later after we left. We went down to Devon in January 1941.'

As I walk through the long hall downstairs, I am reminded of Annalisa's memories of the night the bomb was dropped on Seven Trees. For safety away from the windows, the girls had been relocated to the hall to sleep on rows of mattresses rather than in their dormitories, but Annalisa disobeyed and crept upstairs to her comfortable bed. 'Apparently, I didn't hear a thing. The house and all of us were saved, the only damage being the roof of the garage and a lot of oil-soaked mattresses in the hall, which I discovered when I woke up the next day.' Later Amanda shows me the garage, now intact.

Amanda has done her own research on the history of her house, but when I tell her that my father was just eight years old when he arrived here, she tears up. Her own son is the same age, and she can't imagine as a mother having to abandon him and then the little boy struggling on his own. Only I very quickly realise in Seven Trees and later at Mount Zion, Dad wasn't alone. These homes were filled to the brim with children who just seemed to muck in and get on with it.

Annalisa says in the early mornings she would make her way over to Mount Zion to help in the kitchen – even during the raids, which looking back she realises was pretty dangerous. 'I wasn't really scared of the bombs, I don't know why. I remember picking up a saucepan and putting it on my head to walk across the road. But they shouldn't have allowed it. I would help with the breakfast, being a girl, and you can imagine porridge for all those boys in great big pots was quite a task. I had to stand on a box so that I could reach.'

Annalisa keeps in touch with Inge Plitzka, who appeared in the Czech documentary and now lives in north London. The two of them used to drive here together to check on the bench. The filmmaker Jiří brought Inge back to Seven Trees and filmed her visit. She looked delighted to see the house again, where she recalled 'happy sunny days playing in the garden and running along the pathways'.

After the bombing, the majority of the children were evacuated to the large country house the Mission found in Devon called Craddock House. Despite its slightly dilapidated state, their time there sounds pretty halcyon. Seven Trees remained in use as the BMJ offices and staff quarters, and home for a few children until after the war everyone returned.

Since he boarded at the private schools he was sent to, Dad, of course, was only in the BMJ homes in the school holidays, which is a shame. I think he would have enjoyed this communal life with children who shared his journey and understood what was really going behind the scenes for all of them. But at least he had some time here.

Seven Trees' history is really important to Amanda, who has her own folder of cuttings and research, including a 1937 sale advertisement from *Country Life* magazine boasting 'central heating'. The red brick, wooden gable and big bay frontages haven't changed a bit. As we speak, Amanda tells me that her teenage daughter is about to set off on a school trip to Auschwitz and wants to present a project on the role of her house in saving the lives of Jewish children, including my father, many of whose families were murdered in the death camps. When I bid farewell to Seven Trees it feels right that this family are here now, appreciative of what went on inside their walls.

Back at Charing Cross station a violinist is busking, playing Mozart's Violin Concerto No. 1. I know it well. This was one of Dad's favourites. As I stand to listen, I realise that in many ways my father did find himself here in England, and that however much I battle with the Davidsons' evangelism, they gave my father the loving, comfortable home he so desperately needed. Chislehurst became his auspicious place of refuge.

———

My next stop is the reading room of the British Library. I want to find out what sort of world my father was now a part of, what England was like and how the government was supporting these vulnerable refugees. What I discover makes pretty depressing reading. In the British House of Commons, politicians bickered over refugee policy while Hitler proceeded to close the door to emigration and strip all Czech Jews of their livelihoods. The path of Nazi terror in Czechoslovakia was well known to the British people, and the next step of rounding up Jews and sending them to concentration camps reported widely.

I quickly realise that my father had been lucky to be permitted entry and his parents smart to grab this opportunity. I can also see that it would have been impossible for my grandparents to have accompanied him. My grandfather's war wound would have hampered any application, but also Britain simply wasn't letting in many adult Jews. The nation was nervous of adult Jewish refugees flooding in and taking British jobs, even though it officially condemned Hitler's anti-Semitic persecution. For my father, heading to British private school to morph into an Englishman was probably the safest course of action.

And just in case I was in any doubt that the extent of the horror in Eastern Europe was somehow hidden, I come across a Foreign Office report in the National Archives in

Kew from the British section of the World Jewish Congress held on 1 December 1942:

ANNIHILATION OF EUROPEAN JEWRY.
HITLER'S POLICY OF TOTAL DESTRUCTION.

The Jews of Europe are being exterminated by the Nazis. It is not merely that atrocities are being committed against the Jews. They are being quite literally slaughtered in masses, in pursuance of a systematic plan and in accordance with a deliberate policy.

This is Hitler's 'final solution of the Jewish problem in Europe'. He has openly proclaimed his design. He is now executing his policy with a diabolical fiendishness unknown in the whole history of human savagery.

I continue to trawl through the newspapers and government archives and then, suddenly and unexpectedly, I came across a record in the British Home Office archives in a box called 'Personal Files of Refugee Families' under the name of Rieden.

The catalogue tells me that the records relate to the period 1949–69 and were created or inherited by the British 'Home Office, Ministry of Home Security and related bodies' within the division 'Aliens and Immigration, Denization and Naturalisation'. They are part of the 'Czech Refugee Trust' records, subseries 'Personal Files of Refugee Families', subseries 'Refugees with Restricted Choice of Employment'. Dad's is not the only file in this subseries. There are boxes under other Czech- and German-sounding names, and these are all closed to public access.

Very mysterious.

The Czechoslovak Refugee Trust, I later discover, was a fund set up by the British government specifically to offer financial assistance in the emigration and settlement of refugees from Czechoslovakia. Only the box is closed . . . locked to public access until 2040 – that's 12 years away!

This can't be right. If there is a file in there about my father I must see it. I register a Freedom of Information request to have the box opened and cross my fingers. I hurriedly fill out the forms and put my case. What could be in this box and will I be granted permission to see these documents about my father?

CHAPTER FOURTEEN
UNLOCKING DAD'S DOSSIER

My time has run out on the ground in England, and with still no response to my Freedom of Information application I return to Sydney. It has been an immense journey. I feel happy that I have discovered so much, but after my grief I am starting to enter the anger stage when I consider the many iniquities perpetrated on my kin. Of course I knew what went on in the Holocaust, but now this is my story too.

Over the next few weeks all I can think about is the box sitting on a shelf in the British National Archives in Kew with my father's name on it. The documents inside this box must reference what happened to my father after he had left the care of the BMJ and after his parents had told him they were neither coming to England to join him nor thought it prudent for him to return to Prague to be with them. Dad was on his own. I assume Rudolf and Helena would have been unable to renew their son's Czech passport in Prague, and nor did they want to. They had made it clear that they wanted Hanus to change his name to John, become a British citizen and leave Czechoslovakia for good.

On my father's part, his hands were tied. Since his parents were still living he couldn't apply for British nationality until he turned 21, and even then, the fact that they, his only family, were alive and in Prague wouldn't have helped his application. While he was incredibly lucky that his parents had survived the Holocaust, it did land him in a kind of wilderness where British refugee policy was concerned.

I don't know what my father wanted back then. He had been moved about so much throughout his childhood and adolescence and had become hardened to rolling with the punches. But that doesn't mean he found the constant lack of stability easy. The father I knew craved order and forward planning, and I can imagine this uncertainty would have made him extremely anxious.

In 1948 Dad's situation was compounded when Communist rule took over in Czechoslovakia. Many Czechs tried to emigrate in the window between the end of the war and the beginning of Communism. I wonder if Rudolf and Helena had sought refuge and were again knocked back. Both still suffered ill health from their time in the concentration camp, and as before Grandpa's disabled status would have been a major barrier to any visa application. Even with their son living in England, I can't imagine they would have fulfilled the UK requirements for emigration at the time. Oh ... and of course they were still Jewish, and the last thing Britain wanted was to be overrun with post-Holocaust Jewish immigrants carrying wartime trauma.

As for my father, clinging on to his life in England and trying to pursue his dream of going to university would have been the priority for both him and his parents. But as a refugee with limited rights and support in Britain, this wasn't easy. Dad's status was murky. While he had been in the Mission,

Reverend Davidson had been his official guardian. Now he was an adult with no one to turn to for help.

Aunt Annalisa tells me that the day she turned 21, she immediately applied to become a British citizen. She felt that 'English people were very generous', because the authorities approved her application quickly without fuss. Her brother Theo was naturalised when he was 16, 'by special dispensation for orphans,' he tells me. By this time, brother and sister had discovered that their mother had been killed, so they definitely saw England as their home and were both keen to ensure their future there was secure. 'Hoss [the name Theo used for my father] didn't qualify because his parents were alive . . . But the disadvantage of being naturalised was that you had to go for national service when your time came,' Theo explained.

This would have been a major concern to my father. Not only had he grown up seeing his father cope with a debilitating war injury, Dad was a pacifist through and through. He never believed armed conflict solved anything. While Britain was now in peacetime, in this era conscripts were often sent to the decolonisation wars in Kenya, Malaya and Cyprus, where they were used as part of the colonial forces through troubled negotiations. Dad wanted to pursue his education, study for a degree. National service would have involved 18 months in the armed forces followed by four years on the reserve lists, available for call-up in times of national emergency. I am certain this would have influenced his decision not to apply for British citizenship during this period.

But although military service ended in 1960, my father still didn't apply for citizenship until 1968, by which time he was a 38-year-old father of three. My eldest brother Nick says that Mum had talked about the cost of naturalisation being a barrier – he recalls her mentioning a figure of £25.

But then, when in 1968 Dad found he needed a passport to take the whole family on holiday abroad, he finally bit the bullet and applied.

Of course, with a steady job, a wife, three children born in Britain, a home and 30 years now as a resident, achieving citizenship should have been a foregone conclusion. But my mother told me that after Dad put in the application, the Home Office posted detectives outside the house watching us. She used to take them cups of tea.

My brother Nick, who would have been aged nine at the time recalls 'a visit from a man who looked around the house and had a long talk with Mum and Dad from which we were excluded. He was a policeman, Mum always said, from Special Branch, who was interviewing them to see if they were spies. This was the height of the Cold War, and there were a few notorious Soviet spies who had been uncovered assuming false British identities. So a sudden passport application from a man born in Prague, educated in England and suddenly, at the age of 38, wanting to go abroad, which was only just becoming a common thing for ordinary people to do, was regarded as suspicious.'

Once again, my father's heritage was raising alarm bells, only this time it wasn't about being Jewish, but about being Czech. Rudolf had died in 1965, but my grandma Helena was still living in Prague, which would have been noted by the British authorities. It was all starting to sound like a plot from a John le Carré novel, and while I quite love the idea that my father was a suspected spook, the notion still makes me laugh out loud. But naturally I wonder if this could have something to do with the locked box.

Until this time, I believe Dad's legal status in the UK would have been that of an 'alien'. He didn't want to go back to Czechoslovakia either immediately after the war or at any point later on. He felt it was unsafe, and even though his parents were there, he no longer belonged. As far as I know, he spoke very little Czech any more, and having been educated since the age of eight away from his fellow refugees at English private schools, he was totally assimilated into British life. As I said, he spoke the best English of all of us. Even his diction was impeccable. We used to joke about it as adolescents when our father would – constantly – correct our grammar.

But in many ways, I guess after my father left the guardianship of the BMJ, he became what we would now call an asylum seeker in Britain. He had fled Czechoslovakia because it was a place of danger for him and that was still the case; and the risk of going back and then not being allowed to leave to come 'home' to England was very real.

He didn't go back then, not even to visit as a young man, but he did travel in Europe, and to do this he would have needed what, after 1951 (following the Geneva Convention relating to the state of refugees), was called a 'certificate of identity'. Since asylum seekers are unlikely to be granted a passport by the nation they have fled, this refugee travel document acted in lieu of a passport, so the bearer could travel outside their new homeland and still be allowed back in. Dad used this to go to Europe with friends and later with my mother. But my brothers tell me that it was only when he wanted to take us – his family – on a holiday to Spain that he finally applied for naturalisation. He needed a family passport to cover his children and possibly his wife (though my mother had an Australian passport of her own), since the certificate of identity could only cover his travel.

The naturalisation was granted, but Nick says that when

Dad went to pick up the passport, he 'was warned not to travel East of the Iron Curtain . . . and of course he never did, only returning to Prague after the Velvet Revolution'.

I was five years old when we went to Spain, and I remember it well because as a freckly redhead I suffered my first bout of serious sunburn and I can still recall the pain. My brothers have a different memory involving a different sort of pain. 'It was while we were actually in Spain that the Russian tanks rolled into Prague, crushing the Dubček regime. I can still remember the hotel manager telling us about it over breakfast, miming a man with a machine gun,' says Peter, my second brother, who would have been aged seven at the time. Both he and Nick recall Dad going pale and he and Mum being very worried about Grandma, who from this moment on was stuck behind the Iron Curtain.

The timing of his naturalisation was perfect, but I think coincidental, for my father. As the Soviets took over Czechoslovakia, he was safe in the knowledge that he was now British. But what about Helena?

While I wait to hear from the National Archives, I start to explore the Czech Refugee Trust Fund. What was this organisation, and why did my father have his own dossier in its archival records?

In the autumn of 1938, the British and I think French governments (though reports differ as to whether both nations were involved) awarded a gift of £4 million to Czechoslovakia for refugee assistance. It's hard not to see this as anything other than blood money following the Munich Agreement. The Allies had signed the Sudetenland over to Hitler in the full knowledge that many of those living in this area, especially Jews and German and Austrian intellectuals and political activists, would be thrown out of their homeland.

This cash was to help the inevitable fallout of refugees the Allies' actions would engender.

Once the Czechoslovak government fell under German domination only five months later, the grant was placed under the control of Her Majesty's Treasury so it didn't fall into Nazi hands. And so the Czech Refugee Trust Fund was created, with the remaining funds directed to the support of Czechoslovakian refugees in Britain and its dominions. This support continued after the Communist takeover of Czechoslovakia in 1948 and in 1975 the remainder of the fund was turned over to the Trustees of the British Council for Aid to Refugees. In the UK this trust especially supported the education and training of refugees.

But this wasn't all the trust did. On further investigation I discover that the trust was also under close scrutiny from MI5. The body was considered a potentially dangerous hotbed of Communism harbouring and supporting spies, and an investigation was launched. There it is again, that link with the dark world of undercover agents and counter-intelligence. I am starting to believe there really could be some plausibility to my father's involvement in espionage.

The National Archives is unable to open the box until 2040 because the material is personal in nature and protected under Section 40(2) of the *Freedom of Information Act 2014*. Such information, I am told, must remain closed during the lifetime of the subject of the file or, where a date of death is not known, until after the 100th birthday of the subject.

I write back, pointing out that my father died in 2006 and as his daughter I feel justified in seeking access to the contents of his file. The National Archives requests evidence in the form of a death certificate. This I send and in consultation with the Home Office my application is approved. The box can be opened and this will happen on 8 August 2018, two weeks away. Once it is opened I will be notified of the extent of the contents.

I am on tenterhooks and hoping that the contents won't just turn out to be bureaucratic forms. When I call my brothers to discuss it they are equally intrigued. Could our mild-mannered father really have been a spy? The next two weeks can't go fast enough.

On opening I am informed that there are 172 documents, all relating to my father. What?!

After a long process of ordering copies, my locked box of 'secret' documents pertaining to John Rieden finally arrives, and I am still reeling from what I find.

═══

24, Landseer Close,
Edgware,
Middx

10/2/49

Dear Miss Goodchild,

You may be rather surprised to get a letter from me, but I am in a little difficulty and I wonder if you could do anything to help me out. You may remember that I came to see you twice last summer, when I was not certain as to what I was going to do. Soon after that I got a post as a teacher in a Preparatory school, but for various reasons I left the school at Christmas, and I have now got a clerical job in London. At the moment I am staying with relatives of mine in Edgware, but I want to move further into the centre of London. I wonder therefore if you could help me to get some lodgings or a place in a hostel in London. If you could do this, I would be most grateful. I am already trying to get a place in a hostel belonging to the London Hostels Association, but it appears to be rather difficult at the moment.

I hope you will be able to do something for me, as the matter is getting rather urgent.

Yours sincerely

(Mr.) J. Rieden

This was the first document in the file, handwritten by my father. The last letter I had seen from him was in the BMJ file to Mrs Davidson, written three months before this. In it he talked about settling into his life as a teacher at Winbury School in Maidenhead. He'd said, 'I like it. I am actually finding the teaching a lot easier already,' and added that in his spare time he would be studying for the entrance exam to London University. And yet from this letter it seemed that just two months later he had left the school 'for various reasons'.

How had it all gone so wrong?

I had already tried to trace records from Winbury School, which closed permanently in 2011, but because it was a private independent school, there was nothing in the local council archives nor in the libraries. I did uncover a Winbury old boys' website and managed to track down a previous pupil, Michael, who had been there when my father was a teacher. But he had no clear memory of my father. I was surprised at the time, but now I realise Dad had only been there for a few months.

The pupils' memories of school life recorded on the website seemed to depict an old-fashioned, warm-hearted institution, but Michael described one teacher at the school as 'an enigma with two sides to his character'. This man could be 'very severe and frightening at times' and he also boarded, so my father would have been in close contact with him. Perhaps Dad had a personality clash with this man, or perhaps he had simply decided he didn't want to spend his new life with people he didn't like or admire. This is pure speculation, of course, but I know my father wouldn't have just thrown in the towel, and certainly there was no implication that he had been sacked. The spectre of anti-Semitism, which was still felt in some pockets of reactionary Britain, enters my head, but without any evidence I push it aside.

Reading this letter I feel sad for Dad. He would have been so vulnerable and alone at this time, and the tone of his letter suggests he was getting desperate. I am interested to see that he was living with 'relatives', since I had no idea he had any in Britain. But Edgware rings a bell. We did know people who lived there. I knew them as 'Aunt' Fine (short for Josefine) and 'Uncle' Lud (short for Ludwig). My understanding was that this couple was part of my grandparents' inner circle of friends. They would go to coffee houses together in Prague and talk about everything that was happening. As I said, Fine and Lud were the only two in the group to get out of Czechoslovakia in time – I believe they left in early 1939 – but to do so they'd had to leave all their possessions and money.

In a later document in Dad's dossier of paperwork, I find that Fine and Lud's surname was Samisch, then I start searching in global archives for their connection to our family. After many days of trawling, I hit the jackpot. Ludwig was my great-grandfather Emil Rieden's nephew, the son of his sister Pauline. This would have made him my father's second cousin. As he wrote this letter, Dad was obviously living with Fine and Lud, but it was a temporary measure. I can't imagine they would have had much room to spare, and both the cost of transport to get into central London and the time involved would have also made this situation untenable for Dad.

My father wrote that he had already been to see the Czech Refugee Trust, presumably when he had realised his support from the BMJ was coming to an end; and as I read more of his file it became obvious that my father's greatest need was financial. Since the trust was set up precisely to help refugees like my father, I feel his enquiries were entirely appropriate, however awkward he may have felt posing them, and behind the polite requests I can feel Dad's discomfort in having to ask. This was government money given to help those Czech refugees who were the victims of part of British foreign policy, a policy many believe deliberately appeased Hitler in order to give Britain time to arm itself and prepare for inevitable war. Dad was a pawn caught in the middle of a dangerous diplomatic game. He had lost his home and the majority of his family, and now he badly needed assistance.

He was certainly right to ask for help with London hostels, for during the war the Czech Refugee Trust rented and adapted hostels for the use of Czech refugees, and after the war used some of their funds to meet the refugee need for furnished accommodation, offering subsidised or at least non-commercial rents.

But the trust's reply to my father was disappointing. In a letter back to him five days later, a Mrs Henry delivered the bad news that Miss Goodchild was no longer working there (a further handwritten note in the file showed that no one actually recalled seeing my father on the couple of occasions he had visited) and that they 'could not do anything more in the difficult problem of finding lodgings'. Mrs Henry's rather patronising suggestion was that Dad should go along personally to see the warden – 'it is often more successful than writing'.

The next item in the file was another letter from my father. He seemed to have found lodgings in Maida Vale in west London, and this time was asking for assistance with his education – another area the Trust Fund was expressly set up to assist.

5, Lanark Rd,
Maida Vale,
W.9.
10/6/49

The Czech Trust Fund
Rutland House,
Rutland Gardens, S.W.7.

Dear Sirs,

I am a young man of 18 and entered this country from Czechoslovakia in 1939. As my parents are still in Prague I am entirely on my own, and I am writing to you in the hope that you will be able to help me in solving a certain difficulty of mine.

At present I am earning my own living as a clerk in an insurance office, and I manage to make my salary of £200 p.a. pay for my food, lodgings, clothes etc. In my spare time I study through a Wolsey Hall postal course with the eventual aim of gaining a B.A. degree as an external student of London University. I am taking the Intermediate examination next November, and it is here that I have come up against a difficulty, for, apart from the 10 shillings registration fee which I have already paid, I find that I must pay a £3 matriculation fee and 6 guineas entrance fee before I can take the examination. I am now wondering if you would be prepared to give me any financial assistance, as I can see no other way of paying these fees.

Please let me hear from you at your earliest convenience, as the Matriculation fee is already overdue.

Yours faithfully,

John Rieden

Dad had obviously passed the entrance exam for London University and was now studying for the first year of a degree by correspondence while also holding down a full-time job. The sums of money he was asking for seem small to me, but when I run the numbers £3 is the equivalent of approximately £100 today, which would have been insurmountable for him at the time.

Again, reading this letter, I can feel the sense of panic and urgency in my 18-year-old father. Since he wasn't eligible for a state education grant, he was doing everything he could to broker his own further education, but he kept on hitting brick walls. His isolation is palpable.

I recall heading off to university myself at that age. It was my father who drove me to my halls of residence and my parents who supplemented my state grant, so that I could live away from home and enjoy campus life as a full-time student. Dad was always generous with his support, and at the time I barely gave it a second thought, but reading about his struggle I realise how lucky I was and how determined he was to make things different for his children.

I am surprised that my father doesn't mention what had

happened to his family in this letter. Perhaps he still didn't know about his aunts and uncles, but his parents' parlous situation following liberation would have added weight to his request. This silence is, however, something I recognise.

In their reply a few days later, the trust asked my father to fill out a personal questionnaire and make an appointment for an interview with Mrs Henry that week. Handwritten on the bottom of this letter I can see additional notes from Mrs Henry's superior advising her that in the interview she must ascertain what my father's parents were doing in the war, who paid for his education, his history with the BMJ and who his UK relatives were.

The completed questionnaire was also in the file and was fascinating to me. It charted my father's exodus from Prague on 8 March 1939. He wrote that his reason for leaving was 'the coming German invasion' and in the question about his landing conditions he quoted directly from his travel document, which was a 'Home Office Permit Card': 'Leave to Land granted at Croydon [the airport at which the KLM charter had landed] this day on condition that the holder does not enter any employment paid or unpaid while in the UK.' It was then noted that the regulations regarding employment were cancelled by the Home Office Circular No. 189, in 1947.

On 29 July 1946, when he was living in the Mission home in Devon, my father, then 16, was given a Police Certificate of Registration number. Just seeing that reminded me of the numbers that had ruled his family's lives. Here in England, my father was now also a number in a file.

Under languages my father had written 'English and a little French'. He didn't mention Czech, nor his mother tongue German, which he always spoke well, even years later. It was clear my father was ready to shed his past. I can't decide if this was an emotional decision or a pragmatic one – probably a bit of both.

When asked about his plans for the future, including 'emigration plans', my father cited: 'Probable career as school-master on obtaining full B.A. Degree.'

Finally, in the section that asked about relatives in the UK, before Mr & Mrs Samisch, my father listed Dr W. Hoffer as a 'distant relation', with an address in the affluent area of St John's Wood in North London. This was the Uncle Willi my brother Nick had faintly recalled from our childhood. Willi became a relatively famous psychoanalyst in the UK, having worked with Sigmund Freud in Vienna before he fled to London in 1938 with Freud's youngest daughter Anna, who saw Willi as a mentor. He became a consultant at the Hampstead Child Therapy Clinic, which Anna founded, the president of the British Psychoanalytical Society and also very well known internationally on the lecture circuit. Willi was married, but I don't think he had children, and I am wondering if it was he who paid for my father's preparatory school education. The benefactor wasn't noted in any of the documents in the file, even though the trust had noted their interest in this information.

While my father had obviously gone in for an interview from the notifications within his file, again no one at the trust could remember seeing him. The woeful level of minuting and filing systems must have been truly aggravating, espe-cially considering my father's desperation. Mrs Henry had been ill that day and Dad saw someone else. But from his subsequent letter to the trust it seemed that whomever he managed to talk to had promised to pay the six guineas fee for his university exam.

Annoyingly, Dad had to follow up with a begging letter asking that the promise be acted upon and swiftly. The notes from a Mr Dudding approved the payment but sounded rather dismissive. 'I can't recollect seeing Rieden myself though I may have done so,' he wrote.

In her letter confirming the payment, Mrs Henry asked that my father come in for 'a chat'. My father wrote back saying that he was at work during the week but could come in on a Saturday. Mrs Henry's typed notes from that chat revealed a couple of key things. She wrote that my father had been 'refused a Major Country Award on account of his nationality'. So my father had tried to apply for a grant to go to university but as an 'alien' was knocked back. This feels particularly unjust since he had been a scholarship student at Blundell's. Having won that place, he was now being denied the education every other English child was offered. Mrs Henry wrote that my father had been taking a correspondence course for the 'Intermediate B.A. examination' and that 'He feels he cannot take his finals in this way. He is therefore writing to the Home Office to find out if it would be possible for him to be naturalized before he is twenty-one. He could then apply for a grant to study full time at a University for a B.A. (hons.) degree.'

So if being naturalised could get him a university grant, my father was prepared to accept being later called up for National Service. His Home Office request must have also been denied, which I suspect would have added to his reluctance to reapply for naturalisation until much later on.

Mrs Henry had recorded a detailed breakdown of my father's personal finances right down to the cost of his rent and lunches, and the fact that he cycled to work (no doubt to save money) and at the end of the week had just 20 shillings (the equivalent of £33 today) left over to meet all his other expenses. 'He just manages to carry on,' she wrote.

Mrs Henry's conclusion of my father's future plans was: 'He is completely anglicized and he intends to remain in this country. He will probably become a Schoolmaster after he has obtained his degree.'

Three months after this meeting, my father was writing again to the trust.

5, Lanark Road,
Maida Vale,
W.9.
3/4/50

Mrs. B. Henry,
The Czech Trust Fund,
Rutland House, S.W.7.

Dear Mrs. Henry,

You have not heard from me since I came to see you last November, just before taking my Inter B.A. exam; and I am afraid that I cannot give a very good account of myself, as I have failed. However, I am still anxious to get a B.A. degree, and I intend to take the examination again next July, so I am now hard at work once more. I only failed in French, getting a pass in Geography and Latin, but unfortunately I have to take all three subjects again, and, what is worse, the Latin set books are different. Still, by paying a little more attention to the French I think I should be able to get through this time.

I am writing to you now because I will shortly have to send in my entry papers and pay the fee of six guineas, and I should be very grateful if the Trust Fund would again help me by paying this on my behalf. I should find it very difficult to raise this sum at the moment, and I am sure it would make very little difference to the fund, so I hope you will be able to arrange this for me.

Thanking you for your past kindness, and hoping you are in the best of health,

Yours faithfully,

John Rieden

I really feel for my father as I read this letter. He had been working so hard with no support and had only just failed, and yet seemed to be so hard on himself. I recognise a lot of myself in him, and recall how I would castigate myself if I slipped a grade or flunked an exam.

Fortunately, the trust was prepared to help Dad once more, but aside from failing the exam he had made a grave error in this letter. My father's casual remark 'it would make little difference to the fund' fell on exceedingly stony ground. Mrs Henry thought it was 'rather unfortunate' but did add in her report to Mr Dudding, her superior: 'Apart from this I should be inclined to recommend that we give him another chance; it is pretty tough going to study for such an exam in spare time and do a full time job as well.'

To which Mr Dudding replied: 'Yes, but as I reacted to his letter in exactly the way you did I think we are right in disapproving of his "manners" even if it does not reflect his real "attitude". To this end therefore, would it be possible for you to speak to him – perhaps on the telephone? And tell him his expression is unfortunate and that if he looks to people for help he cannot afford to be ill-mannered.'

As I read this I am seething on my father's behalf. How dare Mr Dudding be so patronising and pompously patrician.

Here was a boy torn from his parents at the age of eight, whose family had been massacred in the Holocaust, whose parents had survived but told him they weren't coming to get him, highly educated in England's private schools but forced by the system's attitude to refugees to beg for support as he tried to put himself through the further education freely available to 'English' children, being told he was 'ill-mannered'. Where were Britain's manners when they handed his homeland over to Hitler, when they refused entry to adult Jews so this little lad could stay with his parents, when they allowed him to be stripped of his religion by a group of evangelical missionaries capitalising on misery in the pursuit of fresh converts?

Mrs Henry duly wrote to my father. 'I should like to have a word with you with reference to your letter. Would you please telephone me between 10 and 1pm.'

I can't imagine how my 19-year-old father kept his cool when he was being reprimanded by Mrs Henry on the telephone but I know that he managed it, for in his next letter he sent a further request for the six guineas he needed, which Mrs Henry had obviously approved, and added: 'I apologise also for the faux pas that I committed in my last letter, and assure you that I did not mean to offend in any way.'

I don't know how my father did in his exam but I do know that he didn't complete his degree. I suspect the pressure of work and study just proved too much.

Nine years passed before my father engaged with the trust again. Dad was now married with a baby son, my brother Nick, and was again struggling financially. His letter was 100 per cent the man I knew – calm, rational, detail-focused, eminently polite and dignified.

159 Southborough Lane,
Bromley,
Kent
22/2/59

The Administration of the Czech Trust Fund,
Rutland House, S.W.7.

Gentlemen,

I am writing to you in the hope that you will be able to give me some financial help over a matter of accommodation.

I was born in Prague of Czech parents in 1930 and I came to this country as a refugee – March 1939. My parents stayed behind and spent most of the war years in Theresienstadt; they survived and after the war my father returned to his old job as an official of the Czechoslovak Treasury (finanční rada). He has now retired and is receiving a pension from the Czech government. Both my parents are still living in Prague.

I have been a permanent resident in this country since 1939 but I have not been naturalised. Last year I got married and we now have a son. Before his arrival my wife and I were quite content to live in two furnished attic rooms without running water, but with the baby this was naturally impossible and we moved to furnished rooms at the address at the heading of this letter. The rent is as much as I can afford but our position here is not satisfactory, partly because the owners of the house, who also live here and with whom we share the kitchen and the bathroom, naturally objects to having these cluttered up with baby's nappies and the like. We must therefore make another move.

We have looked around a good deal, visiting flats and accommodation agencies, and we have been driven to the conclusion that suitable rented accommodation is simply beyond our means. We have therefore decided to buy a house, as with a good mortgage this is not only cheaper (in terms of weekly outlay) than renting a furnished flat but it is also a much more suitable place for a family with a small child to live. Besides, we shall probably have more children in time.

Negotiations are in progress over a house in Camberley which is on sale for just over £2400. We have been offered a 90% loan on mortgage (subject to additional collateral security to the value of £250), and we ourselves have £250 in the bank, which is just enough to cover the remaining 10% of the purchase price. We must therefore find money to pay for the legal costs, fees and expenses (which I think will come to about £80), removal costs (£20), the premium for a mortgage indemnity policy to provide the additional security demanded by the Building Society offering the mortgage (£18-15-0), and furniture. As we have been living in furnished rooms we have no furniture of our own and the cost of buying even the absolute minimum we need is frightening.

I work for an insurance company in the City at a salary of £735 p.a. After deduction of income tax and National Insurance contributions I am left with £12-15-0 a week. To give you an idea of my problem I will set out my estimate of the weekly outgoings on the house and my fares to and from work.

Mortgage repayments	£3-5-6
General rates	14-0
Water rate	2-6
Insurance	2-3
Schedule A tax	5-0
Fares to and from work	£1-3-6
TOTAL	£5-12-9

This leaves us with just over £7 a week for food, heating, gas, electricity, clothing, general fares, pocket money and saving for holidays etc. Neither my wife nor I smoke, but even so we consider this a pretty tight budget with not much room for additional expenditure. I could probably obtain a short-term loan of the extra money I need, and furniture can be bought on hire purchase, but I could not afford the heavy repayments that these courses of action would involve. That is our difficulty.

I shall be grateful if you will let me know whether you are able to offer us any help.

Yours faithfully,

John Rieden

I had no idea my parents started their married life with so little money. Their reminiscences from that time always sounded romantic to me. I knew they had struggled to make ends meet, but here are the cold hard facts. In this letter my father paints a vivid picture of life in furnished rooms in Bromley where he and my mother and new baby Nick were now living in very cramped conditions, and also of their previous life in west London in attic rooms with no running water.

Bromley is on the outskirts of south London, and Nick recalls our mother telling him about the landlady there with whom she got on very well. So while they may have been moved on because of the baby, it wasn't acrimonious.

Mum earned a reasonable wage at the Flour Advisory Bureau, and it was always a family joke that when they married Mum earned more than Dad. But at this time, she would have been on leave to look after my baby brother, so money would have been doubly tight.

Moving out to a house of their own in Camberley, where we were all raised, 55 kilometres from London in Surrey, was a sensible solution that changed my parents' life significantly. It was also brave, since it involved my father sinking every penny of their savings in the house.

Two and a half weeks after writing this letter, my father heard back from the trust. In the file was a note of calculations written I suspect by a trust administrator assessing my father's outgoing expenditure. It came to a proposed sum of £120 for legal fees, removal expenses and mortgage indemnity, but then noted further money would be needed for furniture.

Mr Dudding and Mrs Henry were no longer the correspondents, which was good for my father, for the new person he was dealing with seemed much more businesslike and helpful, without demanding the forelock-tugging their predecessors required. In his reply, the assistant director offered my father a loan of £200 'to be secured by a second mortgage of the property' with interest to be charged at five per cent per annum and repayments made of £2 per month. While this was a generous offer – although I can't help wondering why it had to be a loan rather than an actual sum of money – my father, knowing that his mortgagee was unlikely to approve a second mortgage on the property, started negotiations.

After a whole suite of letters with various different suggestions on both sides, a resolution was agreed. The trust would award my father the loan, with a legal undertaking attached that should he default on the £2 monthly payments a second mortgage would be executed. The five per cent interest was to be paid quarterly, but 'during the first year or two at our discretion' interest payments could be waived. The trust also agreed to pay the legal costs of drawing up the undertaking.

My father was meticulous at every stage of negotiations,

which went on for six months (an indication of how the property market has changed!). This was the John Rieden I knew and recognised here, dogged in his pursuit of the fairest and most beneficial deal, dotting every 'i' and crossing every 't'. On the ledger it stated that the assistant director had waived the interest for the full term of the loan so long as it was repaid in regular instalments, but in actuality the issue of interest payment was revisited annually, which would have been a little annoying for my father as each year he would have to wait to hear if he would be charged or not. In any case, I know my parents would have been over the moon to receive this loan. It changed everything.

In his letter to the assistant director on 20 February 1960, I can feel the joy in my father's heart. Finally, things were going his way: 'We have now settled down in our new home and for the first time I have the opportunity to write and thank you for your help in enabling us to buy the house. We are delighted with it, and without your kind assistance the purchase would not have been possible.'

The file was now filled with credit receipts and accounts ledgers recording my father's monthly £2 repayments for close to ten years. While I am thrilled that Dad was finally receiving the support he deserved, I am still a little perplexed that there was never any question the trust might offer a gift of money rather than a loan. But isn't this what the trust was for? I am reminded of the £50 surety that someone – possibly my father's family who were later murdered – paid in order for their Hanus to be allowed entry to England. This money would have been very useful to him as he battled to make a home for his family.

But the house was a huge success. Dad commuted to London every day. Mum retrained to be a teacher. My brother

Peter was born and finally, in 1963, I came along. Add our collie pup Polly, and my father had achieved a typical suburban English family life.

Then five years into their domestic bliss in Surrey, my father wrote a lengthy letter to the trust in which, for the first time, he talked in depth about his mother Helena and revealed what had happened to his family. This was the only time my father had referred to the events of the Holocaust, and for me it showed that yes, he knew what had happened to them all and that yes, the wrongs that had been wrought on his family cut exceedingly deep. The fact that my father was so candid was testament to the desperation of his situation. In the following 1000 words Dad poured out his heart. It was the only time I believe he did this and, considering the result, I could appreciate why he never did it again.

25, Robins Way,
Camberley,
Surrey.
September 20, 1965.

The Trustees,
Czech Refugee Trust Fund,
Rutland House, Rutland Gardens, S.W.7.

Dear Sirs,

I am writing this letter about my mother, Mrs Helena Riedenova. She is a Czech citizen, domiciled in Prague and is now 72 years old.

She and my father (J.U. Dr Rudolf Rieden) remained in Czechoslovakia during the Second World War, and spent 3 years together in Terezin. They probably owe their survival to the fact that my father served as an officer in the Austrian Army during the First World War, and lost one leg. After the last war he returned to his job as a civil servant (Financni Rada) in the Ministry of Finance in Prague, and later he retired on a full pension. In recent years he suffered from a gastric ulcer which could not be satisfactorily operated on, and my mother looked after him during his illness. He died in March of this year.

Both my parents came from large families, but almost every member was killed during the war. Apart from myself the only survivors are my mother's youngest brother, who lives in Israel, and an elderly sister-in-law, who lives alone in a village well away from Prague. I am the only child of my parents.

In effect my father's death has left my mother entirely alone in Prague. She has a small flat and receives a State pension of about 1000 crowns per month, partly on her own account (she worked in a bank before the war) and partly as a civil servant's widow. Materially she can manage, but I think that being alone with no real friends will make her very miserable.

She is at present on a temporary visit in this country. It is the first time she has been to England and the first time she has seen me since 1939, when I left Czechoslovakia at the age of 8. She speaks a little English and manages to make herself understood to strangers. My wife is Australian (of British parentage) and none of us speaks any language other than English, so real conversation with my mother is not easy. However, she seems happier now than when she first arrived, and I have suggested to her that she should consider living permanently in England. It is, of course, a difficult decision for her. She would be leaving a familiar city to live in a strange country with a strange language and customs. On the other hand she would see us frequently, watch her three grandchildren grow up, and know that she had someone to turn to in an emergency. She has not made up her mind yet, and will probably not do so until some time after her return to Prague.

If she should wish to take up residence in England finance will be a major obstacle. My mother has virtually no savings. I understand that the Czech Government has on rare occasions, in cases of hardship, agreed to pay a State pension to a pensioner resident outside of the country. Obviously my mother would begin by making an application for the payment of her pension in this way, and if the Czech Government agreed to pay the full amount in England there would be no further problem, as I am told that it would amount to about £50 a month in English currency. But if, as is more probable, the Czech Government refuses to continue her pension if she leaves the country, she would have no income whatever. I am writing this letter to ask you whether, in such circumstances, you could help my mother, either financially or by way of accommodation. If you can consider giving her some assistance I think my mother's present visit is a good opportunity for her to discuss the matter with you, so that she knows exactly where she stands before finally coming to a decision about her own future.

My position is that I live with my wife and 3 small children in a small semi-detached house which is not large enough to give permanent accommodation to another adult. I bought the house six years ago with a mortgage of 90%. I cannot afford either to move to a larger house or to maintain my mother in a flat of her own. My mother is still mentally alert and well able to look after herself, and I think she would prefer to retain her independence by living in a small flat of her own, close to us, rather than be completely dependent on us by living with us, even if the extra space was available in our house. It might even be better for her to live in a building or locality where there were other German-speaking people, as it is a strain for her to speak nothing but English all the time.

My mother has now been in this country for two months and will probably stay for another 3 or 4 weeks before returning to Prague. So far she has been with us in Camberley, but from Wednesday, September 22 for about 7 days she will be staying with a friend in London. I shall be grateful if you can see her at any time, but it would be most convenient if you could fix a date for an interview with her during her stay in London. If you wish to make arrangements for this interview at short notice you can telephone me during office hours at MANsion House 5410. My mother speaks some Czech and a little English, but I think it would help if a German-speaking member of your staff could be present during your talk with her.

I have omitted to mention that neither of my parents has received any compensation from the German Government, and it is most unlikely that my mother would have a valid claim if she now established residence outside Czechoslovakia. No doubt you are familiar with the legal issues involved. Of course I also have received no compensation payments from Germany.

I shall be most grateful for your consideration of the matters I have raised in this letter, and look forward to hearing from you.

Yours faithfully,

John Rieden

As soon as I read this letter I call my brothers. My grand-mother's one and only visit to see us in 1965 was embedded in family legend. I was a two-year-old toddler and scared of this Eastern European old lady in mourning who wore black and spoke in a foreign language. As I mentioned earlier I screamed until I was sick when I saw her smoking in my bed, but after that we got on famously. It was when Grandma went home that my mother told me I stopped eating properly, living on a diet of raw cabbage, nuts and chocolate for a while, and subsequently developed into a very faddy eater. Helena had a lasting effect on me. But I had no idea she had stayed with us for so long and definitely knew nothing of this behind-the-scenes bid by my father to bring her over to be with us in England. My brothers, who would have been aged seven and five at the time, fill me in on the details.

Rudolf had died on 30 March 1965, and Helena had obviously come over as soon as she could manage after his death. She arrived in England four months later. Had Rudolf's injury and the gastric ulcer my father described in his letter prevented them from both coming earlier I wonder? Or did Rudolf not want to come?

Now I knew the date of Rudolf's death I asked Julius Müller, my Czech researcher, to put in applications for Rudolf and Helena's death certificates. He found Rudolf's quite quickly. My grandfather died in hospital in Prague of sepsis caused by haemorrhagic necrosis of the pancreas. He was 70 years old.

Now it was time for Helena to find her boy. I can't imagine what it must have been like for Helena to see her son after 26 years apart, and for my father to be reunited with his mother. Did they talk about what had happened to the aunts, uncles and grandfather to whom Hanus had bid goodbye in 1939? Did they discuss Theresienstadt?

My brothers can't remember what language Dad and Grandma spoke to each other, but I imagine it was a bit of German and a bit of English. Dad would also have been at work for much of her visit, so it would have been left to my mother to look after Helena.

My mother had always said that the visit was troubled. She felt Helena was critical of everything. My father by this time was working as an insurance underwriter in the City of London, a job that became his lifelong career. Helena had the archetypal Jewish expectation that he should have achieved more, perhaps as a lawyer or a doctor, and voiced her feelings. I was about to turn two and my parents had honoured Helena with my middle name of Helen. But my grandmother said that this was against Jewish tradition, which says it is bad luck to name a child after a living relative. It was as if my parents wished her dead, she said. Mum was nevertheless desperate to please her mother-in-law. She'd heard that continental women washed their sheets every day, rather than weekly as was her regular routine. So she set about daily laundry, only for Helena to turn around and posit: 'Do you think I am dirty?'

I had always assumed that these issues, coupled with a sense of abandonment that I had imagined my father felt, though he never expressed, meant that too much water had gone under the bridge for mother and son, that being together was just too hard. But here in this letter I learned that my father had actually fought to bring his mother over.

When I talk more to my brother Nick about the visit he says he understood that after visiting us Grandma went off to see her relative in Israel and that she would decide with which of her relatives – her son or her brother – she wanted to live. We have photos in our family album from Israel, taken in the coastal resort of Hadera in 1966. We knew the pictures were of distant family, but didn't know of whom, and I had always thought that the teenager in the photos bore an uncanny resemblance to my brother Peter. When I read Dad's letter I immediately pull the photos out. I now realise that they show Helena in a swimsuit on a beach with presumably her youngest brother. This must be Josef Hoffer and his family. Nick recalls Mum telling him that Helena also didn't get on with Josef and that in the end she decided to live out her days alone in Prague. But now I am not so sure.

I am certain that we would have photos of Helena in England. My father used to take photographs on colour slides and then we would watch them as a family gathered around the slide projector, the images focused on the living-room wall. He was also meticulous in his filing of these photos by date. Now I have a date, Nick agrees to go through our family slide archive.

And then suddenly there they are: the photos of everyone with Helena. There are six photos of various family groups, the most poignant of mother and son. Helena has her arm around my father and is gripping on tight. She looks happy and proud. My father looks anxious and is holding on to his mother's cigarette packet, which is a strange sight since he never smoked. The top of my head is in the far corner of the shot as I hang on to my father's leg. In another shot Dad is holding me in his arms smiling, with Helena by our side. This reunion with my grandmother is what I later dreamed of, not realising there was a time when we were together, if only for a few months.

In the letter, for the first and only time, my father talked about lack of compensation from the German government for both his parents and himself. Typically, Dad did not labour the point, but this was a pertinent issue. The Nazis, via the Protectorate of Bohemia and Moravia, had stripped Rudolf and Helena and the whole family of all their wealth. With the vast majority of their siblings murdered, all of whom were adults with jobs and personal wealth, aside from their own assets, Rudolf and Helena's inheritance would have been substantial. My father's university education and his accommodation could easily have been underwritten, and Rudolf and Helena could have had a more comfortable life, perhaps even have emigrated to be with their son. Everything would have been different for my father. Here was another war crime, which became a hot political potato later in Czechoslovakia and has still not been resolved.

But the trust's response to Dad's impassioned request was clinical. They didn't write back but telephoned, and there is a note recording the conversation:

> I phoned John Rieden and told him that we were unable to help his mother as we have never been in a position to give guarantees of maintenance and accommodation to cases such as this.
>
> Furthermore we are no longer accepting new tenants in new cases for maintenance. I suggested he might contact J.R.C. [Jewish Refugee Council].
>
> JW
>
> 22/9/65

I am sure my father tried every organisation he could and fear he found no support. What's more, Helena's visit had plunged him into a financial quagmire and the trust was on his back. Dad had defaulted on his loan repayments from January 1966 for a number of months, and in a series of curt letters Mrs Henry, back in her position as Welfare Officer, was threatening to make the trip from London to come to the house to demand payment. On 4 June 1966 my father gathered himself and wrote with an explanation. Yet again, my father is forced to go on bended knee and apologise, and I can feel his pain and disappointment between the lines.

> 25, Robins Bow,
> Camberley,
> Surrey.
> June 4, 1966

Czech Refugee Trust Fund
Rutland House, Rutland Gardens,
London S.W.7.

Dear Sirs,

I must apologise for my delay in replying to your letter of April 29, and for omitting to keep up my loan payments since January.

My mother, who is a Czech citizen resident in Prague and now aged 72, spent three months with us towards the end of last year. As the result of expenses connected with this visit I am now in temporary financial difficulty. It will help me considerably if you will agree to postpone the remaining loan repayments for a further 3 months, after which they will be resumed at the former rate of pound 2 per month.

I hope you will find this proposal acceptable, and shall be most grateful if you will agree to it. I am afraid that your suggested visit by Mrs Henry on June 7th will not be convenient, as I do not usually arrive home before 7pm. Alternative arrangements can be made if you wish, but I do not want to put Mrs Henry to the trouble of such a long journey out of town and you may feel that it is no longer necessary for her to call to see me.

Yours sincerely,

John Rieden

My father must have paid for Helena's flight from Czechoslovakia, her travel visas and costs in the UK, and it pushed him over the financial edge. The trust agreed to the extension and called off Mrs Henry's visit. My father didn't manage to resume his payments until December 1966. He finally paid off the loan in October 1969, almost ten years after it was granted. That day must have come as a great relief to him. Dad always hated being in debt, and this loan, which also tied him to the pain of his past, must have weighed heavily on his shoulders. Jubilation would certainly have been in order.

The papers in the box finish with the loan settled. I don't know if Helena decided not to move to England or if England wouldn't have her. In any case, when the Soviets invaded Czechoslovakia in 1968, the door slammed shut for Helena and it was this no doubt that my mother and father looked so concerned about on our holiday in Spain, his first trip abroad as an Englishman.

It takes Julius quite a bit longer to find Helena's death certificate. It arrives in my email inbox late one night and I feel quite teary opening it. Helena was in the same hospital where Rudolf had died when she left this world. I fear she had no one by her bedside. She was alone behind that Iron Curtain I had imagined so vividly as a child when she died on 11 March 1973 from heart failure due to ischemic heart disease. She was 79. I have been unable to find details of her estate in the Czech records, but my brothers both recall my father receiving notification that the Czechoslovak state had liquidated his mother's estate and that there was a sizeable sum of money left to him. But accessing this inheritance was going to be tricky. Transferring hard currency out of Communist Czechoslovakia was extremely difficult, and then there was the inheritance tax, which consumed half the estate.

My father had to appoint a Czech notary at great expense, cross his fingers and hope. A year later a sum of money, which my brother Peter believes was around £5000, arrived in my father's bank account. This was the equivalent of £40,000 today. It had reached England via a circuitous route through different currencies, such were the dark arts used to take money out of Soviet-ruled Czechoslovakia. My brother Nick recalls Dad's bank calling him late one evening announcing the arrival of a foreign bank transfer. The bank suggested that since it was a large sum, the money should be placed in a high-interest account overnight.

Helena's bequest was a great help to my cash-strapped parents, and enabled them to buy their first ever brand-new car among other things. But I am totally perplexed by this sum. My father had stated in his letter to the Czech Refugee Trust that Helena had no savings, and I am certain he wasn't hiding anything. It wasn't in Dad's nature to lie and, especially where issues of finance were concerned, he was always scrupulously honest.

Helena must therefore have had assets, most likely a house. I know from my land and property record searches that she didn't own the Prague flat she died in, and it appears that she and Rudolf also didn't own the flat my father was born and raised in. There may still have been the one-eighth of the Hoffer property in Žlutice, but this wouldn't have amounted to much. Could it possibly have been that mountain holiday home my father had been searching for on his visit with my mother more than a decade later?

In one of his letters to Reverend Davidson, written in 1946, Rudolf talked about difficulties regarding compensation for 'confiscated property' and 'the flat'. Maybe the executors had achieved compensation, or maybe Helena had herself managed to do this in the last decade of her life.

The sad truth is that even if she had finally been recompensed for thefts wrought by the Third Reich, under Communist law at the time, my grandmother would have been unable to access this money herself to fund a new life, either in England with us or in Israel with her brother.

CHAPTER FIFTEEN

POSTCARD FROM A TRAIN

In my father's letter to the Czech Refugee Trust he had said that Helena's youngest brother, who now lived in Israel, and her elderly sister-in-law, who now lived in a village away from Prague, were the only family survivors from the war aside from himself and his parents. Here, finally, was some certainty, and from a very trustworthy source – my father. This was thrilling news at last.

Helena's youngest brother was of course Josef Hoffer, who, as I had earlier discovered in the cadastre records from Žlutice, had returned to his sister in Prague in 1945 from Israel, his refuge during the war. He and my father were the only members of the family who had managed to flee Czechoslovakia out of Nazi clutches. After spending time with Rudolf and Helena, Josef had then moved in to the Hoffer family home in Žlutice. But I had been unable to discover what had happened to him after that.

Here, though, I had proof. Josef had left his homeland one final time to make his life away from the chaos of postwar Eastern Europe in the Jewish state of Israel. On 14 May 1948,

David Ben-Gurion, head of the Jewish Agency, proclaimed the establishment of the State of Israel 'open for Jewish emigration'. At last Jews around the world had a homeland. They no longer had to go on bended knee to nations that didn't really want them, begging to be let in, and I imagine Josef moved quickly to secure his future. A few months earlier, in February, the Communist Party of Czechoslovakia's coup d'état had ushered in another harsh regime. Yet again, life became very difficult for Czech Jews, and as someone who had lived in Israel during the war, Josef would have been a target. Nevertheless, it would have been difficult for Helena to lose her brother a second time.

Had Rudolf and Helena gone with Josef, their lives may have been easier, though from my father's letter I can see that Rudolf had managed to return to his job with the Ministry of Finance and that he had been awarded his government pension, so perhaps he and Helena maintained some of their protected status even then.

I assume that the sister-in-law my father had referred to in his letter was Hedwig Jungova, who would have been almost 65 then. Before the war, Hedwig had already moved away from the Rieden family to make her own life with a German, non-Jewish husband, Erwin Jung, so I imagine of all the Rieden siblings she was the most distant and possibly didn't even know Helena. But Hedwig had been liberated from Theresienstadt with Helena and Rudolf, and lived in the same barracks as Helena at one point, so postwar there would have been the closeness of shared experience and of family loss.

While it is great to hear that Josef and Hedwig were safe, I am disturbed to see that there had been no mention of Anna Ungermannova, Rudolf's sister, and her husband Rabbi

Samuel Ungermann in Dad's letter. Did he just not know about them or had they also perished?

In Prague my researcher Julius is still looking for the Ungermanns, and a few days after I read Dad's letter, Julius discovers a document in Hebrew, a testimony from the Yad Vashem digital archives in Israel. Julius doesn't read Hebrew but he says he thinks the testimony listed Aliza Rakhel Ungermannova, who he believes was the daughter of Samuel and Anna. So my father did have another cousin in addition to Vera and Johanna. But, Julius adds, she seemed to have been killed in Auschwitz. While I bury my head in my hands, Julius points out that the testimony had been submitted by another member of the family who was alive and, at the time, living in Israel. Hard though it is to hear that yet another member of the family has been killed, the notion that others might be living is indeed encouraging. Could there be descendants of Samuel and Anna living in Israel?

I send the document to the Sydney Jewish Museum, where one of the staff kindly agrees to translate it. The testimony had been submitted on 18 November 1955 by a Kalman Hagari, who at the time of submission was living at Kibbutz Givat Chayim, in Israel. It was about his sister Aliza and her parents Shmuel and Anna. This was Kalman's testimony:

Shmuel Ungermann
Family situation: married
Birthdate: 30/7/1881.
Birth place: Hungary.
Belonged to Postelberg community in Czechoslovakia.
In 1939 lived in Tsart.
Occupation: Rabbi
Died in: Auschwitz, Poland, death camp

282

Wife's name: Anna

Died Auschwitz.

Maiden name: Rieden

Children's names: Aliza Rakhel – 17 years old.

Last known place of residence of the registered: Bratislava, Czechoslovakia

This is a shock. I had hoped that Anna and Samuel had made it to Israel and now I knew they had a daughter too. But all three had been killed in Auschwitz. This means that eight of my relatives ended their days in that place, most probably in the gas chambers. Their names had not appeared in any of the many Holocaust digital archives I had searched, and the Auschwitz archivist also couldn't find any trace of the Ungermanns, which suggested that their records must have been among those destroyed by the Nazis.

Kalman's testimony threw up an explosion of questions in my head. First and foremost, who was he and how did he know what had happened to Anna, Samuel and Aliza? Secondly, if he was Aliza's sibling, as he stated, did this mean Anna and Samuel had at least one other child and possibly more, and why was his surname Hagari? Thirdly, how did Kalman escape without his parents: could he have been on some sort of kindertransport like my father?

I now had proof that in 1955, there had been a relative of Anna Ungermannova living in Israel, so this is the next place to focus my search. Having found every other member of the family I don't want to leave Anna's story untold, nor ignore the opportunity to find her kin. But I am confused by the surname Hagari. Why was Kalman not an Ungermann?

On the internet I come across a Ben Hagari. He seems to be a rather edgy artist of considerable renown, working in film

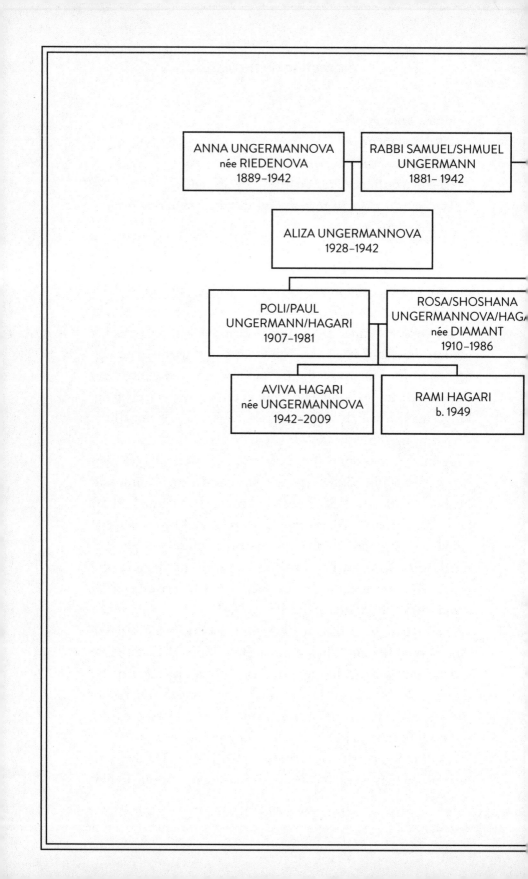

ANNA UNGERMANNOVA
née RIEDENOVA
1889–1942

RABBI SAMUEL/SHMUEL
UNGERMANN
1881– 1942

ALIZA UNGERMANNOVA
1928–1942

POLI/PAUL
UNGERMANN/HAGARI
1907–1981

ROSA/SHOSHANA
UNGERMANNOVA/HAG/
née DIAMANT
1910–1986

AVIVA HAGARI
née UNGERMANNOVA
1942–2009

RAMI HAGARI
b. 1949

THE UNGERMANN/HAGARI FAMILY TREE

FANNY
RSCHKO
84–1922

NA/DIONYSUS
NGERMANN
1908–1942

KALMAN/KOLOMAN
HAGARI
né UNGERMANN
1909–1983

ILAN HAGARI
b. 1942

SHULA HAGARI
1943–2007

DANIEL HAGARI
b. 1976

BEN HAGARI
b. 1981

JONATHAN HAGARI
b. 1984

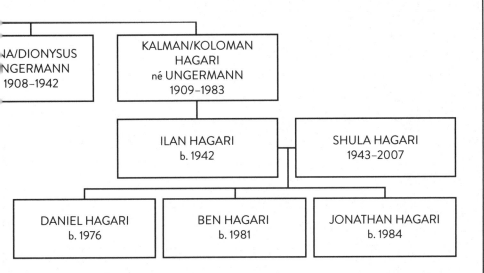

and video installations and living between New York and Tel Aviv. His work is thought-provoking, looking especially at the human condition, unpicking issues of identity and territory. There is a contact for him on his professional site, so in a wild stab in the dark I compose an email.

Ben replies the very next day. Kalman was his grandfather. He kindly puts me in contact with his father, Ilan Hagari, a graphic designer with his own studio in Tel Aviv. And from Ilan I finally learn the truth about Anna and Samuel.

Ilan is surprised and happy to hear from me, and extremely generous with his family story. Kalman was his father, Samuel Ungermann his grandfather. Over a series of emails we share what we know, and Samuel and Anna's lives start to come into focus. It feels slightly surreal but amazing to be finally talking to a relative who is alive and well, but what he has to tell me is harrowing.

Kalman had two older brothers, whom Ilan called 'Poli' and 'Dina'. (Charged with this new information, I later put a fresh research request for Samuel Ungermann into the Liberec archives, and am sent records for Samuel that list his sons as 'Paul', 'Dionysus' and 'Koloman'.) The mother of these three boys, however, wasn't Anna Ungermannova but Samuel's first wife, Fanny Herschko.

Samuel and Fanny were from Hungary, where Fanny had died in 1922 when Kalman was 13. But by this time Samuel had already left Hungary for Czechoslovakia. According to Ilan, Samuel was a Communist activist and had been sentenced to death in Hungary, so fled across the border to Czechoslovakia. Ilan told me that he believed Samuel had taken his family with him, but from the Liberec records I think Fanny must have stayed in Budapest.

In Liberec, Samuel became a rabbi, married Anna sometime

after 1912 in the local synagogue where he was a teacher, and the couple had a daughter, Aliza, who would have been raised alongside her three half-brothers.

Samuel's son Kalman emigrated to Palestine in 1933 to live in the Kibbutz Haim (Meuhad). This collective had been founded just a year before in 1932, so Kalman would have been among its earliest members. Kibbutzim were popping up all over Palestine at the time, and were often a rite of passage for Jews, many of whom were raised in the communities or joined them as teenagers. The founders of this kibbutz had mostly been trained in the Zionist Youth Movement in Europe and moving into the next decade were joined by Jews fleeing the Holocaust and their families. For Kalman the kibbutz would have been a place of safe refuge, where Judaism was at the heart of life and could be practised freely. As the son of a rabbi and an activist, I imagine he was more religiously aligned than my other relatives. Over the course of the next five years, Kalman returned twice to Czechoslovakia, and on each of these visits married a woman and took her back to Palestine and the kibbutz. Shortly after they arrived safely, he divorced each woman. In doing this, Kalman saved their lives and fought Hitler's impending genocide with cunning and courage.

Ilan explains that Ungermann – which literally means 'man from Hungary' – ceased to be the family name in the 1940s, after Samuel had advised Kalman to change it to Hagari. 'Kalman wanted to change the name so it would sound like a Hebrew name with biblical roots,' explained Ilan who was born in 1942 with the name Ungermann, which was shortly after changed to Hagari. This means Samuel and Anna were still alive in 1942.

It's ironic that Emil Rieden had just three decades earlier changed the family name from Rindskopf to Rieden to avoid being recognisably Jewish, and here the opposite was happening. When I look up Hagar, aside from being the Hebrew name for Hungary, I see that it derives from the story of Hagar and her son Ishmael, and means 'one who flees' or 'one who seeks refuge'. Ishmael is, of course, a Hebrew variant of Samuel, so it seemed poignant that Samuel had asked his son to change his family name to Hagari.

I now have a burning question. I need to know how Ilan's father Kalman had known that Samuel, Anna and Aliza had been killed in Auschwitz. His answer is agonising, painting a picture that will remain with me forever.

In Israel in the 1940s Kalman received a postcard from his father, who at the time was recorded as living in Bratislava in Slovakia. On the card Samuel wrote that he, Anna and Aliza were on a train to Auschwitz.

This was the last communication Ilan's father ever received from Samuel.

It is chilling. In my research I had read stories of victims throwing letters out of the gaps between the slats in the side of the cattle carts when they paused at train stations, hoping that the onlookers would do the right thing and post this final message to their loved one. Had Samuel done this? Ilan says the family no longer has the card and that his father, who died in 1984, was 'too traumatised to discuss it at length'. Like my father, Kalman spoke very little about the Holocaust to his children.

Bratislava was one of the few places where Jews had mobilised resistance to the Nazis, and considering Samuel's background as a political activist, I now imagined that he might have been one of those who fought back. The Bratislava Working Group gathered large sums of money both from international Jewish groups and Jews within Slovakia, to literally bribe Nazi and Slovakian officials to stop deporting Jews East. Their efforts may have slowed the process of deportation, but eventually failed.

Armed with this new information I embark on more archival searches for the Ungermanns and, finally, I find them. In 1942 Samuel, Anna and Aliza were living in Nitra, Slovakia, where there had been a sizeable Jewish community before Nazi occupation. From here, along with several thousand Jews, they were deported east to Poland. They were together when they were piled onto trains for Lublin, Poland, on 15 April 1942 and perhaps it was from this train that Samuel sent the postcard thinking they were headed for Auschwitz. In fact, Samuel was murdered in Majdanek concentration camp in Lublin on 25 June 1942, most probably in the gas chambers. There is no record of Anna and Aliza's death but it is highly unlikely that they survived this vicious camp where inmates were either shot, gassed or died from starvation, cold or sickness.

Ilan was right about his grandfather's murder, though not about the place of death. He tells me that he believes his uncle Dina (Dionysus) was also killed in Auschwitz and again I start my search. After many false starts, I find him listed in two places in the Yad Vashem archives, and the sources for once are conclusive. Dina had been on a transport of Jews deported directly from Sered concentration camp in Slovakia to Auschwitz that left on 13 April 1942. Then, just over a month later on 28 May 1942, he was killed in Auschwitz, the murder recorded in the death books that were later compiled from the fragments of the death registers found when the camp was liberated.

I suspect it was after watching one of his three sons being deported that Samuel hastily advised Kalman to change the family name to Hagari so he couldn't be traced, and maybe it was on that postcard.

'Poli' had followed Kalman to Palestine in the early 1940s and then moved to the United States in the 1950s. Desperate to find some light at the end of this tunnel, I start looking for Paul Ungermann, and after an extensive search I find him listed in the United States Holocaust Memorial Museum archives.

On 3 July 1939, just three and a half months after Hitler occupied Czechoslovakia, Paul boarded a ship illegally bound for Palestine. He was part of an unstoppable wave of Jewish refugees flooding out of Nazi-occupied Europe any way they could. He joined the SS *Naomi Julia* in Bratislava, where the Ungermann family was then living. The ship was intercepted by the Palestinian authorities and, together with an estimated 1600–2000 others, Paul was forced to dock at Haifa on 25 September 1939, where he was promptly arrested by the Palestinian Police Force and sent to the Sarafand Detention Camp. On his records it states that Paul was 'destitute' although he had 12 gold teeth, which at that time would have been a sign of wealth. The papers also say that Paul had a wife, Shoshana, and that she was living in Haifa.

Britain ruled Palestine at this time under a League of Nations mandate supposedly to prepare the area for a 'Jewish national home'. But to appease Arab opposition to a mass influx of Jews, in the 1930s Britain imposed strict quotas on Jewish immigration, which remained in place until 1948. Once the quota was reached, any Jew trying to enter Palestine was declared an illegal alien and deported. This feels like an extremely inhumane policy to enforce during the war, when Jews subject to persecution by the ever-increasing Third

Reich were running for their lives. But it seems the whole world was petrified of allowing Jews the chance to settle and rebuild their lives.

The Sarafand Detention Camp was a ghastly place, and bore some similarities to the European concentration camps these refugees were fleeing. Conditions were poor, the camp was overcrowded with bad sanitation, guards patrolled the wire fencing, and inmates often suffered sickness or died. But this was not an extermination camp, and ultimately some of the inmates were released into Israel. Others were deported to a camp in Mauritius. But I can find no record of what happened to Paul.

I go back to Ilan to share these newly discovered records. In response he introduces me to his cousin Rami Hagari, Paul's son, who currently lives in Chicago where he works as a violinist. The warm and gentle Rami is distraught when I tell him our family story. He knew nothing about the postcard his grandfather had written to his uncle, nor of his grandfather's subsequent murder. 'My parents spoke very little of the Shoah,' is his familiar reply.

Rami says that his mother was called Rachel Rose Diamant, and since Rose in Hebrew is Shoshana, he imagines this was the wife referred to on the documentation. His uncle Kalman had left for Israel in 1933 just before his brother Paul's wedding. 'I never knew the name of the boat, but I understand that soon after they disembarked from Czechoslovakia they were all transferred to a freighter on which they spent the next three months. My mother was very ill when they arrived and they were separated for quite some time from each other,' Rami explains.

I imagine Paul was sent to the detention camp and his wife, whose deportation details I quickly find among the same records from the arrests made by the Palestinian Police Force on the arrival in port of the SS *Naomi Julia*, may have been sent to hospital in Haifa.

'We were told by a cousin of my mother that they actually were rejected by the British and were sent to Cyprus rather than staying in Palestine, and had lost a baby,' Rami continues.

Jews were deported from Palestine to Cyprus by the British between 1946 and 1948, so the Hagaris may have been sent then or earlier. Poor Paul and Rose were being shipped all over the place. But Rami's story doesn't end there. Following Kalman's lead, Paul also changed his name to Hagari.

'My handicapped sister, Aviva Hagari née Ungermann, was born with cerebral palsy in 1942 in Israel and I was born in Tel Aviv as Hagari in 1949. We emigrated by ship to America, coming through Ellis Island, in 1951.'

Ellis Island, situated at the mouth of the Hudson River between New York and New Jersey, was the notorious US immigration station. Notorious because of the gruelling selection process immigrants faced after their arduous voyages. Anyone unfit for entry – physically, mentally or politically – was sent straight back to where they had come from. Rami says that here Paul and his wife were again separated, 'as Aviva had to be tested for diseases and mental retardation, neither positive'. This process could have taken weeks and was reportedly very unpleasant. Eventually, the family was let in and their new life in America began. Paul died in 1981, Rose in 1986 and Aviva in 2009, and while Rami is thrilled we are now in contact, knowing more about his family's journey, he says, 'brings to mind the everlasting pain that my parents suffered'.

When I set out on this pilgrimage, one of my missions had been to find surviving family members. Though Ilan, Ben and Rami are not blood relatives, it is encouraging to at least discover that another branch of my family had managed, through dogged endurance and strength of character, to escape Hitler. Both welcome me into their families with open arms and hearts, which for the complaining little girl who longed to have relatives is a wonderful feeling.

And while I have yet to find descendants of Josef Hoffer, I hope that somewhere in Israel his family continues to thrive.

DAD, THE MAN HE BECAME

In March 1982 our family home went up in flames. It was the early hours of a Sunday morning and I was woken by my brother Peter screaming 'fire'. I was 18 years old and in my final year at school, due to be taking my A levels in a few months' time. I had been out late with friends and was fast asleep and rather annoyed with my brother for waking me up. My eldest brother Nick was away at college, my parents were asleep downstairs and our dog Toby was in his kennel in the garage.

I pulled back the covers and walked to my bedroom door. As I opened it, the rush of air fed the flames, which had begun in the corner of the living room below. We found out later that this was an electrical fire that had started from the television. I tried to close the door against the impending inferno but the backdraft was too strong.

Terrified, I rushed to the window. As I opened it, the glass of the double glazing shattered in the heat. I yelled out into the darkness: 'Help! Help!' It felt like an eternity as I stared out hoping someone would come, but it would have been barely a minute. Time had run out, and as the flames licked up the side of the house I realised I had to jump. From above I thought I could reach the soft grass of our Surrey garden lawn, but I must have passed out in flight and landed on the concrete patio below.

I was found unconscious by my mother, who with Dad had climbed out of their ground-floor bedroom window and had immediately run to the back of the house to find me. Mum prodded me and told me to get up, and then panicked when I didn't move. Peter meanwhile was hanging out of his window – literally – singeing his wrists and waiting for the fire brigade, who raised a ladder to bring him down. I was carried next door by the neighbour, wafting in and out of consciousness. I woke up fast when Toby, grabbed by Mum on the way from his kennel, jumped up to lick me . . . The right side of my body was a mess and I was rushed to hospital and into surgery. I had broken my hip, wrist and elbow, and slashed my right eye, but I was alive. Peter had burns and cuts, but was otherwise okay. Toby was barking and shepherding the family together – he was a sheepdog! I was in hospital for a month; my arm was in plaster, I had three metal pins in my hip, and my right eye, a kaleidoscope of yellow and dark purple, was covered with a patch.

The house was gutted, a shell with the charred remains of our family's life soaked by the fire hoses. We lost pretty much everything, and anything that hadn't been destroyed was thick with black ash.

We were all in trauma, but the fire hit my father the worst.

My mother was wise and pragmatic, but Dad was shaken to the core. He made lists. Lots of them, methodically trying to work through the new chaos that had engulfed the Riedens. I have a vivid memory of finally coming out of hospital on crutches to see him in the kitchen of my parents' best friends' house – where he and Mum had been living temporarily until rented accommodation was found – manically scrubbing the soot off wire coathangers. Mum said she had tried to tell him that we could buy new ones, but Dad *needed* to wash and preserve these and nothing could stop him. And as I stood next to him, I realised that if I tried to interrupt, he might break down.

I think for Dad, losing the house was somehow intrinsically linked to losing his family. He thought everything was at risk again. In the bricks and mortar he had paid for with his own sweat and tears, Dad felt safe, but now all that had gone up in smoke. Since he worked in insurance, we were well covered, so it wasn't even about the money: this was a deeply emotional response from a man who rarely let his emotions take over. In the end my parents decided we couldn't rebuild the house – it would always be the home that burnt down – so they eventually moved to a new one.

In writing this book I wanted to find out everything I could about the relatives I never knew, to unmask their suffering and to see if any survived the Holocaust. Then on the way it morphed into a journey all about the father I loved so much and thought I knew so well. What I learned, at 55 years old, has made me understand what made Dad who he was and fully appreciate his immense courage and resilience against what at times seemed like unsurmountable odds. It has also made me deeply ashamed of how Western nations responded to the plight of the Jews in the Second World War and then how England failed to support Dad. He always felt grateful for being taken in, for being allowed to become an Englishman, but what I discovered showed how hard he had to battle for everything he achieved. Survival and endurance are the lessons of the Holocaust, but I think what has troubled me most about my father's experience was the indignity he was made to suffer along the way.

Although he didn't talk about it, my father's past revealed itself in everything he did. Education was paramount, and he used to check over my homework rigorously and give me French and Latin tests twice a week. My brother Nick recalls Dad's extreme dislike for borrowing money and paying interest, which is hardly surprising given his experience with the Czech Refugee Trust. 'He once told me that paying interest in any circumstances was senseless, and Mum told me that when I got my first mortgage (a 100 per cent mortgage for £40,000) he had sleepless nights worrying about my taking on such a loan in my late twenties.'

All through my childhood, Dad used to suffer from bouts of depression, usually linked to money worries, when everything in his world went dark. My mother was the antidote to these moods. Mum was a fixer; problems were to be solved, not worried about. I like to think that Dad shared some of the difficult moments from his past with Mum, but I think he also kept a lot of it to himself. He didn't want to pass on the pain.

When my brothers and I were clearing out the family home after my mother's death, I found a number of books about the history of the Jews earmarked with lots of bits of paper, with detailed notes in Mum's handwriting. I remembered that she had taken a course looking into both Judaism and Islam at Reading University in England, one of many she took in her retirement following the PhD she completed in the 1990s. The sections on the Holocaust were heavily annotated.

Mum was eager to understand as much as she could about her husband's past, a desire I have clearly inherited.

One of Dad's closest friends, Richard, with whom he went camping to the South of France in the 1950s, tells me that my father barely mentioned his childhood to him, nor did he talk much about his schooling. He certainly never talked of the annihilation of his family. 'It's obvious to me now that John had a pretty harrowing upbringing, lonely and in solitude. It must have been pretty bad news all round. But he kept it all very quiet,' says Richard. 'Your mother was very upset with John's mother because she didn't make much effort to contact him after the war. But the thing about John was that he was a true intellectual, absolutely. His knowledge was incredible and he was a very talented individual.'

———

In May 1993, my father returned to Prague with my mother to go on an extensive road trip around Bohemia, Moravia and Slovakia. They took their camcorder – the favourite amateur recording device of 1990s middle England – and Dad turned tourist in his birthplace. They visited medieval castles, epoch-making chateaux, ancient town squares flanked by Renaissance houses with ornate ice-cream-coloured façades, spa towns, and the crisp beauty of the High Tatra mountains streaked with white expanses of dazzling snow. They were not on a tourist bus, but on their own, driving in a hire car through the Czech Republic and Slovakia with the sense of freedom I imagine my father recalled from childhood.

I knew that the recording of this holiday still existed in our family boxes, and asked my engineer brother Peter to see if he could somehow convert the old tapes to a format I could access. Peter has never been bowed by a technical challenge, and when two DVDs arrived in the post I knew he had pulled it off!

Together there were close to two hours to watch. My parents' journey started in Bohemia, in the elegant spa town of Mariánské Lázně and then moved to nearby Karlovy Vary and Františkovy Lázně. This was Hoffer country, where Helena, Dad's mother, was raised and I know my father visited regularly as a young boy. I was hoping he might reveal some family memory about his murdered aunts and uncles in the recorded soundtrack, but true to form Dad's resolute silence was golden.

I recall, on their return, my mother telling me that they had attempted to find the family's holiday house in the countryside where my father used to go with his parents. Mum said they thought they'd found the village, but when they asked the locals for help, they hit a brick wall. In fact it was more than that; Mum felt they had been viewed with suspicion. As I looked through Dad's recording I wondered if any of the many, many houses he focused his lens on might be him trying to remember if 'this could be the one'.

They had made their trip just four years after the Velvet Revolution, at a time when relatives of Jews killed in the Holocaust felt the new regime might finally support restitution justice. All over Czechoslovakia, Jews were searching for their property, which in some cases had been taken by Nazis, but more often had been 'appropriated' or 'given' to non-Jewish Czechs, who were now living in what amounted to stolen goods. My father wasn't on such a mission, but Mum felt that the people they had asked assumed he'd come to claim his family home, which was why, she said, they had quickly abandoned the search.

But this was a happy holiday. My father was revelling in the historic architecture, the handsome town squares, and most of all the rivers, lakes, forests and mountains. In the High Tatra Mountains I could feel his rapture. Was this where he skied as a lad? With the glacial streams rushing along the roadside, my mother by his side and almost no one else in sight, my father was having a wonderful time.

Back in Prague he filmed the famous anatomical clock in the Old Town Square playing at noon, and on the soundtrack I can hear him say to Mum, 'Where's the skeleton?' as he tried to focus the lens on each figure. The skeleton is the most popular of the clock's medieval personalities, and as I sat and watched Dad's movie I could imagine Hanus asking the same question of his mother back in the 1930s, in pre-Hitler Prague.

It felt good to witness my father reunited with his homeland, and was the perfect end to my own pilgrimage.

My parents travelled a lot in their retirement – to Kenya, Jordan, China and all over Europe. They lived and loved every minute. My father especially enjoyed his granddaughters, Peter's two girls Kathy and Annie, who have both developed exceptional musicality from my sister-in-law, Vivien, their mother, but also I like to think from their Czech blood.

When my father died on 24 January 2006 from prostate cancer at home it was too soon. He was just 75. On the day he died my mother sat with me and my brothers in her kitchen and she regaled us with her favourite story of how she clutched on to Dad on the back of their Vespa, swooping around Hyde Park Corner in London as they headed off on their honeymoon to Spain. She later discovered she was pregnant with Nick.

My mother died seven years after Dad on 19 November 2013. A few months before her death, she told me she missed him every day – he was her soulmate.

RESOURCES

BOOKS

Adler, H.G., *Theresienstadt 1941–1945: The Face of a Coerced Community*, trans. Belinda Cooper, Cambridge University Press, New York, 2017 (first published 1955)

Bondy, Ruth, *Elder of the Jews: Jakob Edelstein of Theresienstadt*, Grove Press, New York, 1989

Davidson, Lucy V., *For a Future and a Hope: The Story of the Houses of Refuge in Chislehurst*, annotated John S. Ross, CWI Publications, Chislehurst, 1989

Barbican Mission Homes for Children, Barbican Mission, Chislehurst, publication date unknown

Eban, Abba, *Heritage: Civilization and the Jews*, Summit Books, New York, 1984

Elias, Ruth, *Triumph of Hope: From Theresienstadt and Auschwitz to Israel*, trans. Margot Bettauer Dembo, John Wiley & Sons, New York, 1998 (first published 1988)

Engelmann, Isa, *Reichenberg und seine jüdischen Bürger: zur Geschichte einer einst deutschen Stadt in Böhmen (Reichenberg and its Jewish Citizens: The History of a Former German City in Bohemia)*, LIT Verlag, Berlin, 2012

Jaegermann, Judith, *My Childhood in the Holocaust*, Mazo Publishers, Jerusalem, 2004

Johnson, Paul, *A History of the Jews*, Phoenix, London, 2001

London, Louise, 'British government policy and Jewish refugees 1933–45', 1989, *Patterns of Prejudice*, vol. 23, no. 4, pp. 26–43

Pressburger, Chava (ed.), *The Diary of Petr Ginz 1941–1942*, trans. Elena Lappin, Grove Press, New York, 2007 (first published 2004)

Redlich, Gonda, *The Terezín Diary of Gonda Redlich*, trans. Laurence Kutler, ed. Saul S. Friedman, University Press of Kentucky, Lexington, Kentucky, 1992

Świebocka, Teresa et al., (compilers), *Auschwitz-Birkenau: The Past and the Present*, 2nd edn, trans. Adam Czasak, Auschwitz-Birkenau Museum and Memorial, Oświęcim, 2007

Thomson, Ruth, *Terezín: A Story of the Holocaust*, Franklin Watts, London, 2011

Valavková, Hana (ed.), *... I never saw another butterfly ... Children's Drawings and Poems from Terezín Concentration Camp, 1942–1944*, Schocken Books, New York, 1993

Weiner, Pavel, *A Boy in Terezín: The Private Diary of Pavel Weiner, April 1944–1945*, trans. Pavel Weiner, ed. Karen Weiner, Northwestern University Press, Evanston, Illinois, 2011

WEBSITES

Auschwitz-Birkenau Memorial and Museum –
  en.auschwitz.org
British Library – bl.uk
Christian Witness Israel – cwi.org.uk
Czech Holocaust Database – holocaust.cz/en/main-2
Lidice Memorial (Památník Lidice) – lidice-memorial.cz/en
The National Archives UK – nationalarchives.gov.uk
National Archives Czech Republic (Národní Archiv) –
  nacr.cz/en
Sir Nicholas Winton Memorial Trust –
  nicholaswinton.com/WintonMemorialTrust.htm
Sydney Jewish Museum – sydneyjewishmuseum.com.au
Terezín Memorial (Památník Terezín) –
  pamatnik-terezin.cz/?lang=en
United States Holocaust Memorial Museum – ushmm.org
Vedem – vedem-terezin.cz/en/home_en.html
The Wiener Library for the Study of Holocaust and
  Genocide, London – wienerlibrary.co.uk
Yad Vashem, The World Holocaust Remembrance Center –
  yadvashem.org

TV DOCUMENTARY

Barbican: A Forgotten Mission, directed by Jiří František
Potužník, 2018

ACKNOWLEDGEMENTS

I spent 18 months researching this book and along the way received extensive help.

First and foremost, I would like to thank my publisher, Ingrid Ohlsson at Pan Macmillan Australia, for giving me the wonderful opportunity to walk in my father's footsteps, and editor Nicola Young for her advice and sound guidance. Thanks also to Ariane Durkin, Lucy Inglis and Belinda Huang. Thanks to the hugely talented Alissa Dinallo for her inspired cover interpretation.

And thank you also to Katie Ekberg, who worked beside me as researcher, proofreader and sage editor, throughout Europe and then back in Sydney, as I lived through this journey.

A million thanks to the endlessly inspiring Magda Szubanski, who wrote the powerful foreword to this book. It was Magda who first encouraged me to investigate my father's family history and without that initial spark of mentoring I wouldn't have had the courage to embark on this investigation.

To my brothers Nick and Peter Rieden, thank you for being my family archivists, searching through photos, videos and paperwork to discover valuable gems. Thanks also for trawling your memory banks, and Nick for accompanying me to the CWI archives – sorry you pranged your car en route!

Huge thanks to the tireless Julius Müller from Czech archival research service Toledot, who was a charming guide and indefatigable researcher, always going the extra kilometre on my behalf.

My special thanks to Tomáš Fedorovič, the historian at the Terezín Memorial, who was so generous with his time and sensitive to my pain; to John Ross at CWI for opening up the organisation's archives and being so giving with your own research and work; and to Adam Shah at the CWI offices for putting up with me.

Thanks to the brilliantly efficient Ilona Dvořáková at Národní Archiv, the Czech Republic National Archives.

Endless thanks to Jiří František Potužník, the director of *Barbican: A Forgotten Mission*, for sharing his research and being so generous with his time in Prague when I know he was fighting his own deadline.

Thanks to Vida Neuwirthová from Wittman Tours for her deeply affecting guide to Auschwitz. Thanks also to Sandy Hollis and Professor Konrad Kwiet at the Sydney Jewish Museum for their continued guidance, advice and translation services, and for introducing me to amazing Theresienstadt survivors Litzi Lemberg, Tomas Fleischmann (now Flemming) and Paul Drexler, all of whom kindly shared their stories with me.

Thanks to: Lea Květ and Robert Filip at the Liberec Archives; Mike Sampson, the archivist at Blundell's School who unearthed photos of my father in the cricket team and his house reports; Michael Williamson, an old boy from

Winterdyne School; and Michael Chapman, an old boy at Winbury School, for sharing his pertinent memories.

Thanks to my father's great friends Annalisa Mayer and her brother Theo Mayer for going back to those dark days and sharing their story, and to Richard Long for reminiscences of his friendship with my father.

To Barbara Winton, thank you for talking to me about your father Sir Nicholas Winton's courageous Kindertransport; and thanks to the hospitable Amanda Jagger for welcoming me into her home, Seven Trees, where my father spent so much time.

Thank you to Dr Piotr Setkiewicz, head of research at the Auschwitz Museum, for checking my manuscript for factual accuracy; and to Krystyna Leśniak, Ewa Bazan and Sara Ranogajec at the Auschwitz Museum for their archival searches.

Immense thanks to Conor Gregan, the Freedom of Information Assessor in the UK National Archives in Kew, England, for opening the box of material on my father that proved to be the key to unlocking my father's struggle.

Thanks to Kaya Stainton, my Slovak neighbour, for her wonderful help translating my grandfather's Czech records.

And finally ... warmest thanks to my newly discovered family: Ilan, Ben and Rami Hagari.